British Television Advertising

Cultural identity and communication

British Television Advertising

Cultural identity and communication

Renée Dickason

UNIVERSITY
OF LUTON

press

British Library Cataloguing in Publication Data

A catalogue record for this book is available from the British Library

ISBN: 1 86020 571 2

To Rebecca,
To my relatives and friends,
To my students

Published by
University of Luton Press
University of Luton
75 Castle Street
Luton
Bedfordshire LU1 3AJ
United Kingdom

Tel: +44 (0)1582 743297; Fax: +44 (0)1582 743298
e-mail: ulp@luton.ac.uk
website: www.ulp.org.uk

Cover Design Gary Gravatt, Gravatt Design Consultancy
Typeset in Van Dijck MT
Printed in United Kingdom by J W Arrowsmith Ltd, Bristol, UK.

Contents

Acknowledgements

I should like particularly to thank

- the library staff at the Advertising Association and the Independent Television Commission
- Mr Michael Brodie, former Director of Advertising at the Central Office of Information
- Film Images (Paris)

for their invaluable help and advice.

I am most grateful for the patience, understanding and support of my whole family – especially my daughter Rebecca.

I express my profound gratitude to Professor Manuel Alvarado for his confidence and encouragement in the accomplishment of this project.

Renée Dickason
December 1999

Introduction

TV ads are an inescapable cultural phenomenon whose importance, now in the late 1990s, would seem to have been proved beyond all reasonable doubt. In 1998, according to figures supplied by the Advertising Association, the total value of advertising time sold on terrestrial and cable and satellite television was of some £ 3,867 million. What is sometimes not realised is the sheer range of commercial goods and services whose attributes and benefits are now presented to the general public, while the 1980s and 1990s have seen an unquestionable trend towards the extension of advertisements for public bodies as well as for charitable and generally 'good' causes. Moreover, the influence of ads is growing with the ever-increasing number of satellite and cable stations carrying paid advertising and even BBC Prime and BBC World transmit a limited number of commercials in their international broadcasts. In the early years, British television advertising was faced with the thorny problem of combining the effectiveness required by advertisers with viewers' acceptance of publicity in a world where the BBC was already well-established and where the quality of broadcasts was a major criterion. It was necessary to resolve the question in a particularly British way and the solution reached in the 1950s formed the basis for much of subsequent practice. More recently advertising has become a fully emancipated partner in the audiovisual media and has come to be an accepted part of the spectacle offered by television.

Although this study will consider the stages of and developments in practice, its primary purpose is neither historical nor chronological. While it is necessary to examine the context of ads (both past and present) to understand the techniques employed, the creative logic of commercials is organic and synthetic rather than historical and simply derivative. The situation is complicated by the fact that television advertising is a medium of communication in its own right and has the dual role both of reflecting and interpreting society and of influencing and leaving its mark on it. The social and economic historian, Monica Charlot, reminds us that television as a whole may play this role. She declares:

> British television may be regarded as a reflection of the British people at the present moment, provided we bear in mind that television and people are conditioned by their traditions while remaining open to change. Television is able to contribute to this change, not by trying to impose it, but by openly revealing and presenting it.[1]

Martin Davidson, a journalist with experience of working in advertising and publishing, maintains that advertising is both a powerful and a varied medium, with its own separate and identifiable qualities:

> *Advertising is not a static entity, but a series of quite different things [...]. It is a commercial tool, a social language, a genre of spectator/reader experience, a technique of persuasion ; in fact, it is almost a world in its own right, with its own languages, customs and history, one that sets the tone and place for large parts of our lives.*[2]

Advertising Executive David Putnam's remarks are more succinct, for him as for many others in the business, commercials are nothing less than a statement of identity:

> *Ads are a barometer of the age. If you want to know how a country perceives itself, look at its ads.*[3]

Recent years have seen a growing interest in television advertising, which emphasises that it is both a means of communication and an essential element in society, while remaining open to various interpretations. In 1978, Judith Williamson's *Decoding Advertisements* studied the semiology of commercials, applying to them some of the tools of textual analysis, a technique which aroused some critical reactions from advertisers themselves. Four years later, Gillian Dyer's *Advertising as Communication* treated both communicational and historical aspects, while Brian Henry's *British Television Advertising – The First Thirty Years* (1986) added the professional advertisers' creative and commercial points of view to a substantial historical outline. Kathy Myers' *Understains* of the same year was the first of a number of works to cover the advertising and the consumerism of the 1980s and the reactions they aroused. In 1990, the BBC screened a series entitled *Washes Whiter* which contained a compilation of early and later adverts, along with comments, from advertisers and academics, on their sociological implications. It seems to me that, beyond the argument that all such approaches are potentially valuable, it is the very complexity and mutability of the interwoven strands making up TV advertising which constitute its fundamental interest. Ads communicate in the here and now, appealing to and comprising part of what might be called a common cultural context in which they present themselves to the consumer (in the extended sense of the term). The word 'culture', when applied to commercials, is perhaps best taken in its large and all-embracing sense, as used by T. S. Eliot. In *Notes Towards the Definition of Culture* (1948) he defined the term as 'all the characteristic activities and interests of a people', going on to add his own examples in the English context:

> *Derby Day, Henley Regatta, Cowes, the 12th August, a cup final, dog races, boiled cabbage cut in sections, beetroot in vinegar, nineteenth-century gothic and the music of Elgar.*[4]

What seems peculiarly relevant to the argument is both the diversity of social classes and groups implied by Eliot's illustrations and the fact that so many of the references would now seem particularly dated. Culture, in this sense, is, as Monica Charlot suggests for television, both anchored in the past and susceptible to change and evolution.

TV advertising is influenced by its own recognisable and identifiable norms. While the techniques employed are determined to some extent by the product or service to be promoted, they are also influenced by the nature of the medium and by the context in which the transmissions take place. Such details as lighting, sound effects, camera angles and so on, are those employed by TV and borrowed, at greater remove, from cinematographic methods. Conventional methods of communication have developed over a considerable period of time, certain promotional norms are created for specific products and abrupt divergence may be a high-risk strategy since familiarity is part of the conditioning process. At a different level, British TV ads (like TV itself) are subject to strictly defined and generally observed parameters, established over the years by the various bodies controlling independent television, most recently the ITC, and are screened only after consultation with the Broadcast Advertising Clearance Centre (BACC). While remaining outwardly inflexible, the ITC codes can and do change, with the legislative framework varying to reflect changes in society, or more precisely, modifications in cultural attitudes. This explains, at least in part, the role of and need for innovation in advertising. Cultural identity or self-representation is undergoing perpetual alterations, whether or not these meet with the approval of a given individual or group of individuals. Advertisements cannot stand still (although it seems that many frequently purchased goods are promoted in a consciously restricted number of ways) not only because new products and services have recourse to new techniques as well as tried and tested methods, but also because existing products may need to be *re*presented to reflect new marketing requirements or cultural appreciations. This much is certain, the legislative and conventional frameworks do not function in the same way, but both reflect aspects of cultural identity and imply different elements of cultural communication.

Viewed in this way, TV ads are a kind of living archive of a society, indicating the concerns and interests of a given culture at a given period in a particularly immediate way, as chapters 2 to 4 of this book will attempt to show, by relating the ads broadcast from the 1950s to the 1990s to the social, political and economic developments of the time. Each of these sections starts with a brief outline of the historical context, including developments within television itself. Since the material is always evolving, the archive is subject to accumulation, variation and reconstruction, as ideas are confirmed, swept away, rediscovered and modified from moment to moment. Most significantly, ads go beyond the representation of a culture: they serve to restructure and to recreate it by influencing and determining not only immediate behaviour and habits, but also underlying attitudes and opinions. Government ads are especially strong on the transmission of information but now seem to be moving away from this traditional role and even away from broadcasting warnings of specific health and welfare dangers, towards a wider objective of education, that of preparing and moulding the citizen for life within the community. Commercial ads have different perspectives, of course: they are adept at creating new solutions and at creating new wants, but the goods and services they promote may prove acceptable and even essential or be rejected as the culture evolves. Equally, rhythms need to be respected in the promotional process: intensity and novelty must be associated with convention and to some extent must match with expectations. Shock tactics are a double-edged sword: sudden impacts may be short-lived and even counter-productive, the consumer and the citizen need to be persuaded and cajoled as well as bullied, although exactly who or what this consumer is, or more properly these consumers are, is of course a major question, for they too are constantly being influenced and modified both quantitatively and qualitatively by the ambient culture.

From these remarks, it would seem clear that the techniques of communication need to evolve to meet differing circumstances. Some things have not changed, of course. From the start, British television ads have appealed to elements of a common cultural heritage, (identifiable scenes, national customs and everyday activities for instance) as a means of gaining viewers' confidence and inviting their more or less willing and conscious complicity in the process of transmission and understanding of the commercial message. The growing 'literacy' and awareness on the part of the public of the way in which they may be manipulated, along with developments within the medium of television itself, have led to advertising adopting new tactics or integrating different techniques into established strategies. Most early commercials were firmly product-orientated, concentrating on basic performance claims, and slowly extended to include the benefits that the consumer could expect from the use of the goods in question. Gradually, the more innovative of ads moved away from these methods to develop the idea of more indirect, more subtle and perhaps more insidious promotion, accompanying the brand with favourable images to give it an added value. The final stage of development was reached when advertising became an element of quality in its own right, for example thanks to its innovative or aesthetic features, thereby indirectly giving a positive reflection of the goods or services in question. Such progress has not been uniform or universal. Each advertiser may choose to promote his products in the way he judges most suitable: the length of adverts and the technical devices employed depend on a careful assessment of the best way to achieve satisfactory communication with the target audience. Although the main innovations in technique are indicated in the following chapters, many commercials still content themselves with the application of the most obvious and least imaginative methods.

The broad definition indicated above of 'culture' explains much of the appeal and interest of TV ads. The more limited definition of the term 'cultural', 'of or relating to artistic or social pursuits or events considered to be valuable or enlightened' is, however, also relevant. Television commercials are certainly very rarely elements of 'high' culture, but the inevitable association of the two media, advertising and television, indicates that commercials do indeed represent a form of 'popular culture' in their own right. The aesthetic qualities of ads are frequently limited, if undeniable, while their recourse to intertextual allusions enhances their status as 'magpie genre', referring to and exploiting elements from a whole range of recognisable and related sources. Similarities between television adverts and the programmes that surround them enhance the familiarity and communicational power of the commercials themselves, while they make it increasingly clear that adverts are part and parcel of the spectacle of television and therefore an intrinsic part of this aspect of popular culture.

TV ads are therefore subject to duality and ambivalence, attributable partly to their status as a double medium, but equally to the fact that they are conditioned by the inherently incompatible dichotomies which they try to reconcile. One may immediately think of the individual and the collective, of the realistic and the fantastic (a substantial field for debate and analysis in its own right), of innovation and convention, but it is equally true that each or all or none of such divergent poles may be present at any given moment. Ads are infinitely variable and flexible and may be memorable or effective, or both or neither according to the subjective judgement of sections of the viewing audience, or again may have a deliberately ludic quality, inviting the public to participate and finally be caught up in a half serious game where the rules are known in advance but which nevertheless traps the unwary. They are also ephemeral: today's innovation may be tomorrow's commonplace, since intertextuality is another constantly growing field and, although direct plagiarism is rare, good ideas circulate rapidly. Similarly, the shocking rapidly becomes familiar, anodine and even politically correct. Very few things, and certainly not TV ads, resist the pressures of cultural change, although it is arguably the desire for self-image and self-projection which has helped British commercials to remain largely national in a world of global communications. The following chapters will endeavour to explain and to analyse the particularities of British commercials and to consider how far they are a motor, serving to further cultural change or simply a mirror, reflecting and illustrating changing cultural identities.

Notes

1   My translation of "*La télévision britannique est peut-être à l'image du peuple britannique d'aujourd'hui. À condition de bien voir qu'il s'agit d'une télévision et d'un peuple ancrés dans une tradition, mais ouverts et changeants. Une ouverture et un changement auxquels la télévision peut contribuer parce qu'elle les montre sans prétendre les imposer.*" Monica Charlot (Ed.), *La transmission des valeurs par la télévision britannique*, Paris, Presses de la Sorbonne Nouvelle, 1989, page 12.

2   Martin Davidson, *The Consumerist Manifesto, Advertising in Postmodern Times*, London, Routledge, 1992, page 3.

3   Comments made in *The Getaway People*, in the BBC series *Washes Whiter*, May 1990.

4   Quoted here from F. Kermode, *Selected Prose of T. S. Eliot*, London, Faber & Faber, 1975, pages 297 and 298.

I
Codes and proprieties

The nature of television advertising today is the product of numerous factors. The financial interests of advertisers and the ambient economic climate have long exercised a strong influence, consumer and consumerist pressures have been experienced and are being felt in various degrees and, in different ways, the concerns and preoccupations of government and its constituent ministries can be more or less easily observed and identified. In addition, the legislative framework and the decisions and functions of the various regulatory bodies governing television advertisements have played a substantial role both in determining the characteristics of commercials themselves and in moulding the consumer's attitude to them. At the simplest level, the various codes and guidelines have been instrumental in deciding what may be advertised and, more significantly, the way in which this may be done, thereby determining for the advertising professional the limits of creativity and suggesting to the viewer the boundaries of acceptability. It could moreover be argued that the regulations were initially drawn up in such a way as to correspond to and to inculcate a certain vision of 'Britishness', both in the apparently indirect way in which the control was to be exercised, by a government-nominated body rather than by a ministry, and by the reference to such socially – and culturally – defined concepts as good taste and decency. The treatment of such subjective notions undoubtedly gives an insight into the way in which the British television viewer was expected to situate himself and to react with regard to society and social phenomena. At the same time, the presence of codes offered the viewer a number of parameters by which to interpret and evaluate the propriety of what he was being shown.

Public attitudes to such questions as morality, religion and sexuality have, not surprisingly, moved on since the appearance of the first commercials in 1955 and, with the current growth of the world-wide media scene, today's norms and criteria will almost certainly prove to be much less long-lived than those of the past. It would seem that both evolution and permanence are abiding features of the regulation of television advertisements, for case histories and past judgements count for much in a domain where regulation reflects, sometimes inaccurately, but continues to influence popular perception in matters of taste, decency and acceptability. There is, moreover, greater public awareness of the issues involved. The first regulations were devised primarily to help advertisers and their agencies to come to the correct decisions, but the process has become increasingly open to public scrutiny, discussion and criticism. Despite its regular recourse to expert advice, the decisions taken by today's regulatory body, the ITC, are frequently called into question, the channels available for the registering of complaints are more widely known and permit the viewer to become involved, if not in the drafting of codes, then at least in their interpretation. The development of codes has generally been slow and conservative, consultation and transparency have been key notions, but we may still wonder the extent to which decisions have been made in the interest of the public as a whole or for the benefit of particular special interest groups and how closely they have reflected actual cultural trends and attitudes.

The preparations for commercial television

British commercial television has been closely regulated from the outset, but this control has taken place 'at arm's length' from the government of the day. The successive organisations responsible for independent television have been duty bound to ensure that the broadcasting companies conform to Acts of Parliament and have been required to produce their own regulations and guidelines, ensuring that transmissions are in accordance both with the law of the land and with the general standards of propriety. Television advertising, in fact, is broadly required to obey the same rules as television programmes, in such matters as taste and decency and the portrayal and protection of vulnerable sections of the community. Beyond these common points, however, it has always been subject to more stringent control than the programmes themselves: the techniques of advertisements, with their repetitions, their brevity and the impact caused by the use of sound and picture, not to mention their supposed intrusiveness, have led to the abiding perception that, in this field, the public needs specific and more rigorous protection. This stance was no doubt a reaction to the very real fears expressed, at the time of the introduction of independent television, about the presence of advertisements on a medium so far untainted by financial gain. Certain influential sectors of British society opposed the introduction of a commercial service, which was likened by Lord Reith in a notable outburst in the House of Lords to a pestilence.[1] For some, even the name 'Independent Television' was a deliberate ploy, craftily conceived to hide the venal interests of the new channel behind a flattering exterior. The arguments on both sides of the debate are of some interest in the consideration of independent television, with its advertisements, as a uniquely British institution. The desire on the part of the supporters of the new service was clearly the advancement of material progress and prosperity after the gloomy austerity of the war and the early 1950s. Their vision of what 'Britishness' was, and needed to become, was typical of what the optimism of the day termed the 'new Elizabethan era'. The opponents of commercial broadcasting were activated above all by desire for the maintenance of the standards of public service broadcasting as exemplified by the programmes offered by the BBC. The divisions between the two groups ran broadly along party political lines with the Labour opposition even threatening to put an end to the commercial experiment if the party was returned to power in the 1955 General

Election. Even though this menace did not materialise, there was clearly strong pressure for British television to distinguish itself from the sole advertising-financed model known at the time, the American TV networks. Opponents of commercial broadcasting pointed to the excesses of the American way of advertising, quoting the legendary transmission of an advertisement for a brand of tea, featuring a chimpanzee, one J. Fred Muggs, during NBC's coverage of the Coronation of Queen Elizabeth II. The feeling of shock and intrusion was even greater as it was the young queen herself who had pleaded for the cameras to be allowed into Westminster Abbey for the ceremony. Those concerned with the quality of television at the time did not hesitate to evoke the manifest failings of the American example. Many shows in the United States were directly produced for and controlled by sponsors and he who paid the piper undoubtedly called the tune. Broadcasts were often of a banality calculated to avoid offending even the most susceptible of potential consumers, while the frequent intrusive and inappropriate promotional messages mentioning the name and products of the paymaster further limited the coherence of the programming.

On the other hand, if such commercial extravagance was to be avoided, there was also a danger in the new British service being too closely controlled by the government. If one accepts the notion of ITV as 'independent' television, then, by inference, the BBC must be 'state' television, with undertones of a strong measure of government control. What has often been referred to as a 'British compromise' in the constitution of independent television, and in the regulation of advertisements has, it may be argued, managed to avoid the extremes of unrestricted freedom or of over-rigid restriction. The Television Act of 1954 ordered the creation of a regulatory body which was responsible for the control of commercial television, the Independent Television Authority (ITA). The names and scope of the regulatory Authority have evolved over the years. In 1972, the ITA became the Independent Broadcasting Authority (IBA) with a larger remit requiring it to supervise not only commercial television but also the newly created Independent Local Radio stations. In 1983, further technological progress led to the birth of cable television, which was to be overseen by the Cable Authority and, following the Broadcasting Act of 1990, there are now two bodies respectively responsible for independent radio and independent television, the Radio Authority (RA) and the Independent Television Commission (ITC) which regulates terrestrial television services along with the ever-growing number of cable and satellite operations originating in the United Kingdom. It is also to set the norms for the newly-created digital services. In both cases, the new bodies are responsible on a day-to-day basis for the regulation of programmes and advertisements, as well as for weighty questions such as the choice of franchise holders and the maintenance of technical standards. The 10 members of the ITC, including the Chairman and Deputy Chairman are appointed by the government minister responsible for broadcasting; the Commission itself then chooses its own executive employees. This indirect relationship between government and broadcasters in the independent sector is broadly similar to the model created for the BBC with the appointment of its Board of Governors, who then select the

Director General. Care is taken to ensure the representation of regional, national and sectional interests, by the appointment of members specifically chosen for their affinities with Northern Ireland, Scotland and Wales or for their ability to represent ethnic minorities.

The status of television as a feature of national life and culture has continued to grow throughout the years of existence of commercial television. Initially and for largely historical reasons, broadcasting was under the control of the Postmaster General, whose department also collected radio and television licence fees, the proceeds from which were then paid to the BBC. In 1969, the minister was renamed, more appropriately, Minister of Posts and Telecommunications. Five years later the Home Office took over responsibility for television, which passed in 1992 under the control of the newly-created Department of National Heritage. The title of this ministry was characterised by some critics as backward-looking, indicating an exaggerated concern with the nostalgia and tradition of the past at the expense of the vigour of the future. The change of name which the ministry underwent in 1997, when it became the Department for Culture, Media and Sport, would seem to answer these criticisms and appears to link the media even more cogently with other more dynamic aspects of cultural identity, reflecting the interests, attitudes and concerns of the nation's citizens on a daily basis.

In 1954, when the first Television Act was passed by Parliament, and in the following year, when the fledgling ITV started its broadcasts, television advertising in the United Kingdom was an unexplored and largely unknown field. The task facing the television system set up by the Conservative government was therefore to explore and define unfamiliar territory, with potentially hostile observers on every side. The American model had been judged unworthy of imitation while elsewhere in Europe the channels with advertising were essentially hybrid creations which drew their resources both from the national equivalents of the licence fee and from commercial advertising. The United Kingdom, with its creation of a fully independent channel to rival the fully government-financed BBC, was truly facing a new, exciting but potentially risky challenge. If nowadays, television advertising is taken for granted in Great Britain, then it should be remembered that this was not always the case and, more importantly, that the acceptance which TV commercials enjoy today has been achieved over a substantial period and that the first controls on advertising were essential steps in this process of credibility. The administrative and legislative solution to the problem of intrusiveness, the much-vaunted notion of 'British difference', went beyond specifying the type of publicity allowed (spot advertisements and not sponsorship), to cover the limits which should be imposed on commercial freedom and ultimately to define the tone and content of the commercials themselves. The polite applause from the invited Guildhall audience, which greeted the first advertising break on commercial television on 22 September 1955 was motivated, no doubt, as much by relief that the worst had been avoided as by satisfaction at the creative qualities of the spots themselves. John

Betjeman referred to these first offerings as 'reassuringly British', while Brian Henry notes their rigorously un-controversial tone.[2]

The 'British difference' was equally noticeable in the controls and regulations to be imposed on the new service. The Television Act of 1954 granted a substantial number of powers to the Independent Television Authority, while imposing on it, for the control of advertising, considerable restrictions and obligations and leaving the ultimate responsibility with the Postmaster General. It is easy to forget after over 40 years of largely uncontested commercial broadcasting, just how experimental the new service was and to what extent questions were decided on an ad hoc basis. The ITA's specific obligations, as laid down in the Television Act of 1954 in matters of advertising, were of various sorts. It was to appoint a committee (duly established in January 1955 as the Advertising Advisory Committee or AAC), to ensure that misleading adverts were not broadcast and to draw up a series of principles governing the acceptance of advertisements. Paradoxical though it may seem, the ITA was itself obliged to comply and assure compliance with the decisions of this committee which it had itself appointed,[3] but it should be remembered that the AAC contained members specialising in certain fields, notably medicine, in which the members of the ITA were unlikely to be adequately versed.

The Television Act itself set out the latitude available to advertisers, emphasising in somewhat ambiguous terms that sponsored broadcasts were not acceptable, insisting that advertisements should be clearly distinguishable and separate from the remaining programming and that advertising proposed by religious or political bodies, or directed to religious or political ends, was not allowed. The second schedule of the Act went on to indicate other (considerable) fields where the ITA was to have the final say. The Authority was left to decide on the amount of time to be allowed for advertisements and the gaps to be observed between advertising breaks, subject to the somewhat vague stipulation that '... the amount of time given to advertising in programmes shall not be so great as to detract from the value of the programmes as a medium of entertainment, instruction and information'.[4] Religious services were, according to the Television Act, not to be interrupted by commercial breaks, but the Authority was charged with determining to which additional classes of broadcasts similar restrictions should apply and what interval should separate such programmes from preceding or following advertising. Finally, the Authority had the general duty to appoint the different contractors licensed to provide services in the various regions and to oversee the tariffs for advertising slots proposed.

From these details it is clear that, although advertising was an area in which Parliament judged that particular vigilance was necessary, the supervision of commercials was, for the most part, left to the discretion of the ITA and its AAC. The Television Act was striking for its failure to give precise guidance on matters of principle and interpretation, and it is tempting to surmise that the politicians were relatively pleased to leave to their nominees in the ITA the tricky task of managing the day-to-day operations and establishing the overall ethos of ITV. There may be various reasons for this reticence, but it seems a clear sign that commercial broadcasting was something of an unknown quantity and that its advocates were unwilling on both ideological and practical grounds to become too involved in the daily management of the new service. The ITA had the distinct advantage of being able to rely on the professional recommendations to be obtained from its Advertising Advisory Committee whose members were chosen for the most part because of their specialist knowledge in the fields of advertising or of medicine. The presence of medical specialists on the AAC was specifically required by the Television Act and all the codes and regulations drafted by the AAC and later by the ITA and its successors have contained sections dealing with the promotion of goods and services in this field where the consumer might be deemed to be especially vulnerable. The chairman of the initial committee was an advertising executive, R.A. Bevan, and the professional associations, the Advertising Association (AA), the Incorporated Society of British Advertisers (ISBA) and the Institute of Practitioners in Advertising (IPA), were all represented on the committee, along with the Ministry of Health, the British Medical Association (BMA), the British Dental Association and the Pharmaceutical Society. What is interesting to note is the absence of consumer representation, a point which was to be raised with some vigour by the Pilkington Committee in the early 1960s. In the mid-1950s, of course, such interests were less widely recognised than nowadays and the consumerist movement was not even in its infancy when commercial television was first broadcast in the United Kingdom. This was just one of the new phenomena with which television advertising would have to cope in coming years.

First 'Principles'

The AAC met for the first time in January 1955, still some eight months before ITV took to the air, and faced the difficult task of drawing up the first code for television advertising which appeared on 2nd June 1955, after approval by both the ITA and the Postmaster General. The document, entitled *Principles for Television Advertising*, sensibly took into account the voluntary codes in application in other forms of advertising and opened with the statement that 'all television advertising should be legal, clean, honest and truthful', criteria which remain enshrined in regulations to this day.[5] The *Principles* took the form of a general code with two appendices, the first devoted to detailed rules about specific categories and methods of advertising and the second dealing with medicines and treatments. Misleading claims, disparaging references, testimonials, guarantees, competitions and advertising in children's programmes were all specifically mentioned and regulated.[6] Critics generally accept that this document was relatively unrestrictive, agreeing with Bernard Sendall's judgement that it was 'boldly liberal'.[7] The forbidden categories of products and services were, in fact, very few in number. Money lenders, fortune tellers and matrimonial agencies were deemed unacceptable, smoking cures and products for the treatment of alcoholism were also banned, while, curiously, the promotion of tobacco and alcohol in all their forms was not. Significantly, the committee failed to reach any immediate conclusion about betting and football pools, a field which, as we shall see, was to be the source of some heated debate. In general terms, the evolution of codes is typical of what has happened in television advertising as a whole. The amount of legislation relating to the subject has grown at an ever-quickening pace over the years: questions which at one time appeared straightforward can no longer be handled with the manicheistic simplicity of a blanket ban and greater liberalisation has brought with it increased complexity in the formulation of codes and regulations. It is nevertheless striking, and typical of the progression and continuity in British television advertising, that so many of the initial decisions, which were taken at a stage when the medium was in gestation rather than in infancy should have proved to have been so accurate and so long-lasting. The desire to build on what has already been established rather than to overturn or revolutionise the whole process has characterised the medium as a whole, at least until comparatively recently. The initial years of commercial television were formative in every way: ITV's programming has always tended to attract particular socio-economic groups and the decisions concerning advertising, taken in the distant days of the 1950s, still influence regulation and practice today.

At the same time as the AAC was formulating its first document, the ITA was also faced with important decisions on advertising which were duly accepted in May 1955 by the new Postmaster General, Dr Charles Hill.[8] It was the Authority which suggested that all appearances of the Royal Family should, along with church services, be insulated by two minutes from advertising and that there should be a minimum interval between consecutive commercial breaks. Programmes could be interrupted at points marking 'natural breaks', a term which has never been clearly defined and which has been a periodic source of debate. Furthermore, the ITA proposed, to nobody's surprise, that the amount of advertising time should not exceed 10 per cent (or 6 minutes per hour). This figure was judged to be sufficient for advertisers and programme companies without being considered excessive by the viewing public. In fact, this regulation was applied with some flexibility: the six minutes of advertising time was to be an average over the whole broadcasting day and up to eight minutes of commercials were to be allowed in any one hour. Extra advertising capacity was to be offered by so-called 'advertising magazines', broadcasts of programme length in which various, sometimes unconnected, products were promoted within a recognisable framework created either by a physical setting or by the presence of regular presenters. In 1956, another body which was to exercise control over advertisements saw the light of day. The three programme companies created the Television Programme Contractors' Association (or TPCA),[9] which also set up its own advertising committee. The objectives of the ITA and the TPCA were necessarily divergent and conflicts and differences of opinion arose later between the Authority and its contractors but, in the early days of advertising, the TPCA represented another element of the self-policing method set up following the 1954 Television Act.

Early decisions

So far we have examined the rules concerning advertisements which were drawn up before broadcasting itself started. Once ITV went on air, the limitations of and omissions in these regulations at once began to be felt and the ITA was called upon to take a growing number of decisions and was subject to a number of conflicting pressures. It had to uphold the values of 'public service broadcasting' by ensuring that, while viewers were entertained, standards of taste and decency were both set and maintained. It was further required to defend the viewing public against misleading advertisements (as specified in the Television Act), while allowing adequate opportunity for the programme companies to sell advertising spots. Public acceptance of advertisements was likely to be conditioned not only by the nature and quality of the promotions themselves, but also by the extent to which they were perceived as a natural part of television and not an unwanted intrusion. A substantial number of important decisions were taken in the initial years of commercial television which attempted to steer a course amidst these various obstacles and hazards.

Whether, in the controlling of television advertising, it is possible to see the presence of a consistent policy is, however, quite another question. It should not be forgotten, when we come to examine the late 1950s, that the preliminary estimates of the profitability of the programme companies were wildly exaggerated. Associated-Rediffusion (A-R) and Associated TeleVision (ATV) both lost enormous sums of money[10] and the fledgling network was only able to achieve financial stability as rapidly as it did thanks to the deliberate choice of popular programming. As Roland Gillett, the Controller of Programmes at A-R put it, in a now famous observation:

> Let's face it once and for all. The public like girls, wrestling, bright musicals, quiz shows and real-life drama. We gave them the Hallé orchestra, Foreign Press Club, floodlit football, and visits to the local fire station. Well, we've learned. From now on, what the public wants, it's going to get.

The lesson concerning advertising was similar: the ITA could not afford to be too rigid in its approach. If advertising air time was occupied to an undue extent by commercials for washing and cleaning products and certain medical preparations, then this was the price that had to be paid for commercial viability. Advertising magazines, although their legal status remained questionable in the light of the rules against sponsorship in the Television Act, were not only a useful source of revenue, but they were popular and provided opportunities for smaller businesses to gain access to the medium at relatively modest cost. Frequent commercial breaks were another way to allow programme companies to achieve higher revenues. These observations only represent part of the picture, however, for ITV was still in the process of creating its own programming identity, a task in which advertising came to play an accepted part. Increasing emphasis was put, in the late 1950s, on ITV as being what the Director General of the ITA, Sir Robert Fraser was pleased to call 'people's television'.[11] From this optimistic viewpoint, advertising could be regarded not only as the necessary paymaster of the new service, but its contributions were considered as part of the popular spectacle itself. Advertisements brought to the medium their own aesthetic and creative qualities, while the regulations on timing imposed by the ITA did not prevent advertisers, in the early days, from ensuring, by judicious purchasing of air time, that their commercials were broadcast during, and became intimately associated with, certain well-loved and popular broadcasts. If not always welcomed, commercials were thus part of the entertainment offered by ITV. Supporters of television advertising were pleased to emphasise that it could be and was 'controlled' (Sendall) or 'domesticated' (Potter) and held that a major part of this discipline was due to the standards imposed by parliament and by the ITA's readiness to enforce them. This positive view was voiced by Anthony Bracknell, former Secretary General to the ITA's Advisory Committee and later Deputy Director-General of the Authority, in the following glowing terms:

> *Through the exercise of its statutory powers and with the cooperation of the television companies and the advertising business the Authority has shown that the savage beast of advertising which it was once feared would stalk through our living rooms can be domesticated.*[12]

There are of course contrary opinions. By the end of the 1950s, the notion of 'people's television' was itself under pressure, while the poor quality and excessive frequency of many advertisements was undoubtedly causing adverse public reaction.

The first years of the controlling of television advertising were inevitably as experimental as the creation of rules which had preceded the launch of ITV. The inevitable new ideas in programming, along with unexpected commercial constraints presented the ITA and the AAC with a number of questions to be resolved. When schools television was first broadcast, a notable scoop for ITV incidentally, since Associated-Rediffusion's first programmes in 1957 preceded the BBC's service, it was decided that the programmes should be isolated from advertisements in the same way as those involving the Royal Family. Similarly, the Authority declared that news bulletins were also to be free of commercial breaks. It is possible to see here both the effects of the notion of public service broadcasting and the need to protect vulnerable groups in society. The financial effects of these decisions were not entirely negative, however. All programmes counted as broadcasting time and even in cases where commercials were not directly permitted, they 'earned' advertising time, which could then be exploited at other moments of the day. It was not until the controversial launch of *News at Ten*, in 1967, that the rules were relaxed and news bulletins were interrupted for the first time.[13]

The supposed need to maintain moral values was behind a number of decisions made in the early years, which were also an indication of what 'good taste' was deemed to be. In February 1957, the Advertising Committee of the TPCA decided to ban advertising for haemorrhoid remedies and to restrict the advertising of toilet paper until after 9.30 p.m., while the question of betting raised other, perhaps more profound, issues. The AAC's *Principles for Television Advertising* specifically forbade all forms of betting. In 1957, ITV's first broadcast of a horse race, the St Leger from Doncaster, was accompanied by the indication of starting prices. Some television companies seized on this apparent tolerance or encouragement of the practice of gambling to urge that advertising the widespread and relatively innocuous betting on football matches, by football pools, should be allowed. The AAC thought otherwise, however, and the ban was maintained. Subsequent attempts in 1970 and 1983 to allow adverts for football pools were no more successful, even though betting shops had been opened in Britain's high streets after the passing of the Betting and Gaming Act of 1960. At much the same time as these first attempts to change the *Principles*, the need to protect the public against the wiles of advertisers was recognised by the decision of the ITA to forbid advertisements featuring well-known television personalities within thirty minutes of programmes including them appearing on screen. In 1958, a case of considerable significance arose. General messages of thanks and goodwill from industrialists to their customers were a common feature at the festive seasons of the 1950s, but when the chairman of J. Lyons and Co. made a two-minute commercial to be broadcast on New Year's Eve, which was to expound his company's aims of providing the best possible service to the customer, the ITA was concerned that this kind of 'opinion advertising' could rapidly develop into an invitation to the public to invest in the company concerned, at a time when the advertising of stocks and shares was expressly forbidden by the *Principles for Television Advertising*. The Authority duly banned such commercials, but the problem, as became apparent over the coming years, was how and where to draw the line between the legitimate promotion of individual products, the careful nurturing of a brand image and the implicit recommendation of a well-presented company to prospective investors.

As part of the desire to protect the public came the formalisation of control arrangements. When we consider the machinery for examining advertisements in these early years, the striking thing is the relatively modest degree of day-to-day supervision. Before 1963, the ITA had no machinery in place to view advertisements and the provisions of the *Principles for Television Advertising*, despite their clear and categorical nature, were limited in scope. The task of advising advertisers, agencies and television companies on matters of presentation and of content (concerning the claims which could or could not be made for products) fell not to the Authority, but to the Advertising Committee of the TPCA, which had in 1955, formed a working group to check commercials at the pre-transmission stage. By 1957, the Copy Committee was organised on a full-time basis, with a regular staff and, two years later, it appointed members representing the BMA, the pharmaceutical industry and the fields of pharmacology and nutrition. For its part, the ITA was slowly becoming more involved. In 1958 it issued a formal document, *Advertising Rules and Practices*, to cover questions of the timing and organisation of advertising breaks and, the following year, the Authority appointed its first Head of Advertising Control.

While, by the end of the 1950s, the task of controlling and supervising advertisements was becoming more and more complex, the novelty of commercials was beginning to pall and the ITA and television companies were obliged to take into account the opinions not only of advertisers' bodies, the ISBA and the IPA, but also of professional specialist interest groups such as the BMA which wanted much stricter regulation of medical claims[14] and of certain Labour Party politicians.[15] Viewers too were becoming more critical. These adverse pressures were tacitly acknowledged by a number of measures taken in 1960. The maximum advertising time per hour was reduced from 8 minutes (8.5 minutes on weekends) to 7.5 minutes in September and to 7 minutes in December. At the same time, so-called 'qualitative' advertising improvements eliminated some 20 per cent of advertising breaks within programmes, with documentaries and children's programmes being transmitted uninterrupted. The ITA had realised that viewers were becoming less and less tolerant of the sheer repetitiveness, not to say the banality, of advertisements promoting washing powders and household cleaning products, the vast majority of them from two advertisers, Unilever and Thomas Hedley (a subsidiary of Procter & Gamble). Antagonising such major advertisers was a high-risk procedure for ITV companies,[16] but a decision had to be reached. In September 1960, the Authority decided to act by producing lists of what it called 'kitchen' or 'laundry' products and only allowing advertisements for one of each to be broadcast in any given hour. This restriction was subsequently relaxed to allow more than one product to be promoted within the hour, provided the commercials were not transmitted in consecutive breaks.

It is tempting to see in this decision both the ITA's greater awareness of the interests of the viewer and its need not to be perceived as favouring simple commercial considerations at the expense of all others. In the light of the appointment of the Pilkington Committee to investigate the whole future of television broadcasting, the Authority's action seemed, if somewhat belated, an eminently sensible step. Nevertheless, as critics did not hesitate to point out, the actions of the ITA were not solely altruistic. Even the changes concerning programme breaks could be said to have been motivated by financial interest. Companies were aware that, on the occasions when BBC and ITV programmes began or ended at the same time, a certain amount of changing of channels occurred, which was not necessarily to ITV's disadvantage, but which did lead to fluctuations in the number of viewers, whose loyalty to the commercial channel was the television companies' ultimate argument in negotiations with advertisers. 1960 brought other changes. High advertising rates led to 30-second commercials becoming the norm, while the Conservative government realised that television advertising was a potential source of income to the Exchequer which had so far remained untapped. The introduction in May 1961 of Television Advertisement Duty, at the modest rate of 10 per cent, was the beginning of a long-running dispute over taxation between the ITV companies and successive governments.

The early years of television advertising control went through various stages. The underlying rules and principles which exist today were established during the first formative years, but it was already clear that the new medium was to be subject to permanent but varied pressures and that unexpected difficulties were always likely to arise. Nevertheless, the accuracy of the initial evaluations made by the legislators and the ITA remains remarkable and if the Authority erred on the side of proposing measures and delivering judgements helpful to the launch and extension of the new network, at the expense of consumer interests, then this was understandable. The ITV companies had also shown, through their own decisions on matters of good taste and the temptations of gambling, an occasional ability to look beyond immediate commercial interests. The favourable public climate was, however, destined not to last. ITV was, in one sense, a victim of its own success, the initial programmes and accompanying advertisements had represented a welcome change for a public previously limited to a single and rather stodgy state-run channel. Once the commercial network was firmly in place, this impression of initiative and invention soon began to wear thin, the more so as television companies and advertisers were all-too-ready to content themselves with formulae which had already proved lucrative. Despite the declarations about the importance of 'people's television', there was growing dissatisfaction in some quarters with the lack of variety and quality in programming and with the overtly profit-seeking philosophy of ITV. This displeasure was to be fully voiced by the Pilkington Report in 1962.

From Pilkington to Annan

The Committee on Broadcasting, under the industrialist Harry Pilkington, was charged not only with examining the current state of British television, but also with supplying recommendations for the future. It received evidence for close on two years and was obviously much more impressed by the BBC than by its commercial competitor. Besides advising that the Corporation should be granted the right to run the new third television channel and to introduce colour transmissions as soon as possible, the Committee showed itself hostile to the way the ITA had managed the network and even to the principle of commercial broadcasting itself. The Authority was castigated for its excessively cosy relationship with the television companies,[17] and the Committee proposed that it should take firm control over ITV, by drawing up programming schedules and by taking responsibility for selling commercial air time. In the event, neither of these suggestions for what the Committee dubbed 'organic change' was implemented, but it clearly believed that, while television was a medium with a powerful influence for good or ill, with ITV it was the latter that prevailed.[18] It concluded that there was a fundamental conflict of interests between public service television and the needs of advertisers. It might therefore have been expected that the Pilkington Report would have a major effect on commercial television, but the public mood was far from being as hostile as that of the members of the Committee and both major parties in Parliament were aware that ITV was sufficiently popular and well-established for intervention to be risky, especially in what was a pre-election period. The loss of the third channel to the BBC was a severe blow of course, but the impact of the Report on advertising was relatively modest. Pilkington recommended the ending of advertising magazines and the Postmaster General decided, having seen that the ITV companies still obstinately maintained them in their schedules for autumn 1962, to ban this type of broadcast on his own authority without waiting for new legislation. The programmes were taken off the air from 31st March 1963 and the 1963 Television Act contained two clauses in its second schedule which were intended to prevent their being resurrected, by specifying that successive advertisements were to be recognisably separate and that advertisements were not to be presented in such a way as to appear part of a continuous feature. The Television Acts of 1963 and 1964 offered greater viewer protection by outlawing so-called subliminal advertising and noisy commercials while maintaining the ban on the promotion of religious or political interests.

The principal changes concerning advertising lay in the role and tasks assigned to the Authority, which reflected the concerns of the Pilkington Committee about the general lack of control and direction of ITV, but the amendments represented rather an extension and a reinforcement of current practice, than radical change. The AAC was to remain in existence, but its role was more closely confined to that indicated by its title, an advisory capacity, and the ITA was also to consult with a panel of independent medical experts. The major difference was that it was now the Authority which was responsible for:

> ...draw[ing] up, and from time to time review[ing], a code governing standards and practice in advertising and prescribing the advertisements and methods of advertising to be prohibited, or prohibited in certain circumstances.

The first *Independent Television Code of Advertising Standards and Practice* duly appeared in July 1964. More importantly, it became the duty of the Authority to 'ensure compliance' with the rules contained within the Code, which required the setting up of new and more complex procedures of copy control. So far, the TPCA and the ITCA had dealt with the viewing and modifying of advertisements before transmission, with reference to the ITA only in cases of doubt. From 1964, relations on advertising were formalised between the ITCA and the ITA by the creation of a new body, the Joint Advertising Control Committee (JACC), which was to meet regularly to ensure uniformity of view. In addition, the ITA also set up its own viewing committee, to operate in parallel with the ITCA's copy committee, to check conformity of the finished advertisements with the proposed scripts and, ultimately, to decide whether or not, and subject to what restrictions, commercials could be screened.

The task of regulating advertisements was becoming increasingly complex and these new measures soon proved to be more than necessary at a time when the need for the public to be protected against unscrupulous or less than truthful claims was a serious concern. There had always been commercials which might have been regarded as misleading and the Pilkington Committee had apparently accepted the evidence it had received from the Advertising Inquiry Council[19] namely that some 5 to 8 per cent of all advertisements fell into this category.

Medical advertising was a particular problem. As early as 1961, complaints from the BMA had led to a more critical examination of terms used in commercials, and such well-known but ambiguous expressions as Aspro's *'One degree under'* were banished, while the public was to be protected from the potential dangers of celebrities persuading them of the benefits of various proprietary remedies. In the climate after the Pilkington Report, opinions became even more critical. By the 1964-1965 television season, some 20 per cent of advertisements for medical products required some amendment, most often by the removal of the impression that the presenters of the products were medically qualified to discuss the preparations they were extolling. Quite another question was raised by cigarette advertisements in the early 1960s. In 1962, the ITA, mindful of medical evidence on both sides of the Atlantic, had determined that cigarette commercials should not be shown before 9 p.m., in an evident attempt to avoid subjecting children to harmful influences. By 1965, the pressure was such that the Postmaster General reached the unilateral decision to forbid all such advertisements on television, a sure sign of the perceived power of influence of the medium, since other forms of advertising did not immediately suffer the same fate.

The 1960s saw a growing complexity in the legislation affecting advertising: the ITA was required to update its codes regularly and there were an increasing number of laws on advertising-related subjects.[20] The boundaries of what was acceptable or desirable were in constant movement. It is true, in the 1960s and 1970s, that certain principles of television advertising remained unaltered: in 1969, commercials for *The Bible Today* were prohibited as being examples of religious advertising, while the Conservative government's attempts to persuade the public to obtain leaflets about EEC entry in 1971 and the Labour administration's efforts to promote its anti-inflation campaign in 1975 both fell foul of the ban on political advertising. The promotion of football pools was still forbidden. Perennial problems arose over such matters as the definition of 'natural breaks' and the use of familiar ITV presenters in advertisements resembling their own programmes. On the other hand, *News at Ten* broke the tradition of news bulletins as advertisement free zones, while attitudes to questions of taste and decency were becoming more flexible. Nudity was not allowed, but greater amounts of flesh were becoming visible, contraceptives and sanitary products would have to wait a little longer to be taken off the proscribed list, but false teeth and lavatory pans could be shown. The sheer volume of advertisements was a challenge in itself: by the mid-1970s, some 9,000 new national commercials a year were being viewed by the ITCA and the IBA.

Fundamental questions resurfaced in 1972, when the House of Commons Select Committee on Nationalised Industries (SCNI) proposed a number of changes which, if implemented, would have completely transformed the regulation of advertisements. The Committee advocated a stricter interpretation of the Television Act's rules concerning 'natural breaks', the broadcasting of government-originated health and safety announcements in peak time, the networking of programmes in which consumer tests and advertising claims could be examined and the grouping of advertisements in blocks of up to 30 minutes, as was the practice in some continental countries. Needless to say, the final suggestion alone would have brought into doubt the viability of the whole British ITV network which, unlike its equivalents in mainland Europe, was almost totally dependent on advertising as its source of revenue and the ITCA, along with the advertisers' professional associations, categorically rejected all such notions. Quite apart from the incentive they would give viewers to change channels, the proposed advertising 'blocks' could only accommodate a third of existing advertising time. As for the other suggestions made by the SCNI, the ITCA in its response to the Minister pointed out that government advertising campaigns were placed on a commercial basis in other media and that the free broadcasting of so-called 'fillers' supplied by the Central Office of Information for use in unsold advertising space had saved millions of pounds of taxpayers' money. The Authority maintained, for its part, that advertising breaks were under permanent supervision, that their number and duration had declined since 1955, while it felt that the consumer interest was best served by printed reports of findings and that the newly appointed government Minister for Consumer Affairs was best placed to judge on the protection of the purchaser. All in all, the Minister of Posts and Telecommunications concluded that the arguments of the Authority and its associates were well-founded, but the important decision on the allocation of the fourth television channel was postponed, as the Select Committee had proposed, until a full review of the future of broadcasting had been made. This was eventually to see the light of day as the Annan Committee which reported in 1977. The IBA, meanwhile, in its first code on advertisements which applied equally to radio and television, tightened up a number of regulations. Private investigation agencies were added to the list of prohibited products and services, ITV programme settings and characters could no longer be imitated in commercials and the use in advertisements of the term *news flash* was judged to be misleading and was therefore outlawed. It is fair to consider that the ministerial reaction to the SCNI's proposals was a vindication of the regulations in force and of their application and pointed again to the maintenance of a 'British approach' to the British situation of commercial television.

The conclusions reached by the Annan Committee in 1977 confirmed this view. The Committee received some 750 depositions from various organisations and groups and paid particular attention to the question of advertising. It finally rejected the notion raised by the Pilkington Committee of the centralised selling of advertising time and supported the existing principle of 'spot advertising'. The Committee was broadly satisfied with copy control procedures and went so far as to praise the originality and creativity of many advertisements which it felt were *an important element in the quality of a good public broadcasting service.* On the other hand, it advised that the public should be helped to have a greater awareness of the questions concerning advertising quality and to this end, expressed its desire that the IBA's Code of Advertising Standards and Practice should be made more widely available. There was, moreover, one area in which a majority of the Committee showed itself harder to please, the field of children's advertising. Additional protection was considered necessary and the Committee came out in favour of the prohibition of the advertising of products and services intended for children before 9 p.m., and of a blanket ban on advertisements in and around children's programmes. In their response to the Home Secretary, the ITCA and the IBA pointed out both that children were constantly subjected to all kinds of commercial promotion in their daily lives and that defining the categories of products to be forbidden before 9 p.m. was an almost impossible task. In the end, the only tangible effect of the Annan Committee's proposals was the outlawing of commercial breaks within children's programmes of less than 30 minutes duration. The Annan Committee had approved of the vast majority of the codes and practices adopted by the ITCA and the IBA, and many of its pleas for changes fell on deaf ears. Its hope that charitable organisations might be allowed to advertise was declined by an IBA working party reporting in 1978, although its firm recommendation that the BBC and the ITV should use the same system and organisation for assessing viewing figures was adopted, thus allowing contractors and advertisers to be more precise in their demands and services. The IBA's new code of Advertising Standards and Practice (1977) showed no revolutionary changes, but continued the kind of gradual liberalisation which had been observed over previous years, by permitting member firms of the Stock Exchange, slimming clinics and local authority lotteries to be promoted. The general pattern of controls remained largely unaltered and it is significant that, when Channel 4 (1982) and breakfast television (1983) took to the air, they were to be regulated in the same way as ITV and no specific adjustments to the existing rules were thought to be required.

Deregulation and Competition

The 1980s and even more the 1990s represented a time of substantial change in British television. The arrival of the new terrestrial services was matched by transformations of greater long-term significance, the advent of cable and satellite broadcasting. Cable television began in 1983 and the slow preparations for Direct Broadcasting by Satellite, under the auspices of the IBA were eventually shattered by the premature arrival of Rupert Murdoch's Sky Television which rapidly became the brand leader and proved itself to be less directly susceptible to requests from the regulatory bodies in force. At the same time the political climate had changed, with the free-market tendencies of Margaret Thatcher's Conservative government becoming ever more apparent and the question of advertising on some of the services of the BBC and privatisation of others being a topic of frequent discussion. In the event, it was the movement towards deregulation which was of the greatest importance for television advertising. The 1986 Financial Services Act led to the so-called 'Big Bang', the deregulation of the London Stock Exchange. This in turn was the trigger for a massive liberalisation of the advertising of financial services and products. These developments were enshrined for the first time in the IBA Code of Advertising Standards and Practice of 1989 which differed sharply from its predecessors in this regard,[21] and has proved sufficiently radical as the transformations since 1989 have been relatively modest in this field.

The creation of the ITC to replace the IBA was another significant step. The Commission has the responsibility for all television services originating in the UK but its legal status is different from that of its precursors. The ITC is the regulator (of programmes and advertisements) but not the broadcaster, in other words legal responsibility for transmissions lies with the individual contractors and cable and satellite operators and the ITC has an advisory and, if necessary, punitive role, in the day-to-day running of affairs. It is, however, still obliged to draw up codes of guidance covering engineering problems, programming, sponsorship and, of course, advertising. The 1990s have been marked by the growing commercialisation of independent television. The Broadcasting Act of 1990 lifted the blanket ban on sponsored broadcasts, which had been one of the most basic of principles of independent television, leaving the ITC with the ticklish task of regulating the effects of this potentially intrusive opening. According to the ITC itself, public reaction to sponsorship is characterised by acceptance or indifference, rather than outright hostility, but the Commission's codes on the subject, running to sixteen pages and, like the advertising code, regularly reviewed and renewed, seek to ensure that the process remains discreet and that no sponsor may gain an unfair advantage, for example by the placing of his products or by their indirect promotion in the course of programmes. Efforts are also made to ensure that the sponsorship of programmes is not used to circumvent the prohibition of advertising of certain products and services, or to arrange their promotion at times when it would not normally be authorised. The separation between the financing of the programmes and the determining of their content has been steadfastly maintained. The 1990s have seen a further general liberalisation of rules governing advertising: not only has the range of unacceptable products and services been progressively diminished, but the average time allowed for commercial promotion on terrestrial channels has been raised, since 1991, from 6 minutes per hour to 7 minutes. For cable and satellite services, the ITC determined not to impose greater restrictions on advertising than those required by the EU Directive *Television Without Frontiers* (of 1989 and regularly amended). Consequently, advertising time on channels other than ITV (including breakfast television), Channel 4 and Channel 5 is restricted to an hourly average of 9 minutes with a maximum of 12 minutes. Teleshopping channels are also authorised while up to three hours a day of so-called infomercials or advertorials lasting a minimum of 15 minutes each are allowed on channels not exclusively devoted to teleshopping.

This does not mean, however, that the fundamentals of advertising regulation have changed irrevocably. The status of the ITC, *vis-à-vis* the ministry responsible for broadcasting, has remained unaltered. The Commission continues to have its own panels of experts and the AAC is still in regular operation, considering suggestions for liberalisation and amendment and conducting its own research into public perception of and attitudes to certain types of advertising and products. The 1990 Broadcasting Act also recognised the need for the maintenance of standards in all forms of broadcasting by the creation of two organisations responsible for investigating complaints from the public into broadcasting standards. The remit of the Broadcasting Complaints Commission (BCC) was largely the same as that of the previous BCC set up on the advice of the Annan Committee, namely to ensure that members of the public were not misrepresented in programmes (and advertisements). The task of the Broadcasting Standards Council was to ensure co-operation of broadcasters in matters of taste and decency, and it was required to draw up its own codes of conduct, against which standards could be judged. These two bodies were amalgamated by the 1996 Broadcasting Act to form the Broadcasting Standards Commission (BSC) which produces codes and investigates complaints raised by members of the public. Advertisements have inevitably constituted part of these complaints, but within reasonable proportions. In 1994-1995, for instance, of 103 complaints upheld by the Broadcasting Standards Council, six concerned adverts, while in 1997, the last year for which separate figures are available, although the number of complaints showed a steep rise, the proportion of advertisements investigated was consistent with the time allotted to commercials, some 13 per cent of the total broadcasting time. The BSC is not the only destination for viewer complaints: these may be addressed additionally to individual programme contractors and to the ITC itself, which is legally obliged to investigate such matters, produces its own reports and summarises its findings as part of its Annual Accounts. Whether because of the perceived facility of raising objections, or thanks to greater public awareness of the question of standards, or perhaps simply as a result of increasing dissatisfaction with the growing commercialism of television, the number of complaints received by the ITC about advertising continues to rise. The figures presented for the last four years in the Commission's Annual Reports are indicative of this state of affairs, although the number of complaints upheld remains very low.

The change in status of the ITC brought with it alterations in the dual system of copy control for advertisements. Once the ITC fully assumed its new role in January 1993,[22] it ceased to play any direct role in the examination of scripts or finished advertisements before transmission, although its services are still available on a consultative or advisory basis and it maintains a panel of experts to advise on the ever more complex regulations concerning, for example, medical and financial questions. The role formerly played by the ITVA has therefore become more significant, and to this end, 1993 saw the creation of a new body, the Broadcast Advertising Clearance Centre, operating on the premises of the ITV Network Centre to vet all advertisements. The BACC was initially responsible for radio as well as television commercials, although the former function has now been assumed by the Radio Advertising Clearance Centre (RACC). Legally speaking, the BACC (rather than the individual companies) is considered as the broadcaster of television advertisements carried by more than one ITV contractor or programme supplier. The ITC Code on Advertising Standards and Practice specifically indicates the responsibilities of the ITC and the BACC towards advertisers, in the following terms:

> *For the purpose of additional guidance on interpretation of the Code, the ITC will*
> *from time to time either issue supplementary guidance notes of its own or indicate*

approval of guidance to advertisers issued by the television companies themselves. Advertisers seeking further clarification of any of these rules should in the first place approach the television company with whom they intend to advertise or, in the case of advertising on all terrestrial channels and most of the main satellite and cable channels, the Broadcast Advertising Clearance Centre.[23]

Advertising Complaints Investigated by the ITC

Year	Complaints by category	N° of advertisements concerned	N° of complaints upheld in whole or in part
1995	misleading : 969 offence : 1,654 harmful : 334 miscellaneous : 475 total : 3,432	560 279 137 228 1,204	36 7 2 17 57
1996	misleading : 1,798 offence : 2,375 harmful : 689 miscellaneous : 56 total : 5,427	915 486 223 263 1,887	73 13 13 19 116
1997	misleading : 1,253 offence : 2,976 harmful : 590 miscellaneous : 518 total : 5,337	703 412 212 192 1,519	41 10 5 17 73
1998[24]	misleading : 1,856 offence : 4,279 harmful : 1,063 miscellaneous : 657 total : 7,855	1,110 742 455 253 2,560	88 9 7 18 122

Details given by the ITC's *Annual Reports and Accounts* (1995, 1996, 1997 and 1998).

The figures for 1996 contain an undefined number of complaints unanswered from the previous year.

The 1980s and 1990s have been a period of ever more rapid change in broadcasting, while at the same time the pace of legislation indirectly affecting the broadcasting sector has also accelerated. It is no longer purely British laws which must be taken into consideration. The Broadcasting Act of 1990 was framed to conform to the relevant European legislation, which, in addition to its effects on advertising time and teleshopping, has led to the prohibition of tobacco advertising[25] and to further restrictions in the field of medicine. The list of British statutes to be respected in UK advertising grows ever longer and is regularly updated by the ITC according to the latest changes enacted. Following the passing of the Motor Vehicles Regulations 1993, for instance, children in advertisements had to be shown wearing front and rear seat belts in vehicles fitted with them. It is fair to say that this kind of evolution has been a standard feature of the regulation of television advertising which has taken pains not to show illegal activities, unless they are clearly indicated as being both undesirable and punishable offences. The pace of change has undeniably quickened, however. The ITC Codes are still published on average every two years, but the Commission may now publish press releases at any moment, on matters concerning programming or advertising, and such decisions, when duly announced, are normally put into immediate application.

From its first Code in 1991 onwards, the ITC has striven to supply as much information as possible, in a form readily acceptable to advertisers, to television companies and to members of the general public. The format of the document was changed in 1991, to point out the statutory responsibilities of the ITC, but also to provide extra subtitles, a table of contents and an index of rules, all with the apparent aim of easier comprehension. In addition, advance warning of likely future amendments is given. The fact remains that the Codes have become increasingly lengthy and complex: changes in one area quite often necessitate amendments in another and, in any case, the authorisation of new fields of commercials often requires further controls and regulations. There has been an undeniable expansion in recent years as public attitudes have altered. The IBA allowed charities to make fund-raising appeals in 1989, while the Broadcasting Act of 1990 paved the way for advertising by religious bodies, which has been the subject of appendices to the ITC Code from 1991 onwards.[26] Developments in public taste and alterations in behaviour have also led to recent changes. Commercials for haemorrhoid treatments and branded condoms were permitted for the first time in 1987, the latter largely owing to public anxiety over the burgeoning Aids epidemic; the promotion of undertakers' services became permissible in 1991. Matrimonial agencies have been allowed to advertise since 1993. Finally, with the coming of the National Lottery in 1994, rules on betting were relaxed. The ban on football pools advertising was lifted in 1995 and two years later Bingo also finally achieved respectability. On the other hand, the belief in the need for continuing consumer protection and the pressure of expert advice still make themselves felt. Following recommendations from its medical panel and in accordance with the government's White Paper entitled *The Health of the Nation*, the ITC in its 1995 Code substantially extended and tightened regulations on medicines and health treatments to include the related but consumer-sensitive fields of health claims, nutrition and dietary supplements. The need to protect the more gullible members of the public is totally in keeping with a series of regulations and rules on the advertising of medical and pharmaceutical products which have been present since the very beginning of ITV. In recent years, the promotion of alcoholic drinks has been subject to greater precision, with a firm indication of the ages of participants in commercials and with the additional reservation, from 1987 onwards, that humour, although a legitimate weapon in the publicist's armoury, must not be used to circumvent the regulations in this sector. The greater need for public protection against unscrupulous practitioners has led to the addition of new rules on mail order and direct response advertising, which oblige television companies to ensure the observance of certain principles of good commercial practice before promotions are accepted. December 1997 also saw a clarification by the ITC of its regulations concerning prices in advertisements for air travel, providing an element of consumer information if not protection, by making it compulsory for airport taxes and all other non-optional charges to be included in any quoted prices.

The decisions of the ITC cannot, of course, meet with universal approval. The Commission regularly receives a number of generic complaints, covering such general matters as the amount of advertising, noise, inappropriate breaks, as well as products or services which are judged offensive or dangerous. Particular problems are caused by changes in regulations concerning taste and decency, which are inevitably liable to trigger protests, the best-known example being that of women's sanitary products. Back in 1972, an experimental campaign on Thames Television had generated an adverse reaction which must be interpreted as meaning that the subject was considered a question of great delicacy, if not absolutely taboo. Although the promotion of such articles on Independent Local Radio was accepted, the IBA judged in 1980 that television advertisements were still not acceptable. By 1988, another experimental two-year campaign on Channel 4 generated 889 complaints, but the IBA nevertheless went against what seemed to be popular feeling by allowing ITV to screen commercials at times when children would not normally be watching. Two years later, the IBA's Advertising Advisory Committee permitted the screening of the products unwrapped and in 1992 an explicit campaign for Vespre silhouettes on Channel 4, without timing restrictions, sparked off a record number of complaints (over 500 in four months, compared with a total of 2,500 for all advertisements the previous year) and the ITC decided to place the same scheduling constraints on Channel 4 as on ITV. Only in 1995 was it decided that advertisements of a less explicit nature might be transmitted from 8 p.m., before the 'watershed'.[27] This case serves to highlight both the strengths and weaknesses of the regulatory system. The decision first to allow and subsequently to liberalise advertisements for such products seems to have been taken in the face of public disquiet if not downright opposition and to have been driven by commercial considerations, despite the claims attributed to research conducted by the ITC. This is only one side of the picture, of course, in other matters, for example gambling, the ITA and the IBA seemed to be extremely heavy-handed by continuing to ban pursuits like football pools and bingo which were generally regarded as less than harmful.

All in all, the various amendments to the regulations and codes covering television advertising are typical of an on-going and evolving process, reflecting, however imperfectly, the demands and requirements of each period. Many of the regulations imposed in 1955 have proved to be outdated and have been dropped, the protection of the public against manipulation has become a more subtle and complicated process, while viewers have shown themselves much more sophisticated and able to recognise attempts to condition their behaviour or influence their opinions. Nowadays too, individual broadcasters and advertisers have to make a greater number of strategic decisions concerning the acceptability of certain techniques and methods. In general terms, the principles of autonomy and self-regulation established in Great Britain at the beginning of ITV have been judged adequate to the task and seem likely to remain the rule for the conceivable future.

Notes

1   *... somebody introduced smallpox, bubonic plague and the Black Death. Somebody is now minded to introduce sponsored broadcasting into this country.* Debate in the House of Lords, 22nd May 1952.

2 *It came of something of a surprise to discover on the opening night that many of the commercials adopted the polite and informative tone of a Crown Film Unit documentary.*
Brian Henry (ed), *British Television Advertising – The First Thirty Years*, London, Century Benham, 1986, page 38.

3 The same principle applied to the decisions of the other statutory committees set up at the same time to deal with religious broadcasting and programmes intended for children and young people.

4 Despite its apparent imprecision, this formula made it clear that commercial television was to respect the demands of public service broadcasting.

5 The Advertising Standards Authority, set up in 1962 to oversee advertising in media other than broadcasting, uses similar terms.

6 The 1997 *ITC Code of Advertising Standards and Practice* still emphasises all these aspects.

7 Bernard Sendall, *Independent Television in Britain, vol. 1, Origin and Foundation*, Basingstoke, Macmillan, 1982, page 102.

8 Charles Hill was subsequently to be Chairman of the ITA before being appointed Chairman of the Governors of the BBC.

9 The TPCA was the forerunner of the long-lived Independent Television Companies Association (ITCA), later rechristened the Independent Television Association (ITVA).

10 In its first ten months of operations, A-R lost £2.7 million.

11 This term had the obvious advantage of avoiding the potentially pejorative overtones of 'popular television'.

12 Quoted in Brian Henry, *op. cit.*, page 326.

13 In this respect at least, television companies misjudged the public mood. *News at Ten* was an almost instant success, outstripping BBC News in popularity, while the central break became a much sought-after advertising slot.

14 In its evidence to the Pilkington Committee, the BMA argued for a complete ban on advertisements for drugs and medical treatments and preparations.

15 In June 1959, six Labour MPs, including the former Cabinet Minister, Herbert Morrison, had tried to introduce into Parliament a Bill limiting advertising time to a maximum of 6 minutes in any given hour, with no possibility of averaging the amount over a day.

16 In the early 1960s, Unilever and Hedley, along with the pharmaceutical group Beecham, accounted for 25 per cent of ITV's advertising revenue. As Jeremy Potter points out, the money provided by Procter & Gamble and Unilever *was the salvation of Independent Television, but their advertising did little for its reputation.* (*Independent Television in Britain, vol. 3, Politics and Control 1968 - 1980*, Basingstoke, Macmillan, 1989, page 204.)

17 *... the Authority ... had misconceived its relationship with the programme contractors; ... it saw itself as advocate for them; ... it excused and defended rather than controlled them. The Authority told us that it saw its relationship with the contractors as one between friends and partners. It sought to persuade and to influence. It sought to carry out its functions by giving friendly advice and encouragement, rather than directions. Report of the Committee on Broadcasting*, Cmd 1753, June 1962, paragraph 572.

18 Richard Hoggart, characterised thus the influence of commercial broadcasting as early as January 1960, even before the committee, of which he was to be the most influential member, was appointed: *We have only to watch the programmes in the peak hours for a few evenings to appreciate which way that organisation [the ITA] wants to push society. They want to push it towards a generalised form of life which looks much like the life we have known and for the rest looks nicely acceptable – but whose texture is as little like that of a good life as processed bread is like home-baked bread.* (Quoted in Asa Briggs, The History of Broadcasting in the United Kingdom, vol V, Competition, Oxford: OUP, 1995, p.273)

19 According to Bernard Sendall, this was a body set up by long-standing anti-ITV campaigners such as Philip Mayhew and Philip Noël Baker and its evidence was purely verbal.

20 By the mid-1970s, according to Jeremy Potter, there were more than fifty Acts of Parliament affecting advertising in the UK (*op. cit.*, page 197).

21 The section on Financial Advertising in the 1989 Code was extended to three pages (out of a total of thirteen). The self-regulatory bodies governing the Stock Exchange may be consulted about any advertisement.

22 Between its creation in 1991 and 1993, the date on which the new programme contractors started operations, the ITC retained the status of 'broadcaster'. This function was recognised in its Code of Advertising Standards and Practice for 1991.

23 *The ITC Code of Advertising Standards and Practice*, summer 1997, page iii.

24 The ITC itself attributes the increase of 47 per cent in this year to a number of factors: a backlog from 1997, greater public awareness of the ITC's role, encouragement of complaints by consumer bodies and the Government and the fact that *advertisers seem more prepared to risk offending or upsetting viewers not in their target audience in an effort to create maximum impact amongst those who are.*

25 This decision, which came into effect in October 1991, meant the end, among other campaigns, of the much appreciated Hamlet cigar advertisements which had won several prizes at international festivals.

26 As the 1991 ITC Code made clear, religious advertising was, in fact, only to be authorised from 1993.

27 ie 9 p.m., the time after which more 'adult' programmes can be screened. The same restriction applies to advertisements deemed unsuitable for a child audience.

II

The first twenty-five years of product adverts

Twenty-five years may be regarded as a considerable period to study at once in such a complicated matter as product advertisements. The justification for this selection is in some senses negative: the first studies done on the interpretations of advertising, such as Judith Williamson's *Decoding Advertisements*, date from the late 70s and concentrate for the most part on what were the most recent, accessible and remembered of ads at the time. There is actually no clearly definable turning point within the 25 years either in the development of television commercials or within the political field as there was in the early 1980s, with the beginning of the Thatcher government and the imminent arrival of Channel 4 and breakfast television, to say nothing of the new cable and satellite services. The period from 1955 to 1979 can be regarded essentially as a formative and in some way a normative phase for television advertising, a period in which the medium established itself in the public mind, set its own standards and principles and became a part of everyday life in the context of an ever changing social and economic background. This chapter will attempt to explore how advertising reflected certain supposed and real elements of British society and contemporary attitudes and trends, while progressively adapting its techniques to meet one of the classic demands of advertising communication, namely the need to find innovative and creative ways to reinforce the message. At the same time, ads had to treat television viewers with the respect they deserved in order to maintain their support.

Historical, political, economic and social context

With hindsight, it is apparent that the period from the mid 1950s to the late 1970s took Great Britain a long way down the road of her decline as a major power. This was not, however, evident when commercial television was launched, a move which supporters of the new service saw as a symbolic and practical gesture, at once illustrating the end of austerity and serving as a vehicle to promote economic expansion. The starting of a second television channel was to give greater consumer choice, but was also an attempt to achieve the same kind of economic advancement which the United States, the inspirational model in this as in so many other fields, had been enjoying almost since the end of the War. Within a relatively short time, ITV did indeed make profits and undoubtedly helped to advance consumer spending and develop the economy, while the way that the control of independent television had been established took it largely outside the direct influence of the politicians into an area where social and economic trends were ultimately of greater significance than political decisions. There are exceptions to this observation, of course. The Suez Crisis of 1956 revealed the hollowness of the United Kingdom's world-wide aspirations, a fact which advertisers scrupulously ignored, but the petrol rationing which followed the Anglo-French military intervention in Egypt and the closing of the Suez Canal put a temporary end to petrol advertising and, more importantly, caused the oil companies to reconsider the way in which they should promote their products. Generally it remains true, however, that, for instance, the ready availability of the Pill from the early 1960s and the arrival of American rock and roll in the late 1950s, followed by home-grown Beatlemania, had a far more liberating effect on public behaviour and advertisers' reflections of supposed social trends than, for example, the substantial amount of legislation passed under the Wilson government of the 1960s, such as divorce and abortion reform and the legalising, under certain conditions, of homosexual acts. More surprisingly, perhaps, economic difficulties, the repeated sterling crises of the 1960s, the pay and price freezes of 1966, the 1967 devaluation, the swingeing tax increases of 1968 and the failed attempt at trade union reform in 1969, had little perceptible impact on the field of product advertisements.

The underlying trend of the years from 1955 to the end of the 1960s was the impression of a substantial consumer boom. Compared with the more solid achievements of Britain's competitors, the 'affluent society' of the late 1950s was something of an illusion fuelled by the availability of credit and inspired by Harold Macmillan's usually misquoted off-the-cuff observation that *some of our people have never had it so good*. In their 13 years of government which ended in 1964, the Conservatives did not build a single new hospital, but the Welfare State had had its expected effects on living standards and even on the quality of life for, as Sked and Cook phrase it, people thought they had earned the right *after so many years of rationing [to] have washing machines, refrigerators, vacuum cleaners and televisions and all the consumer goods which technology could now provide* and that there was nothing inherently wrong *with adopting the lifestyle of the television set or screen movie.*[1]

The spirit of the age was best encapsulated by Richard Hamilton's ironical pop art collage of 1956, *Just What is it That Makes Today's Homes So Different, So Appealing* but his jaundiced viewpoint was not generally shared and certainly not by advertisers. The companies' aim was to persuade customers to buy the necessary everyday goods to go with the refrigerators and washing machines which the homes in commercials regularly boasted. The figures suggest that the image which adverts give of life at the time was not completely erroneous. By 1961, 75 per cent of homes had a television set, the number equipped with refrigerators rose from 8 per cent in 1956 to 33 per cent in 1962 and to 69 per cent in 1971, while by the same date almost two-thirds of homes had a washing machine. In the mid-1960s some 4 million also boasted a private telephone. The growth in car ownership (and the associated decline in public transport) was also a reality. Some 2.3 million cars and vans were registered in 1955, and 10 years later the figure had reached 9.1 million; private motoring had become, for a time at least, a possible and pleasurable activity, while the axe taken to the railway system by Doctor Beeching made the private motor car a virtual necessity in many rural areas. Meanwhile, wage rises, better working conditions and technological improvements were a further incitement to consumer spending. Between 1955 and 1969, prices rose by a total of 63 per cent, whereas average weekly wage rates climbed by 88 per cent and earnings, boosted by overtime, by 130 per cent.[2] Factory jobs were often boring and repetitive, but with technology reducing the relative costs of small cars and even the prices of such items as television and washing machines, people were understandably ready to reap the fruits of their labours. The consumer boom of the 'affluent years' was real enough, although not conducted with the same dedication to excess as that spawned by the enterprise culture of the 1980s. The mood of the late 50s and early 60s was, however, also strangely retrospective. Prime Minister Harold Macmillan gave the impression of a backward-looking, Edwardian figure sustaining the United Kingdom's great power image, while belonging firmly to the one-nation school of Toryism. The failure of his bid to enter the EEC in 1963, along with the stop-go economic policies of his government, find no echo in the advertisements of the time.[3]

The pattern was different during the first Wilson government (1964 to 1970). Harold Wilson was himself a master in the art of manipulating the media and the careful 'packaging' of the future Prime Minister was reminiscent of the attention paid to the image of some commercial products. Wilson had come to power proclaiming the *white heat of the technological revolution* and some vestiges of scientific innovation are indeed present within the advertisements of the time. Much more marked were the transformations due to the spirit of the swinging 60s as a whole, with the rise of pop music accompanying the growing spending power of teenagers and the quest for novelty and independence taking preference over established ideas. On the down-side, the growth in car ownership and the urge for redevelopment of Britain's cities led to the construction of high rise blocks which were indeed part of the brave new world depicted in advertisements. By the end of the decade the froth and effervescence disappeared, as Britain suffered the effects of tax increases and rising unemployment, while the collapse of youth rebellion and the holiday currency limit brought further restrictions on freedom. The 'bleak' or 'sour' 1970s were to witness continuing uncertainties. The Heath government (1970 to 1974) was notable only for achieving the UK's entry into the EEC, 1970 saw the publication of Germaine Greer's *The Female Eunuch*, reprinted in paperback the following year, and the winter of 1973-1974 was marked by massive oil price hikes decreed by OPEC, power cuts, the three-day week and the ruinous miners' strike which all played havoc with television companies' advertising schedules, to say nothing of ordinary people's lives. Britain's economic position worsened dramatically. The country acquired the reputation of being the 'sick man' of

Europe, with chronically low productivity, a disastrous balance of payments situation (with a deficit of over £1,000 million per annum between 1971 and 1975) combining with strikes (almost 24 million working days lost in 1972, 14.7 million in 1974), rising unemployment (around 6 per cent at the end of the decade compared with 2.6 per cent in 1970 and 1.7 per cent in 1960) and rampant inflation (up to over 24 per cent in 1974). The winter of discontent (1978 - 1979), with strikes in the public services, finally brought about the defeat of the Labour government amid an atmosphere of doom and gloom.

This brief overview should suffice to illustrate the social and economic context of the first 25 years of product advertisements, and also the types of influence which these factors might be expected to exert on commercials themselves. The period is, of course, far from uniform and public perception of events was at least as important as the facts themselves. The affluence of the 1950s was indeed fragile, but Macmillan's Conservative government was generally well appreciated, at least until the satire boom and the sex and spying scandal of the Profumo affair cast a harsh light on the lack of integrity and competence of ministers. Similarly, the image of 'swinging London' – not a British but an American coinage incidentally, first used in *Time Magazine* in April 1966 – masked the growing economic uncertainties. On the other hand, the image of the 1970s is perhaps unjustifiably bleak. North Sea oil was beginning to become available, the balance of payments improved substantially towards the end of the decade, sterling appreciated in value and, even between 1971 and 1975, strikes in the United Kingdom cost only half as many working days as in Italy.

Before moving on to the advertisements themselves and to complete the framework for our analysis, it is also advisable to take a brief look at the fortunes and development of television throughout the period, for the two media are inextricably linked and associated, and a greater sense of unity can be observed in this field than in those already discussed. 1956 was the first year in which the number of joint radio and television licences exceeded the total issued for sound radio, and both viewing and transmission hours increased steadily, to the point where, in the 1977 Household Survey, quoted by Marwick,[4] TV was the country's major leisure activity and, for the period 1977-1979, average national viewing figures reached 16 hours per week in the summer and 20 hours per week in the winter. Reliable figures for the relative viewing of the BBC and ITV are not, unfortunately, available, for the two services used different contractors and different rating systems until the creation of the Broadcasters' Audience Research Board in 1981. The ITV network was largely completed by 1960, although certain less populous areas still had to await their own service with the last contractor, Wales West and North, finally going on air only in September 1962. The Pilkington Committee, which reported in 1962, represented a last attempt to halt a process which was already unstoppable. The report's criticisms of programming and of the regulation of independent television were damning. While the BBC received fulsome praise, according to the *Times* of 28th June 1962, the Committee *[could] not even raise one [cheer] for commercial television.*

Pilkington's recommendation that the third television channel, with the possibility of initiating colour broadcasting, should be awarded to the BBC was carried through; the BBC's first colour transmissions were made in July 1967, with the first ITV regions following in November 1969.

Television companies were hard hit by the price restraint of the 1960s, by the Television Advertising Duty of 1961 and even more when the Exchequer Levy was imposed on revenue (as opposed to profits) in 1964, but overall advertising income continued to rise, in each of the first 25 years except 1974 (with its power cuts) and 1979 (when a three-month technicians' strike blacked out ITV). For much of the 1970s, however, company revenues struggled to keep pace with inflation. The 1960s saw the establishment of what became known as the television duopoly, with BBC and ITV each assured of their sources of income and not trying to compete too actively with one another. Artists and presenters regularly moved between the two channels, sometimes also finding their way into television advertisements and generally the creativity of both services was improved by the interaction. The interrelation of programmes with advertisements is also a subject of some interest: while it is obvious that the interests of advertisers were, in general, best served by programmes which attracted large audiences, the entertainment or interest value of commercials also played a part in discouraging viewers from switching channels in the breaks between or within programmes. The report of the Annan Committee in 1977 underlined the importance of advertising as an integral part of ITV. While proposing various, largely unrealised, amendments to advertising regulations, the Committee praised the 'amusing' and 'zany' qualities of some commercials and pointed to the success of British advertisers at international festivals, although not without adding that some adverts were vulgar and badly made. Viewed in this light, advertising was no longer a parasitic or predatory activity feeding on the creative efforts of the television programme makers, but a part of the spectacle offered to the viewer in his own home. If the advertisements of the early years of television sometimes seem to lack creativity and imagination, it is worth remembering that they should be considered in relation not only to the moods, expectancies and aspirations of the time, but also with regard to the types of popular programmes which viewers enjoyed.

Problems and Dilemmas

There are a number of obvious differences between the first television advertisements and those that are seen today. The first and perhaps most evident, apart from the use of black and white which only began to be replaced at the very end of the 1960s, is the length and pace of advertisements. Initial practice in British commercial television was for the basic advertising unit to be of 60 seconds, with shorter time spans being subject to a higher pro rata charge. It was not until 1960 that the most 'progressive' of the ITV companies, Associated-Rediffusion which held the now lucrative London weekday contract, decided to fix 30 seconds as the basic charging unit, a practice which was soon to be followed by other companies and which effectively raised the price of longer advertisements by some 33 per cent. The reason for the one minute basis was partly historical. American commercials were calculated on 60-second lengths and advertisers judged that a lengthy commercial was necessary for adequate communication to be achieved, either to set the scene before passing to the message, or alternatively, to give maximum time for reinforcing and repeating the name of the product and/or its qualities. The belief in the restricted capacity of viewers to grasp the essential of what they were being told and advertisers' lack of awareness of the visual potential of commercials were no doubt other contributory factors. The range of articles presented in the early days was also limited. Between March and September 1956, for example, Associated-Rediffusion carried advertisements for only 406 separate products. Everyday consumer items, washing powders, cleaning materials, soaps and other personal hygiene items along with food and drink, perceived as necessities not luxuries, were the dominant elements, a situation which has not substantially changed. The pitfalls of this state of affairs soon became apparent, as Procter & Gamble and Unilever, which had realised the potential of television advertising and rapidly abandoned most other forms of promotion in favour of the new medium, took the lion's share of available air time. Limiting the number of 'kitchen' or 'laundry' products which could be advertised in a given hour was one way of addressing the problem, but in the longer term the extension of broadcasting time proved to be the real and lasting solution.

Fundamental questions concerning advertising came to a head with the arrival of the new televised medium. How far, for example, could and should advertisements entertain the public, without this entertainment value counteracting the effectiveness of the message. The question may ultimately remain unresolved; advertisements which appeal to the public, or are liked by them, may not for a variety of reasons actually encourage purchases of the product. The classic example from the early years was no doubt that of Strand cigarettes, which launched a campaign in the late 1950s, featuring a man savouring the cigarette alone and bearing the slogan, *You're never alone with a Strand*. The perceived attractiveness of the actor and the realistic outdoor street setting were not enough to counteract the general unacceptability of the 'image' in the mind of the public, for whom a man should not be shown alone but presented in his 'natural' social environment. The advertisement was both liked and remembered, but the brand was a failure. The desire to represent cultural conventions accurately and the seriousness with which advertising purposes and consumers' opinions were treated may also explain the sparing use of humour in the first advertisements. Opinions have changed over the last 40 years, of course, but the danger of humour distracting from the power of advertising was for a long time a dominant argument. Writing in 1971, Jeremy Bullmore, head of the creative department at J. Walter Thompson, London, and subsequently chairman of JWT London and a member of the company's world-wide board and chairman of the Advertising Association, summed up the basic argument as follows:

One of the most important and difficult functions of advertising is to show the familiar and the relatively mundane in a new light. Anyone in advertising who backs away from this inconvenient fact and relies instead on irrelevance and dissociated excitement is abdicating from one of his most important responsibilities [...] If humour is to be used relevantly and effectively, a distinction should first be made between products bought from housekeeping money and those bought from pocket money. Most women buying most products from a limited housekeeping budget like to feel they've bought prudently and well. For them, shopping is part of their profession; possibly enjoyable, sometimes sociable, but serious.[5]

In the 1950s, more than 80 per cent of purchases were made by women, most of them housewives, and the observation about respecting social attitudes was all the more pertinent.

This question, leads on to another general point, namely the basic merits of innovation and familiarity in the domain of television advertising. One argument is obviously that certain types of goods require promotion in certain fixed ways. With few exceptions, washing powders from the 1950s onwards have been advertised using the same basic arguments and techniques, claims, 'improvements', demonstrations, saturation coverage and testimonials. Other products have periodically seen the need for their image to be renewed, brought up to date or more simply reassessed, sometimes in the light of falling sales, sometimes because of changes in society and social attitudes. The rapid development and transformations in advertising agencies are also a factor to consider. Agencies may indeed have their own 'image' or 'style' which they confer on the accounts they handle; equally, the advertising industry has always included a substantial proportion of relatively small-scale operations and the departure or recruitment of a small number of key staff may transform the conception and realisation of its production. In the 1950s, of course, these problems were still in the future. Many agencies in Great Britain were apparently as unconvinced of the likely success of the new medium as they were unaware of the potential it offered. It is therefore no surprise that the 'norms' established in the early days of advertising should have undergone radical transformations in the following years, that 'ideas' discovered for one product should be transferred successfully to the promotion of others, or even that 'traditional' and 'innovative' advertisements should co-exist side by side and appeal to different sectors of the audience. Less predictable perhaps was the fact that advertising can often be cyclical, that old techniques can be reused in modified ways and that the development of product promotion occurs in a form for which the best image is often no doubt not a graph, nor even a circle, but a spiral.

The dominant idea in the 1950s was that of promoting a 'brand', the image of a named product to encourage the purchaser's potential identification of and with it. David Ogilvy, generally believed to have been the creator of the notion of brand image, referred to it as the *personality of the brand*, a quality to which the name, the packaging, the price and the advertising all contributed, in addition to the essential nature of the product itself. According to Kathy Myers, Ogilvy was once quoted as saying: *Sell the name and you've sold the product.*[6] Martin Davidson defines the process of brand advertising thus: *its mission [is] less one of telling people facts about products than of adding value to them, helping them endure as brands.*[7]

In the 1950s, this process was only beginning. In the United Kingdom, consumer choice between various competing products was finally becoming available, and, although supermarkets with their own brands hardly existed, it was essential for advertisers to fix the names of their goods firmly in viewers' minds. After all, in the small grocer's shop which dominated the market in 1955 (54 per cent of the grocery trade was handled by independent retailers), it was necessary to ask for the required product by name.

The problem which faced advertisers in 1955 was far from simple to resolve. Television was a new and untried field and the knowledge acquired in other media or in other places was not likely to supply a ready answer to the difficulty. It was, in fact, much easier to say what advertising should not be than what it actually should. The sole existing television model was that of the United States, where experience and practice advocated the need for 'hard sell' methods, with exaggerated repetition of the product name and no undue respect for the consumer's intelligence. British feelings towards American marketing methods, as far as they were known, were essentially enigmatic. The excessively commercial approach thought to be typical of the United States was considered by many to be culturally inappropriate, somehow indelicate and unsuited to the finer sensibilities of the British. There were, however, no other examples of television advertising to serve as inspiration. Britain did have press advertising but the communication context was different and it was hard to make direct comparisons. Despite the rationing of newsprint which continued until 1959, press advertisements could be long and complicated and take considerable time to read. In addition, the medium could make only limited use of visual effects, restricted to packshots and cartoon strips, and advertisements were essentially static. Cinema advertisements were an altogether closer match for TV as the technicalities of filming for the two media were similar, but substantial difficulties remained. Cinema commercials resembled much more closely short films with a brief advertising message attached at the end. Moreover, colour was already available on the large screen, while its introduction to television was not even envisaged. If this was not sufficient, advertising agencies had to strive to satisfy the aspirations both of their customers and of the television viewer. The former were naturally keen to achieve the greatest benefits from their expenditure in terms of cost effectiveness,[8] but this could not be achieved without the tacit consent of the viewers. Intrusiveness was an ever-present danger: cinema-going or newspaper-reading were conscious choices, while television advertisements entered the viewer's home unbidden, along with the programmes. Moreover, the targeting of a specific audience was impossible, which again caused the danger of hostility and channel switching. The fear of antagonism to advertisements rapidly proved to be justified. Although an ITA survey into public attitudes towards ITV in 1957 showed that only half the population was dissatisfied with advertisements and that almost 50 per cent actually liked them, three years later the novelty value seemed to be wearing thin as over two-thirds of those sampled asserted either that they liked a few advertisements but disliked most, or that they would prefer no advertising at all.

The most successful stratagem advertisers eventually came up with was that of reassurance. Many commercials were certainly closely modelled on press adverts, many others did indeed adopt 'hard sell' methods, but, above all, the first televised advertisements paid due attention to the viewers' sensibilities and to a sense of 'Britishness', or the 'right way of doing things'. Both terms are of course worthy of attention. 'Britishness' is a key if evolving, slippery and ultimately subjective concept, conditioned by social, economic and personal factors, but it is one which can be applied to most television advertisements, in one way or another, throughout their history. 1950's commercials now seem hopelessly stereotyped and old-fashioned, with their slow delivery, middle-class accents and general self-satisfied air. There was, however, equally undeniably something recognisably familiar and therefore 'truthful' about the settings or attitudes portrayed and the tone employed. Brian Henry's comparison with the productions of the wartime Crown Film Unit is far from inappropriate, for various reasons. To modern eyes, the black and white photography, the use of (male) voice-overs, documentary methods and the technique of demonstration are perhaps the most obvious elements, but wartime memories of such practices were still fresh and positive. Many of the outdoor scenes were shot at recognisable places and, even if the exact settings were not themselves known to the viewer, there was a look of authenticity about them. Beyond that, the majority of these commercials made an effort to be psychologically accurate, reflecting the attitudes and aspirations of a people who had just emerged from a period of hardship and suffering and were beginning to have the possibility of spending more freely at last.

The reassuring side of commercials manifested itself in various ways: an attempt to mitigate strident or intrusive techniques and a certain respect for the viewer, linked with an effort at explanation and information. A couple of examples will perhaps serve to illustrate the point. Actress Ruth Dunning appeared in Persil's first commercial on ITV's opening night, to welcome viewers to the new service (thereby soliciting their complicity and involvement) and to present Persil's cartoon characters, taken directly from previous press advertisements, who were to be regular features of the brand's television campaigns. Advertising magazines, officially known as 'shoppers' guides', a title which emphasised their informational role, rapidly became a popular and comforting feature of ITV. In essence, ad mags had a status somewhere between that of programmes and that of commercials, combining promotion with a story-line not far removed from the scenario of a soap opera, and they undoubtedly fulfilled advertising's informational role in a gentle and low-key manner, aided by the appearance of familiar faces as presenters. Ad mags were soon to disappear from the screens, but not before they had played a part in familiarising viewers with the phenomenon of commercial television.

Establishing norms

The period from 1955 to around 1960 can be seen as the period of the fixing of norms which were to guide television advertising, some of which, in direct, indirect or parodied form can be traced through to the present day. The date of 1960 can only be approximate. The techniques used for the promotion of certain articles, like washing powders, remain substantially unchanged and many techniques of '1950s advertising' can be traced well into the 1960s. On the other hand, rock music, which was to make a major impact on television advertising in the 1960s, had already been present in Rice Krispies promotion of RK records (1959) and the following year saw the launch of Cadbury's Lucky Numbers, the first commercial for which was based on music and words close to those of Bill Haley's rock and roll hit *Rock Around the Clock*. In the regulatory field, the ITA's qualitative improvements in advertising (1960) were followed, the next year, by the BMA's submission to the Pilkington Committee favouring the banning of advertisements of drugs and medical products, which led to the Authority's ordering of the re-examination of the scripts of 184 proprietary medicines and by a much increased vigilance in matters of claims of miraculous qualities. The conveniently round date of 1960 nonetheless offers the possibility of distinguishing between the advertisements screened during the creation of the ITV network, with its efforts to achieve high audience ratings, and those of later years, or again of separating the prevailing, largely unquestioning attitudes of the 1950s from the more provocative and demanding age of the 1960s. In 1990, Martin Davidson reproduced his own version of *Campaign* magazine's branding map and firmly placed 1950s commercials in the bottom left-hand corner designating them as 'conventional' and seeking only 'mechanistic contact' with consumers. He went on to describe them as *inherited from America and the progeny of the marketing giant Procter and Gamble, notorious for its creative inflexibility ... the stuff we learnt to love to hate, patronising, brain-shatteringly dull and sexist.*[9] The judgement is harsh, for these commercials were the beginning of British television's advertising heritage and were far from attracting such unfavourable reactions in the 1950s. However despised or derided they may now be, they represent the seeds from which largely home-grown and unashamedly national television advertising has grown.

(a) Communicational criteria

The limitations of camera and lighting, along with those of sound recording made themselves felt in the 1950s. Along with tight budgets, they were one of the contributory factors to the impression of early commercials as being static and mechanical. The packshot, from Gibbs SR's opening offering onwards, was an ever-present feature. Typically, this first advert in fact contained two images of the product, the packshot proper, placed at the end of the commercial, and a second version, which had also been used in the press, showing the toothpaste tube in an iceblock. This advertisement's use of photographs to illustrate the spoken word and the juxtaposition of stills with snatches of film sequence show that the narrative structure was very much in its infancy and that movement was both slow and deliberate. Ford produced a series of advertisements between 1955 and 1958, hardly ever showing the models on the move, emphasising rather the quality of workmanship, price and associations with luxury. The contrast between these commercials and Renault's dynamic 1959 promotion of the Dauphine could hardly have been more marked. In the latter case, two vehicles were shown on the move, one being driven by a woman, and the advertisement used parallel editing techniques while pointing in almost modern fashion to the refinements of the model, with its heater, snappy gear-change and suspension, and suggesting the notions of speed and manoeuvrability. It is tempting to see behind these differences a change in attitudes in society towards the importance of technology and the freedom of movement. Nor was the dynamic quality of the early advertisements favoured by the use of the spoken word. Early commercials relied heavily on voice-over, with the male and female voices being overtly stereotyped: men were employed to give advice and instructions, women to suggest human qualities. The corollary of this was the absence of real dialogue. Characters were seen speaking to camera, answering questions posed in voice-over or asked by an interlocutor who was carefully placed, almost out of shot in order not to disrupt the direct-to-camera transmission of the message. In early ads, it was judged dangerous to attempt to complicate the sales pitch, which should be presented unequivocally and categorically, and with a maximum of clarity and repetition. It was common for the pictures to reinforce the spoken, sung or written word and the use of repeated shots was also a frequent occurrence.

A difference needs to be made between repetition and redundancy. Nowadays it is accepted not only that advertisements should be sufficiently complex to be viewed an almost unlimited number of times but that redundancy can be an essential part of the polysemic approach of the televised medium. In the 1950s, simple repeated messages, reinforced by slogans or jingles were the rule. The appreciation of the mnemonic value of these devices was apparent from the start. *I'd love a Babycham* has stood the test of time as well as any other slogan and dates from ITV's first commercial break, while jingles rapidly replaced nursery rhymes in many homes. A Birds Eye advertisement of 1959 went as far as to consciously reinforce this process by showing children singing the jingle as they turned their skipping rope: *For the happiest way of eating fish, Birds Eye Fish Fingers.*

In the absence of colour, the use of visuals for demonstration purposes was relatively sparing and had difficulties to overcome. Both Harmony Hair Colorant and Camay soap in 1956, for instance, found themselves obliged to describe what was actually being displayed, the various shades of hair colour which the first product offered and, more problematically, an artist's portrayal of the city of Paris in the second case, in an advertisement named *Pastels of Paris*. The difficulty for Camay was quite particular. The pinkness of the soap and its 'shimmering pink pearl foil' wrapping were an important element of brand image, a cultural indicator suggesting luxury as well as indulgence, and this too had to be pointed out in the voice-over. In the end, the verbal description of Paris, the romantic city par excellence, along with the tacit appeal to the viewer's benevolent imagination, served, it might be argued, to reinforce the importance of the colour of the product and to make a virtue out of necessity.

The 1950s introduced techniques which have now long been standard practice. Cartoons, appealing to both children and adults, served various purposes and contained humour and even dialogue which conventional advertisements could not copy. There were also tentative examples of association and objective correlative. Ford's 1958 car advertisement featured the Consul in a rural setting surrounded by equestrians, the horse no doubt here being suggestive of (social) class. The link between beauty and hair-care products and social (if not yet sexual) and professional success was clearly indicated. Favourable moods were created by the almost invariably sunny weather, unless the desire was to portray products countering the effects of inclement British climate, while Babycham's opening night cartoon chamois was surrounded by the trappings of a conjuring trick, with dice, top hat and wand, suggesting the transformation of the grey real world into a magic realm of indulgence. Finally, the principle of endorsement was well to the fore. Numerous artists and public figures were used, with varying degrees of pertinence: world water speed record holder Donald Campbell, a real if rare British 'hero', found the time, in 1958, to expound the merits of Mobil petrol and could subsequently be seen promoting Kellogg's Sugar Frosted Flakes and BP petrol, as well as giving a strongly moralistic message about children's tooth decay and the benefits of Gibbs SR. In the example of endorsement at least, advertisements conformed to a particular characteristic aspect of Britishness, with the accent being put on identifiable figures who inspired confidence in a period when people generally adopted an unquestioning attitude to what they perceived as higher authority and accepted at face value the information they were being given.

(b) Conditioning the viewer – stereotypes

An essential element in advertising communication is the establishment of confidence or at least the creating and defining of a certain bond of trust between the transmitter of the message (advertiser or agency) and the receiver (the television viewer). This 'conditioning' of the viewer was achieved in various ways in the 1950s. One of the most evident was the advertiser's portrayal of himself as a purveyor of 'information', rather than merely as an enthusiastic salesman. In 1955, both Shell and National Benzole produced long commercials, showing picturesque parts of England which could be reached by motor car. Shell's three-minute *Discovering Britain* series was presented by John Betjeman. The picture-postcard scenes were mixed with cultural information, fully exploiting the notion of what National Benzole called *Our National Heritage* and putting the accent on timeless values rather than commercial gain. Such altruistic and lengthy advertisements could not last; branded petrol became unavailable during the rationing caused by the Suez Crisis and when it returned, advertising time was too expensive for companies to allow themselves such luxuries. Archive or documentary-type footage continued to be used, however. BP's advertisement of 1960 showed newsreel film of Donald Campbell's world-breaking run on Coniston Water while in 1956 Persil screened material shot inside its Warrington factory. At the same time, belief in scientific or technological progress was an area used by advertisers to associate their products with the achievements of the United Kingdom's engineers and scientists. In 1960, Wall's *People and Places* series visited the first of the New Towns, East Kilbride in Scotland, in a transparent attempt to associate itself with a redevelopment project considered at the time to be a source of pride and the solution to the problems of slum clearance. The opening of Britain's first nuclear power station was celebrated indirectly by Castrol which gave brief information about the UK's atomic pioneer, Lord Rutherford, before pointing out that its oil too was at the forefront of technology while, two years later, Kellogg's exploited similar prowess by offering children a working model of the world's first nuclear-powered submarine, fuelled by baking powder, with each packet of cornflakes.

More generally, in this age of deference, the use of authority figures was a potent argument to convince viewers of the truth of advertisers' claims. However flimsy the true credentials of these characters were, the general argument was that viewers, even if they did not believe the advertiser, could at least take the word of such people as a policeman or a headmistress, a grocer or later the butcher or the baker. Each of these worthies further reinforced his/her credibility by wearing the clothes clearly identifying his/her status, cap and gown, uniform, white coat, striped apron or chef's hat. Other reliable experts were also available: the scientist in his white coat and with his air of serious erudition was the principal example. One could be seen conducting unidentifiable analyses or examining the flakes of Kellogg's Super K as they left the machine (1959) and subsequently explaining to an interviewer, in pedagogical terms, the substantive ingredients of the product and their benefits. His authority was heightened by his being seated behind a desk with, in the background, a wall on which barcharts and graphs were just visible. Some advertisers were anxious not to exaggerate; SR's opening commercial was keen to associate the dentist, as well as the toothpaste with the fight against decay. In many cases, however, the authority was transparently bogus and relied purely on the fact that the presenter was a man, in a certain age bracket (not too young and not too old), dressed in a respectable manner, sitting behind a desk and speaking with the correct RP accent to convince the viewer. Appearances counted for a lot and until 1960, it should be remembered, National Service and the discipline it imposed, was still in force. A couple of examples of these bogus authority figures should suffice to prove the point. The presenter in a Lucozade advert of 1960 prefaced his words with, *I'm not a doctor* before going on to explain to his gullible female interlocutor the unquestioned benefits of the health drink, with which she wholeheartedly concurred. Less plausible still was the man posing as an expert in matters of washing and it appeared increasingly incongruous for him to advise women as to how to accomplish this thankless task. In the late 1950s, advertisers found a novel solution to this dilemma, the man himself disappeared and was reduced to a disembodied, yet dogmatic, voice asking the housewife questions and casting doubts on her answers from somewhere out of camera shot. This device, ironically known in the advertising industry as the 'voice of God', indicated that the notion of authority continued to hold sway.

If authority figures could serve to convince viewers of the benefits of a product, advertisers further sought to give their commercials the ring of truth by presenting social situations in a way which might have been thought 'authentic', but which was in fact highly simplified and stereotypical. The focus of 1950s life, in advertisements at least, was the family in which roles were clearly defined and in which divergences from the norm were almost unknown. Men, women and children had their allotted functions within the stable and generally happy position depicted. The woman, of course, had the dual role of wife and mother. Her task was to run the home, the quality of her work being judged, according to the item being promoted, by her ability to keep the children's clothes clean, to feed them adequately having due regard to taste and nutritional value, to ensure their good health and to care for them on the frequent occasions when they were ill. She was also expected to do the shopping and make the necessary regular and exceptional purchases with a careful eye to value for money. This picture, for all its stereotyping, had a ring of truth about it. The working mother was a rarity and, despite labour-saving equipment and the growth of convenience foods, looking after a home was a full-time job. Food rationing was still a recent memory and the heating of most homes and public buildings was so inadequate that coughs, colds and childhood diseases were rife. Advertisers did try to attach a more favourable aura to domestic tasks, however. In 1961, Persil was to launch a campaign around the theme, 'What is a Mum?', but in the 1950s 'Good old mum' was already the person who could be relied upon to answer questions and whose decisions, determined the norms of correct behaviour and wise purchasing.

1950s man had few of these responsibilities. His task was that of breadwinner, although he was rarely shown at work unless he was an expert of some kind, and his role in and around the home was limited to gardening, rudimentary D-I-Y, occasionally playing with the children and presiding over the dinner table. In the evenings he was most often to be seen seated comfortably in his armchair, contentedly reading his newspaper while his wife looked after the children. All of course were impeccably dressed, for the home depicted was almost always comfortably middle-class. As for the children, the approved number was two, one boy and one girl, who were well-groomed, well-behaved, smiling, active enough to eat well, appreciative of what was done for them, but sufficiently fragile to need constant care and attention. The only cloud on this idyllic horizon was advertisers' use of fictional children to encourage real children to pester their mothers into buying what they wanted. The enjoinders, *Get Mum to* (Wall's Ice Cream, 1955) or *your mother ought to* (Kraft Miracle Whip, 1957) were powerful selling arguments, but the most memorable of these 'pestering' advertisements was undoubtedly Rowntree's *Don't forget the fruitgums, Mum* (1957) More than any other, this commercial epitomised the dichotomies of the mother's role of disciplinarian and loving parent; the repeated voice-over message, the boy's plaintive look from behind the garden gate, symbolising dependence and hope, all made the granting of a small treat almost inevitable. Stereotypes are by their nature reductive and inaccurate. The children depicted in 1950s adverts were too good to be true and the social values and material conditions shown were far from universal. More significant perhaps were the figures absent from the portrayal, in particular people of relatively limited purchasing power or who were difficult to portray. Retirement pensioners were rarely shown and teenagers would have to wait for the explosion of youth culture and for youngsters to have money in their pockets in the 1960s to find an appropriate place in advertisements. Nevertheless, stereotypes presented the 1950s viewer with a series of norms which he was expected to recognise and perhaps aspire to, even if he rarely conformed to them.

(c) Truth and fantasy

Another aspect of conditioning was the association of goods with a limited number of fantasies, enjoyment of which was tacitly agreed to be acceptable in the light of the sufferings of wartime and rationing and in the attempt to improve one's self-perception or self-esteem. The types of indulgence shown in the 1950s were essentially individual (often based around cleanliness and the well-being it created) and harmless. Babycham, the fantasy of which derived largely from the oxymoronic slogan *genuine champagne perry* came in a convenient glass-sized bottle and substituted in appearance for what it may have lacked in substance. It was shown as allowing a woman to take pleasure in a drink devised for her, but which could also be requested respectably in male company. Soaps went beyond promoting the importance of cleanliness as a way to achieve respect and success (although Lifebuoy's B.O. advertisements still emphasised this primary function) into the territory of fantasy. The immediately conventionalised image of the woman in the bath, luxuriating in the rich foam and lather was a standard feature of ads for up-market brands like Knight's Castile, Lux and Camay. The element of fantasy was clearly present, the bath in which the model sat was large, the water invariably sufficiently deep to foil all attempts at voyeurism and to emphasise opulence and, most of all, the bathroom was huge. The woman could therefore enjoy her (supposed) fantasies, in a narcissistic but private manner, at a time when, in fact, bathrooms were small in British homes and hot water a limited quantity.

It was a short but important step in communicational terms from the article itself to the social benefits it was intended to bring, namely the association of beauty products with attractiveness to the opposite sex. In this field, goods for men hardly existed and the ubiquitous Brylcreem was sufficiently well-known for advertisers to be able to go beyond product claims, which were obvious and could be reinforced simply by pictures, to emphasise the link between the brand and social or professional achievement and recognition. For the woman, however, toiletries were shown as being an essential part of a dream which was both romantic and practical. A woman who looked after her appearance by choosing the correct soap or shampoo, so the message ran, would soon be attractive to the right man, romance would bloom, fashionable invitations would follow and all would end happily in marriage. All that was required was beauty care, modesty and patience, awaiting the moment when, to use the conventional visual and verbal images of the time, an RAF officer decided to enter your compartment (the RAF was definitely the favoured service for charm and elegance), when *the curtain goes up on your romance* or when *romance comes drifting down the river to you*.

Exotic or fanciful settings in the 1950s were, however, rare. Fry's Turkish Delight adopted a variety of decidedly inaccurate settings, featuring desert nights rather than Ottoman reality, but the fantasy was no doubt never expected to be really credible. The viewer's aspirations were most often portrayed as realisable within the local or domestic context and the settings of the advertisements, whether actually shot on location or using studio mock-ups, were intended to be close to the reality of recognisable everyday British life. The neighbourhoods shown were most frequently respectable middle-class districts, with solid pre-war semi-detached houses, tree-lined streets and, of course, in order to maintain the 'home and castle' image, individual, fenced-in and well maintained gardens. Mass appeal items like washing powders did venture into apparently less favoured areas of council housing, but the same conventional images of care and cleanliness prevailed. More important than the externals of the houses themselves was the presence of the close-knit neighbourhood, an echo of wartime solidarity on the one hand, a source of rivalry in matters of good housekeeping on the other, for lines of washing could always be implicitly compared for whiteness. Individual privacy was still respected: neighbours did not intrude or give advice unbidden, a task which was left to the advertiser's announcer. Once the cameras entered the home, however, the realm of realism was left behind, as the viewer gained access to a tardis-like world. Not only were the rooms quite disproportionately large, but they were equipped with all the latest trappings of elegance and ease of living, from the hearth, the centre of the living room and the apparent focus of family life, to the curtains, pictures, table lamps, fitted carpets, chairs and sofas. The kitchens, if anything, were even more remarkable. They contained the obligatory fridge, cooker and washing machine, still had room for a large table for the serving of meals, were impeccably clean and tidy with the washing up always completed and the dishes put away, unless the object of the advert was to present the efficiency of the product in use. Such presentations of the home were to be the norm in advertising.

In all this we may wonder, about the 'truth' of the images portrayed. The externals of the settings are obviously and recognisably British and this remains an abiding feature of television adverts. On the other hand, the extraordinary size and cleanliness of the interiors can only have represented aspirational rather than actual norms. Did 1950s viewers really believe that houses in the next street had amenities which theirs did not, was this an incitement to keep up with the fictional Joneses or did they simply accept this type of exaggeration as being typical of the kind of claims which some advertisers made for their products and which needed to be treated with a large pinch of salt? It is certainly true that in the 1950s the British were inclined to give credence to authority however flimsy and that the force of the visual image, as well as the unrelentingly repeated nature of the message, were potentially particularly powerful. The government soon felt obliged to act to restrict bogus and exaggerated claims, and perhaps its concern was occasioned by the fact that the advertisements were given a deliberately familiar yet deceptively unreal setting. The 'creativity' of the early commercials was limited; on the other hand the viewer was being presented an image of himself and his country to which he was expected to conform and which, crucially, was illusory. Advertising's mirroring of life in the 1950s was less transparently false than at some later periods, but sensibilities and aspirations were nevertheless being massaged in the direction desired by advertisers. In this as in other respects, the 1950s prepared the ground and set the norms for the development of the industry which was to come.

Cultural identity in the ads of the 1960s and 1970s

As commercial television became firmly established, new goods and services came to be advertised for the first time while others disappeared from the scene. Ladies' girdles and brassieres were in, while motor cars, thanks to a cartel arrangement between manufacturers, quietly vanished, until the arrival of Japanese vehicles in the 1970s. Commercials were, with few exceptions, firmly situated in the present and continued to reflect the age in such realistic aspects as fashion, skirt and hair length as well as the rapidly advancing movement in social and economic trends and mentalities. Critics usually distinguish between the effervescence of the early and mid 60s, the disillusion and reflectiveness of the late 60s and early 70s and the gloom and quasi austerity after the first oil price hike. Throughout the period, however, television advertising remained national if not nationalistic and the medium of television gradually became fully exploited by advertisers. Not only were the tones and shades offered by colour a considerable advance, but the thematic excitement of commercials was also reflected in the desire for technical experiment. Polysemy and redundancy were discovered, creativity became a key notion and the viewer was emancipated from his position of meekly absorbing an explicit message to become an active participant in the communication process by being invited to put his own interpretation on the increasingly complex (and rapid) advertisements he was shown. Martin Davidson's chart[9] shows ads moving from the 1960s to the 1970s away from 'mechanistic' towards 'humanistic' contact with consumers.

(a) Change and permanence

The setting conventions of the 1950s ads continued into the new decade. Scenes in the home followed what had now become rules and while decor varied as fashions changed, the hyperboles of size and cleanliness were still present. 'Themed' advertisements continued as before although the settings and characters were brought up to date. Those who failed to wash with Lifebuoy soap still suffered from B.O., as a kindly friend was prepared to indicate in a discreet stage whisper, but the characters whose social prospects were impaired by unfortunate odours now found themselves in different situations, at the bowling alley or in the shared flat, rather than at the workplace or the ball. The experts who, in 1962, were unable to tell Stork from butter included a TV producer, a farmer who sprayed his own crops by plane, a switchboard operator and, a decided step forward in women's emancipation, a female textile-chemist, complete with the white coat denoting the specialist. At the same time, the romantic fairy tale was on the wane: Lux's 1962 advertisement still showed the attractive woman in her bath, dreaming of her Prince Charming, but he proved to be the inaccessible film star George Baker and the advertisement openly admitted, by the technical convention of a dissolve, that this vision was indeed no more than a dream.

More important, although authority figures and known personalities still continued to talk to camera as 'experts', their claims became to appear progressively more hollow: Alan Freeman proclaimed Omo's latest wonder ingredient, *a fabric brightener called WM7* (1964) just after aspiring to honesty by stating: *We're not going to make exaggerated claims.* Trill bird food was alleged to contain *vital iodine* (1963) while the same year's New Whiskas' scientific formula included a linguistically incongruous collection of 'High Protein' *Meat*, 'High Protein' *Liver*, 'Vital' *Minerals and* 'Zest' *Vitamins* (my emphasis). In fact, the days of experts were numbered. Progressively, their function as adviser and counsellor was taken over by role models, some of whom convinced not by their words but simply by their general professional status or competence which had nothing to do with the product being promoted. If Diana Rigg was granted the prestige of a desk from behind which to expound the virtues of Lux in 1966, she was rapidly followed by Lulu and Sandie Shaw whose testimonies seemed more spontaneous and, in any case, the 1960s pop singer was a figure of general appeal than even the TV star. For men, the examples varied from a train driver (Golden Virginia, 1962) to a hovercraft pilot (Manikin, 1968). The very ordinary social backgrounds was another part of the attraction of some of these figures. Their humble origins corresponded to the quest for the classless society which was one of the myths of the 1960s, and the fact that, as Kathy Myers has pointed out, advertisers sought to target especially socio-economic groups C1 and C2 was yet another argument favouring the use of different personalities. In the 1970s, very young children took over the role of presenters for items like Heinz Baked Beans and their lack of polish and the naturalness with which they stumbled over words made a revealing contrast with the impeccable delivery previously required. This was one of the new areas in which children intervened, the other was an extension of their role as mother's greatest admirer or helper. The little girls in the 60s were often shown asking questions relevant to the article being portrayed, which allowed the creation of such pseudo-dialogues as: *Does sleep help Peter to grow? – Sleep and Cow and Gate* (1964) *What's this? – Heinz tomato soup* (1969) or more simply enabled mother to prove her maternal qualities by replying patiently to the repeated question *why?* (Fairy Liquid, 1965). All these trends show a movement away from the notion of explanation or telling to the mode of interpretation which was an important part of the psychology of the rebellious 60s: in advertisements as in life, things would never be quite the same again.

The notion of change was indeed key to the period in hand whether it was more or less voluntary, as in the 1960s, or more or less reactive, as in the 1970s. Historian Christopher Booker, writing in 1969, caricatured the frenzied novelty of the decade by the title of his book, *The Neophiliacs*, a term he defined as *those afflicted by a morbid love of the new*.[10] Certainly, the 1960s were a period when advertising, along with other media, perpetrated the prevalent libertarian myths and ideals, while the 1970s were a decade when both people and advertisers had to react to entirely different and much less agreeable conditions. In such circumstances, change and transformation were essential features. The primary motif in the 1960s was novelty, 'new' became the advertisers' buzz word and things had to be exciting, which often meant moving away from product claims and immediate benefits to a kind of atmospheric free association. The advertising of Wonderloaf, the packaged and sliced bread, in 1966 was a classic example. The slogan *Ain't life Wonderloaf* was in itself revealing, with its familiar language, parody of a proverbial expression and deliberate association of bread and life, *a modern bread for a modern world*.

The home in which the product was observed was, of course, also modern, with the kitchen sometimes containing a portable television in addition to such practical appliances as the mixer, while all kinds of traditional goods found themselves obliged to take on fresh associations or to reposition themselves. The immediate moment took on positive associations and there was a spate of advertisements which went so far as to make the date an intrinsic part of their message. *As new as 1962"* (Persil), *Flawless Make-up 1965"*, the *Mobil Economy Run 1964* and *1966 and Ain't life Wonderloaf* were but a few examples of advertisers seizing on the bandwagon idea of a new order and of long-established products striving to bring themselves up to date. Player's Weights, in one of the last cigarette advertisements, equated the brand with a whole lifestyle, *the time, the place, the cigarette*. The time was, the present, the place was London, with authentic scenes of buses, a railway station, the Underground and busy streets crowded with people, while the only vague product claim was contained within the reference to these being filter-tipped cigarettes, the manufacturers' last effort to counter arguments about health hazards and to stave off what was by now an imminent ban.

It was easier for some brands to adapt than for others. The advertising for Mars in 1968 typified the dilemma, the background to the advertisement was newsreel footage of the Trooping of the Colour, onto which was grafted the necessary degree of excitement and the enigmatic message promising novelty and suggesting regular consumption, *Eaten every day and new and exciting every time*. Genuinely new items or those with a viable marketing claim could afford to be less schizophrenic, but still needed to respect what had become the norms of the age. Changing life styles and the obsession with the physical appearance of the whole body created a new market for slimming foods, for instance. The approaches of Energen, Ryvita and Nimble, in advertisements dating respectively from 1965, 1968 and 1971 are interesting examples. The first accentuated *the march against starch* by featuring young people dancing at a party, the second was more graphic and illustrated the *inch war* by presenting a (slim and attractive) model wearing a tape measure just below her (naked) midriff as she moved around a setting which was apparently that of a Mediterranean luxury hotel. The connotations of the scene (package holidays and sexual adventure) were as transparent as the blue water of the swimming pool. By 1971, the mood had changed and Nimble's campaign conveyed the timeless association of flight and freedom as an air balloon carrying a model floated at a gentle pace over some of the most recognisable and traditional of London's sights.

The advertisements of the 1960s and 1970s were also notable for the new roles and different representations of children as well as for the discovery of teenage and youth culture. The questioning child mentioned above was simply a modest development of the obedient 1950s model, but fresh attitudes to children and to child-rearing brought advertising changes in their wake. Child-centred education and the theories of Doctor Spock were to become the stuff of political correctness and the commercials reflected the transformed status of the child. Little boys, in particular, were no longer expected to be unquestioningly obedient and if their peccadillos like eating between meals were essentially harmless to others, the sense of mischief and fun were shown to be natural and were made into sources of more general good humour. Gangs of children were even shown (the ancestors of Heinz Beans Street Kids), a notable example for Walls Funny Faces (1968) containing an amalgam of comic activities loosely based on the Keystone Cops and Bonnie and Clyde. On the other hand, moderation and patience were diminishing qualities. As early as 1961, Smarties advertisements emphasised the quantity children could consume, *lots and lots of chocolate beans*. Walls research showed that many children were *hungry Horaces* whose major ambition was to eat as much icecream as they could cram down their throats, regardless of its form and presentation, and the picture of children eating what *they* wanted was to become standard. The Smarties girl with her modest enjoinder *Buy some for Lulu* was but the timid precursor of Birds Eye's much more developed character advertisements of the late 1970s, where young Ben and his fellows took on what were close to adult roles and in which genuine dialogues, as opposed to the truncated discussions with a disembodied voice-over, became the norm.

The question of the behavioural age of children was, nevertheless, delicate. 1950s children were young in their obedient attitudes, even when well into their teens, while later advertisements frequently showed a reversal of this process. Rock music was used to encourage very young children to imitate their teenage siblings and as early as 1964 Rice Krispies featured a song specially recorded by the Rolling Stones in an advertisement which closed with a transparent pastiche of the BBC's *Juke Box Jury* programme. Teenagers were a different case, however. The youth culture of popular music was a boon to advertising and found its way into commercials of all kinds, but the teenage market was often targeted directly in deference to the spending power of the 1960s teenage generation who, for a few years at least, had money to match their new independence. It was possible to portray teenagers realistically and not as in the stuffy images of the 1950s where they had appeared only rarely and most often as already grown-up. Advertisements could now depict the freedom and pleasures of youth, party going, dancing, travel, but the message often concentrated on the flip-side of these delights, not the dangers of sexual promiscuity (although this was to come later), but the traumas of lack of social success due to typical teenage physical problems. Thus quite traditional products like soaps and toothpastes were able to extend their message to a new audience by seizing on the disastrous consequences of bad breath and perspiration.

Social historians point to the end of the 1960s as a period of reflection and self-analysis, with growing unemployment and with a movement away from individual satisfaction to a sense of more collective responsibility, in accordance with the 'global village' notion expounded in 1969 by Marshall MacLuhan. In artistically cultural terms, the importance of the United Kingdom was also on the wane with the United States beginning to regain its supremacy in popular music and withdrawing its film production capacity from Great Britain. The turn of the decade was marked by international commercials from Coca Cola, which contained the collective aspirations of world-wide youth, some of the gentleness of flower-power, channelled into the correct mode of thinking under the strong influence of American cultural domination. In the United Kingdom, this mood was destined to be short-lived and replaced by the bleak consequences of the international oil crisis and of the country's own rapidly deteriorating economic performance. The rising inflation figures of the 1970s were reflected even in advertisements which regularly showed packshots displaying recommended prices. In this period of uncertainty, consumers unexpectedly turned back to known brand names rather than seeking the cheapest solutions and advertisers were keen to enhance this image of stable values by playing on the notion of quality. David Niven's impeccable accent and sartorial elegance were used to proclaim, in 1976 for example, that Maxwell House coffee offered *more taste in the cup.*

More effective still was the vein of nostalgia, never far below the surface in British society but now appearing strongly in television advertising for the first time. It had occasionally featured in the 1950s but had been for the relatively recent past, the 1930s, the true horrors of which had been conveniently overlooked. In the 1970s, advertisers turned further back into a more remote, more easily idealised, but probably no more agreeable past, situated imprecisely in the early years of the century. Some of the classic examples of this flight from the present were Galaxy chocolate's farmhouse (1972), the Hovis delivery boy's bike ride filmed at Gold Hill in Shaftesbury (1973), Weetabix's traditional harvest scene (1974) and, incongruously for a foreign product, Mateus Rosé's boating party in an English glade (1974). That the recreation was well done is undeniable, British television and film directors had already proved their prowess in this field, but other articles like Horlicks and Gales honey found an easier way to play on the same emotional vein by evoking in words parental memories of childhood. The nostalgia was nevertheless present and its use is a good illustration of advertising's need constantly to find new arguments, or to discover novel and innovative methods of re-evoking old themes. The same effect of on-going modification can be observed in the treatment of the themes of freedom and responsibility.

(b) Freedom and responsibility

Advertising presented the 1960s as a period of sexual liberation, while the 1970s came over as the age of women's liberation. However accurate these labels may be,[11] there is little doubt that advertisers were at pains to reinforce the social subtext, freedom was after all a concept which could be applied both to the technique of commercials as well as to their messages. The idea of pleasurable sensation had been modestly present in the 1950s, the 1960s were to make it both manifest and desirable. The essence, as far as women in advertising were concerned, was firstly the extension of the idea of private or individual pleasure. Cadbury's Flake, whose advertising soon became a by-word for visually erotic suggestiveness had, for its initial slogans, the innocuous messages, *Have it all on your own* and *sixpence worth of heaven*. Enjoying consuming chocolate or looking after one's appearance with hair care and hygiene products were shown as provoking an understandable feeling of well-being. At the same time, other advertisements, the archetype for which was that by National Benzole in 1963, were promoting the notion of freedom and release from the constraints of conformity into a world of open air, sun, rapid movement and blond girls with their long hair drifting exhilaratingly in the wind. The open air and beach settings were an incitement to scanty clothing and narcissistic presentation of the whole body. Bikini-clad beauties plunging into the water to promote shampoos was one expression of the pleasure of being an attractive woman, running through the grass enjoying the liberating pleasure of undressing (but not beyond the bounds of decency) as a prelude to eating a Walls choc ice (1968) was another hedonistic delight. The pictures of nubile women often alone on horseback in forests or in the open country illuminated by dazzling sunlight were easily identifiable for what they did not quite dare to express openly, the association of the product with freedom and movement which itself implied sexual liberation and the achievement of a quite different kind of gratification. Even staid brands succumbed to this easy-going, free-thinking convention. Lifebuoy soap picked up on the voyeuristic potential of the not quite naked body by the use of a scarcely adequate shower cubicle to cover the modesty of its attractive blond model (1968). None went as far as Cadbury's Flake, which unequivocally associated almost explicit images of sexual desire with the consumption of what was no more than a bar of milk chocolate.

By the 1970s, a different image of women was appearing, just as liberated, but much more assertive. There had been occasional forays into the territory of the aggressive or predatory woman in the 1960s, but these had come too early to break the conventions of the female role. The archetypal young 1970s woman was professionally independent, knew her own mind and was self-assured. Typically it was the American perfume Charlie (1975) which epitomised the new woman; she moved rapidly, was admired and respected and, to heighten her independence, dressed in trousers. Chanel n° 19 (1979) took the development one stage further by showing its heroine breaking the bounds of the sacred bastion of a gentlemen's club, to the evident horror of some of the older members and the apparent delight of some of their younger counterparts. This advertisement not only indicated the woman's (supposed) new found status and the staleness of convention, but also hinted at profound uncertainties prevalent within society itself. It cast doubts on the role of men, of course, but also sat uneasily with what was the reality of responsibility for a large number of women themselves, as they sought to combine a satisfying career and life outside the home with their traditional and still generally accepted primary role of mother. The picture of children as vulnerable was a constant of advertising and many of the remedies of the 1970s were traditional, Bovril to warm the frozen football goalkeeper (1971) or Ready Brek (*central heating for kids*) to keep them secure as they walked through the rain to school. The cosy halo due to the product was the only unnatural feature in what the advertiser had deliberately made as close to reality as possible, and with the sound of morning assembly starting, a convenient cultural reference reminding parents of their childhood. Psychological comfort was also an important aspect of the mother's responsibility, something which she alone could give, but the slogans and the regular final shots of many commercials conveyed the reassuring message that, even when she was not there, the brand was a partial substitute which could at least provide the cleanliness and warmth that she desired.

In the 1970s a sense of responsibility was shown as being something which was expected of all sectors of society and advertising reacted in very different ways to the challenge. The oil crisis put special burdens and even blame on the oil companies which rapidly had to revise their commercials away from being the purveyors of movement, liberty and pleasure into organisations which had a responsible attitude and could offer solutions in a time of national distress. Texaco's solution was to return to an old-fashioned communicational approach, namely a presenter speaking directly to camera telling viewers that they were wasting time and fuel with their weekend drives and proposing a series of itineraries offering maximum enjoyment at minimum cost. Esso's approach was intended to be more comforting: the message in 1975 was *we've been here right from the start* and the commercial talked with a certain glibness of Britain soon being self-sufficient in oil. The scenes in this advertisement, North Sea oil rigs and installations for bringing the product safe to shore, were, as it turned out, the precursors of the images to be used by oil companies in the 1980s to enhance their corporate image, but in the 1970s the intended message was that of a sense of duty and responsibility to the country. At the same period, something akin to the old wartime propaganda techniques reappeared. Oxo's Katie, in one of her last appearances, revived the spirit of her earlier ads by substituting an 'almost roast' and a leek and liver casserole for a real joint in the best spirit of tightening one's belt and making do. Simultaneously a number of advertisements appeared ridiculing those who were perceived as the common enemy, the Arab oil sheiks, which was no doubt as good a way as any other of helping to maintain morale.

Men were perhaps the biggest losers in the commercials of the 1960s and 1970s: at the very least they were the ones upon whom the instability of society weighed most heavily. The secure roles of the expert and breadwinner had largely disappeared and, although strength and size remained a common motif when dealing with goods for men, these qualities were most frequently limited to the nature of man's consumption and not to his performance. He had lost his responsibilities and his failings began to become increasingly apparent. With few exceptions, man did not fulfil any domestic responsibilities in the way in which 1950s man had, for example, cultivated the garden and played with the children. The working role models remained of course, but once back on home soil the man was lazy and self-indulgent: he was never seen cooking, he hardly ever participated in the housework and he had no idea of how to do the washing. Worse, he was well on the way to turning into what he sometimes became in the 1980s, an oversized child and self-indulgent figure of fun, who was unable to keep himself clean, who secretly raided the fridge at night and who needed his wife's forgiveness as much as his children did. The only place in which many of these domestic failures felt secure was in the company of other like-minded spirits in the pub which became an increasingly popular setting as beer advertising grew in importance in the 1970s.

More importantly, when dealing with liberated and unattached women, men were shown as particularly unsure of themselves, the difficulty being heightened by the small number of products specifically intended for them. The use of deodorants risked giving an impression of effeminacy which Old Spice, launched in 1970, avoided by its emphasis on 'masculine freshness' and on sporting prowess. Brut's use of endorsement by Henry Cooper allowed the brand to move away from this defensive attitude to one where the product could be used for its own virtues, namely the agreeable smell. The associations of such toiletries were nevertheless difficult to handle convincingly. Both Denim and Hai Karate suggested that the brand would make the wearer irresistible to women, but the exaggeration of the message was clear and Hai Karate, with its slogan talking of a self-defence kit in the packet, led to a comic and frenetic treatment which suggested nothing more clearly than uncertainty. Some men were shown as being exceptionally successful with women, but in situations where reality had obviously been lost. One of these was the St Bruno man who featured in unlikely quasi-espionage scenarios. For most men, however, seduction was shown as a spectator sport, with voyeurism being a common motif both of the messages and images of advertisements. Simoniz wax polish showed a young woman cleaning a car, obligingly rubbing her breasts against the windscreen as she did so (1970), advertisements for beers regularly showed men admiring passing girls, but from a safe distance, while Manikin cigars began, the same year, a series of commercials, each featuring a scantily clad woman moving through an exotic setting, before removing her bikini top and plunging into a conveniently available piece of water. Whether the 'sheer enjoyment' of the voice-over slogan was that of the liberated woman, or in the eye or imagination of the partially satisfied voyeuristic viewer was uncertain, since no man was visible in the commercial. Even this vicarious pleasure could be parodied, of course, notably in an advertisement in the long-running Hamlet cigar series featuring likeable male failures. In 1976, the voyeur was frustrated at the critical moment when the money for his telescope ran out just as the girl he was watching began to remove her clothes. All in all, men came off second best to women on most occasions in the advertisements of the 1960s and even more in the 1970s, as they beat a marked retreat into uncertainty.

Communication – sophistication or simplification?

The advertisements of the 1960s and 1970s showed much greater technical variety and inspiration than their predecessors. Many more different settings were used; the home no longer held sway and new images were used with quite specifically chosen connotations, London (the capital, the swinging city), real or real-looking holiday destinations (for the many beach scenes or those suggesting escape) and other settings selected for their psychological implications or reminiscent of shots from cinema films. Narrative editing began to be used, the importance of atmospheric music was realised and directors sometimes showed off their ability to use expressionistic camera and lighting techniques. It was increasingly realised that the message, at a time when direct product claims were becoming less significant, could be conveyed in indirect ways such as visual and sound techniques, that humour could play a role and that the polysemic effects of symbolism were not a hindrance to communication, but a way of heightening the impact or leaving ambiguity for the viewer himself to interpret when the commercial was retransmitted. At the same time, not every movement was in the direction of such sophistication. Many advertisements lacked originality and, mainly but not exclusively when advertising and research budgets were hit in the 1970s, crassness and absurdity was sometimes the result.

The symbolism and visual techniques of the 1960s are perhaps the obvious point to start any analysis of communicational methods. The liberating or liberated advertisements of this period also gave directors the opportunity to express themselves. As the whole (female) body became the object of attention, it became desirable to apply more precise photographic techniques than the generalised view and the head and shoulders shots which had been used before. Close-ups served to highlight elements of the provocative or suggestive poses, mouth, tongue and teeth and so on, but camera angles also took on an expressionistic significance: the low-angle shot was helpful to emphasise the fullness or shapeliness of the breasts while *contre-jour* images gave the bright light or halo effect which many advertisements favoured. Diagonals, rotating cameras and shots pointing directly upwards towards the sun were all special effects designed to accentuate the escape from convention and to express movement or originality while the notion of speed was strongly indicated by the regular inclusion of rapid and apparently unconnected but vaguely atmospheric images. Advertisements used up-to-the-moment language and plays on words, but the symbolism was more generally and intentionally ambiguous, in the positive sense of the term used by William Empson in his literary criticism, but equally valid for visual techniques:

any verbal nuance, however slight, which gives room for alternative reactions to the same piece of language.[12] Commercials frequently used the same symbols suggesting naturalness, forests, dazzling sunlight and horses, all of which could be seen as objective correlatives of sexual desire in addition to conveying such other major notions such as wildness, beauty, physical strength or the pleasure of free movement. Water was a special favourite: it might suggest cleanliness and freshness, (many products featuring it were concerned with bodily hygiene), but wet swimming costumes also set off attractive bodies to particular advantage and the association with the subconscious mind and deeply hidden desires should not be ruled out.

Polysemy and redundancy also occurred in other ways. It was only to be expected that arguably the most potent British cinematographic image of the period, the socially ambivalent, half-believable, but undeniably dynamic and virile James Bond should be copied or pastiched, more or less directly in a series of unlikely scenarios. The most abiding of them was the Milk Tray man, dressed in black, who carried out a range of death-defying exploits in order to bring the simple chocolate token of romance to his unidentified lady friend. Music developed from the simple jingle first into something which moved commercials along to the rhythmic beat of the age and then changed into an altogether more atmospheric and suggestive element. Classical music anachronistically accompanied the nostalgic commercials of the 1970s, Beethoven's Pastoral Symphony reinforced the bucolic solidity of Galaxy's farmhouse, while Hovis bread's delivery boy mounted and descended the steep hill with his bicycle to the familiar but incongruous strains of Dvorak's New World Symphony. Special care was paid to questions of colour and lighting of course.

Overall, substantial efforts were made to increase the creativity and the complexity of commercials and the term sophistication does not seem generally out of place. A certain amount of humour was present, from the misadventures of Hamlet's wry and resigned loser to John Le Mesurier's stereotyped British diplomat attempting to prove the nation's superiority over its Arab paymasters by pointing to the efficiency of a Parker pen, to the accompaniment of *Rule Britannia*. The scenes of the disciplined tranquillity of a gentlemen's club being disturbed by liberated or even simply exasperated women contained an amusing element of social criticism while the quick-witted lad, out for a good time and lucky or wily enough to evade the consequences of error became another recurrent motif in Harp lager adverts. Of course, not all the attempts at humour were subtle or even very amusing. The images of male superiority seem to be surprisingly at odds with or are perhaps to be seen as a clumsy attempt to make up for the dominance of female figures in other advertisements. Some might judge misplaced the picture of the board of directors applauding their tea girl who had managed to control her body by the purchase of the correct brassiere or consider as no more than gratuitously offensive the repeated views of clerics and colonels enjoying a sidelong gaze at a housemaid's or waitress's ample bosoms while being served with suitably breast-shaped dairy products. Others might see this as no more than a representation in a commercial of the type of harmless fun purveyed by the *Benny Hill Show* or saucy seaside postcards. Despite the economic situation, creativity and originality became of considerable importance as the competence of the television viewer grew and nowhere was this expertise more evident than in the Fiat Strada's robots advertisement of 1979. The commercial was notable for its clarity, its emphasis on precision, its attractive and well-synchronised music (erroneously associated in the public mind with Italy), amusing and memorable slogan *handbuilt by robots* and echoes of the 1969 film *The Italian Job* which had provided substantial free publicity for British Leyland's mini range.

Uncertainty and contradiction

The advertising of the first 25 years of British commercial television was undoubtedly increasingly varied and raised ever more complex questions. It should be remembered that advertising was a reactive as well as a reflective medium. It is obvious that the aim was not simply to give an objective mirror image of society and that commercials themselves reacted to as well as encouraged trends both in society in general and within the medium itself. Despite growing technical sophistication, the images and messages conveyed were often conventional, in the sense that they tallied with what advertisers wanted to believe were the prevailing values of the time and that once a train of thought was established, it was not always easy to break it and adopt another point of view. It was clear that the vision of a stable and static society of the 1950s was a comforting image, but the tacit self-satisfaction contained in many of the first advertisements nowadays seems both exaggerated and displaced. Similarly, the hyperbolic sexually liberated images of 1960s commercials were undoubtedly exaggerated as well as self-perpetuating, while the roller-coaster effect of 1970s advertisements was probably equally excessive.

By the late 1970s, the actual function of advertising had changed: the straightforward product claim, especially when delivered in direct didactic fashion, was no longer what advertisers believed many viewers sought or were prepared to tolerate. The movement of many commercials away from the purely factual approach to the use of associative techniques was well advanced, and the concept of commercials being an actual constituent of brand image was visible, not least in the series for PG Tips, Hamlet, Oxo and Milk Tray. The development of advertising, however, was not a steady or a guaranteed process. Communication techniques undoubtedly became more refined and complicated, evolution could be rapid, but it was neither steady nor linear. A good idea rapidly became a hackneyed cliché, as the advertisements of the 1960s showed just as much as those of the previous decade; commercials copied from one another and mirrored society in a self-conscious and uncertain way. Nowhere was this introspective tendency more evident than in commercials for the printed media. Newspapers, with their colour supplements from 1962 onwards, were a powerful competitor for television and the commercials for serious newspapers in the late 1960s and 1970s put the spotlight on social and moral questions such as marriage, sexual licence and the feminism to which television advertisements too often gave simplistic answers. In this sense the creation of image and message was itself suspect, especially at a time when society itself was showing growing signs of strain and instability.

In the end, television advertising unquestionably remained a national preserve, despite the growing dominance of American culture and the increasing availability, on the British market, of foreign goods. National pride and patriotism no longer brought the old certainties and this trend was captured by some of the advertisements of the time. The Union Jack in the 1960s was an ambiguous symbol and no longer a unifying national emblem, a fact amply illustrated by Hoover's 1968 advertisement in which the model divested herself of a dress bearing the flag's motif, to place it to be cleaned, and presumably made acceptable again, in the washing machine. In the 1970s, too, national pride could still be treated with a kind of mock seriousness, VP wines, for instance, featured the unlikely figure of Benny Hill in the role of Britannia, although other products played the patriotic card with less reticence. One last point should perhaps be made about identity. The mid- and late 1970s witnessed the beginning of the emphasis on local or regional differences as a promotional argument. Northern accents started to be used, by the children advertising Birds Eye beefburgers, or accompanying the boy in Hovis's bike ride. At the same time brewers began to seize on traditional and often comic antagonisms between northern beer drinkers and southerners who preferred lager, as a means of promoting their range of beverages at a time when the Campaign for Real Ale was getting into its stride. The 1980s were to be a period of remarkable developments in advertising, in which regional and national rivalries and differences were to play their past.

Notes

1   Alan Sked and Chris Cook, *Post-War Britain - a Political History*, Harmondsworth, Penguin, 1993, page 196.

2   According to Arthur Marwick's *British Society since 1945*, Harmondsworth, Penguin, 1996, from which these figures are taken, middle-class salaries showed a similar increase, 127 per cent, over the same 15-year period.

3   Commercials for foreign products or featuring foreign settings are a relative rarity before the 1970s, when the strength of foreign competition and a certain patriotic counterblast begin to make their presence felt.

4   *op. cit.*, page 246.

5   Jeremy Bullmore, *Behind the Scenes in Advertising*, Henley-on-Thames, NTC, 1991, page 66.

6   Kathy Myers, *Understains*, London, Comedia, 1986, page 47.

7   Martin Davidson, *op. cit.*, page 26.

8   Television companies showed themselves sensitive to the question of costs in the initial stages of commercial television. Air time has always been much the most expensive component of television commercials and when the first rate cards of the London contractors Associated-Rediffusion and Associated TeleVision came out, the prices for 60 second peak-time spots were carefully pitched just below the psychologically significant £1,000 barrier.

9   *op. cit.*, pages 43 to 45.

10 Christopher Booker, *The Neophiliacs*, London, new edition Pimlico, 1992, page 10.

11 Geoffrey Gorer's study, *Sex and Marriage in England Today* (1971) revealed that 26 per cent of men and 63 per cent of women were virgins at the time of their marriage. A further 20 per

cent of men and 26 per cent of women had married the person with whom they had first had sex. On the other hand, a study of students at Durham University in 1970 revealed that 93 per cent of the girls had been virgins when they came to University, but that, by their 3rd year, only 49 per cent still were. In the 1960s, Parliament had passed legislation to ease abortion restrictions while the 1970 Equal Pay Act, pioneered by Barbara Castle, had started the process of achieving sexual equality in the workplace.

12 William Empson, *Seven Types of Ambiguity*, Harmondsworth, Penguin, 1961, page 1. The first three of Empson's categories seem relevant here, examples when *a detail [is] effective in several ways at once*, cases when *two meanings are resolved into one* and *examples where apparently unconnected meanings are conveyed simultaneously.*

III

The commercial spirit of the 1980s

The 1980s marked a radical change of attitudes and of self-perception within British society, which was fully reflected and even encouraged by the television advertisements of the period. This chapter will point to the substantial cultural differences between the 1980s and the preceding years as well as illustrate the major trends and new phenomena within the decade itself. The introductory outline of the principal political, economic and social events of the period, including changes within television, is necessary background to the product advertisements discussed in this chapter, but the influence of these historical events can also be felt in the commercials placed by government departments and by non-governmental institutions, which will be discussed in later sections.

Historical, political, economic and social context

To talk of a decade as a more or less uniform period in political and social history is a potentially risky undertaking; nevertheless the 1980s are generally accepted as displaying a substantial degree of unity. At the very least, the differences with the preceding period were clearly marked in philosophical and political terms. Whereas the notion of 'consensus' in many domestic fields could be observed throughout the post-war years, the General Election of May 1979 brought to power a Conservative party whose leader was a 'conviction politician' of radical and definite views who was to remain in office until November 1990. Writing in the *Guardian* shortly after Margaret Thatcher's resignation, Hugo Young commented:

> She spoke as no-one else did for business Britain. Not just for big business but, rather
> more, for small ... expressing the economic but also the social philosophy of little
> England shopkeeping from which she sprang. In entrepreneurship, in profit making, in
> market place success she saw the unalterable foundations of a successful society. She
> never deviated from this philosophy and never tired of reiterating its principles as a
> guide to human conduct. Doubted and even despised during the seventies, these at last
> became conventional wisdom in the 80s.[1]

When she spoke of restoring Victorian values, those she had in mind, were *thrift, patriotism, self-help, hard work, and responsibility to the family. Her watchwords were initiative, duty, independence.*[2] There is little doubt that the situation which the Conservatives inherited was dire and that Britain was not just rapidly becoming a post-industrial society, a tide which the 1980s failed to stem, but equally of being the first country to make *the journey from developed to underdeveloped.*[3] By 1990, despite the failings of the decade, this at least no longer seemed to be on the cards. Progress was far from consistent, however, and although many elements of the political landscape had changed for good, the 1980s ended with many clouds on the economic and social horizon, with the country more divided than ever and with another change of mood imminent.

The decade witnessed a number of momentous events, of which the Falklands War of April to June 1982 was perhaps the most important, in patriotic terms of course, but also in the national and international political arenas. The invasion of this remote outpost of Empire aroused a display of national unity reminiscent of the Second World War. Margaret Thatcher deliberately played on Churchillian and even more ancient images, transforming herself from the 'Iron Lady' into a kind of latter-day Britannia. The successful retaking of the islands was cause for much rejoicing, not least within the Conservative government and the so-called 'Falklands Factor' was undoubtedly a major, though perhaps overestimated, reason for their victory in the 1983 General Election. It is true that, in January 1982, the government's popularity was at a very low ebb and the Prime Minister herself attracted an approval rating of only 25 per cent, but after the war Margaret Thatcher was invincible and, with an overall majority of 144 in 1983, was assured of firm parliamentary support for whatever measures her administration might choose to take.

The year-long miners' strike marked another decisive stage and one which signalled a clear turning point in labour relations which had been a regular source of conflict and discontent ever since the Second World War. The popular memory of the 1974 strike, which had led to the defeat of the Heath government, was still strong and with another Conservative administration in power, one which was actively seeking to strengthen the power of management at the expense of organised labour, another conflict was inevitable. The government had laid careful plans by building up coal stocks', by making contingency plans for coal imports, by introducing dual fuelling in power stations and by preventing the activities of secondary or 'flying' pickets who had so disrupted power supplies in 1974. In the event, the strike came at a time when coal reserves were at an all-time high. Miners' leader Arthur Scargill's refusal to hold a national ballot effectively prevented him from mobilising the whole of the industry's workforce as had happened earlier. The productive Nottinghamshire miners in particular were never persuaded to support, eventually collapsed in March 1985, leaving much suffering and bitterness in its wake.

If opposing overseas dictators had never featured on the Conservatives' agenda, weakening, or some would say, breaking trade union power most certainly had and was an integral part of the concepts of independence and discipline and of the process of 'allowing management to manage'. The Prime Minister's economic policies also contained a number of radical, 'monetarist' measures. One of the beliefs was that taxation was a disincentive to effort and initiative and that direct taxation in particular should be reduced. In this respect at least, policies in the 80s were absolutely consistent with the underlying credo. The basic rate of income tax was cut in the 1979 budget from 33 per cent to 30 per cent, further reduced in 1987, reaching 25 per cent in 1988. At the same time, high wage-earners were particularly favoured by the reduction in maximum tax rates over the same period from 83 per cent to 40 per cent. Similarly, for economic, and ideological reasons, the government was anxious to encourage both share-holding and home-ownership. The former was achieved in three main ways, privatisations, the deregulation of the Stock Exchange and tax incentives favouring savings. The list of privatisations is long and will be more fully covered in a later section. Suffice to say that major loss-making parts of British industry were first made financially viable and attractive to potential investors, including the general public whose participation was encouraged by extensive and expensive advertising campaigns, before being sold off. The Stock Exchange itself was reformed in November 1986, by the so-called 'Big Bang', which abolished the distinction between jobbers and dealers, introduced automatic computerised quotations and was intended to make share-dealing more accessible and to open the market to the beneficial forces of competition. In the home ownership field, the 1980 Housing Act gave tenants of council properties of more than two years' standing the right to buy their homes at a discount. The move was a substantial success (and vote catcher) and by the end of 1987, more than 1.1 million homes had been purchased in this way from local authorities, housing associations or in new towns, changing radically the balance between owner-occupied and tenanted accommodation.[4]

Another tenet of the Conservatives' approach to individual responsibility was the notion that the role of the state, and government spending, should be reduced to encourage individual initiative. The economic conditions made this a relatively hard nut to crack with total expenditure increasing in real terms by some 26 per cent between 1979 and 1992, largely on social security, which accounted for over 30 per cent of government expenditure. Self-employment and jobs in the service sector were on the increase, but generally, unemployment was an intractable problem. From around 1 million in 1979,[5] the toll of jobless rose to over 3 million in 1985 and 1986, with the bulk of the jobs being lost in the manufacturing sector where some 2 million disappeared over the 10 years from 1979. Health was another difficult area: expenditure rose (by some 35 per cent in real terms over 10 years) but so, with an ageing population, with more sophisticated medical techniques and with greater expectations, did complaints. The 'internal market' legislation of 1989 which created independent NHS trusts and fund-holding GP practices was considered as bureaucratic and wasteful of money and was believed by some to be an attempt to encourage private medical care by indirect means.

At the same time government intervention in local administration increased. Some councils were notoriously bad managers and much effort was expended to control recalcitrant local government in areas like Sheffield, Liverpool and several London boroughs. Measures were passed, giving greater independence to schools, by allowing them to opt out of local authority control and run their own budgets, but in many areas, the government's attempts to improve state education and to impose consistent standards through the national curriculum only led to more bureaucracy and expenditure. The most revealing decision of all, and in the end a major contributory factor in Margaret Thatcher's downfall was the introduction of the Community Charge or 'Poll Tax', a measure intended to be the flagship of the government's measures for local authorities, by removing the anomalies of the archaic rating system. The new charge seemed likely to bring benefits to the most favoured classes and attracted vigorous opposition in parliament and protests on the streets. Opinion polls showed that some 70 per cent of the population disapproved of the new tax, notably the lower-middle classes and skilled working class, many of whom were only recent converts to Conservatism.

For a time in the mid to late 1980s, the government's management of the economy did seem to be effective and well-conceived. Wide currency fluctuations were avoided, albeit at the cost of high interest rates, and, although inflation figures were high compared with Britain's competitors, average earnings rose faster than the cost of living, which ensured comfortable conditions for those in work. The balance of payments was less buoyant, however. For the first time, North Sea oil was a major positive factor in the trade figures, and, with invisible exports taken into account, the United Kingdom enjoyed a current account surplus between 1980 and 1985. Thereafter, things deteriorated rapidly, with 1989 recording a deficit of some 20 billion pounds. This was just one of the signs pointing to falling prosperity at the end of the decade.

Despite appearances to the contrary, conflicts within society had never completely gone away. The Royal Wedding of 1981 was the focus for much sentimentality, no little pageantry and even more public celebration than the Queen's Silver Jubilee some four years earlier. Politically, the left had been weakened and the extreme left had become increasingly isolated after the miners' strike and by the creation in 1981 of the SDP, which did for a time seem capable of breaking the two-party mould of British politics. For its part, the government attracted unfavourable comment through its arbitrary decision to abolish the Greater London Council and the other metropolitan authorities. Other problems proved ultimately to be more serious. In April 1981, tension over policing tactics in Brixton led to riots in which some 279 members of the Metropolitan Police were injured. In July of the same year, trouble flared in Southall (sparked by a skinhead concert) and Toxteth (Liverpool), shortly followed by similar events in, amongst other places, Bradford, Handsworth (Birmingham), Leicester, Manchester and Wolverhampton. Further unrest, some of it in the same areas, was to follow in 1985. In these circumstances, the public felt insecure and the British Crime Survey of 1982 showed that 60 per cent of elderly women and 38 per cent of middle-aged ones felt 'very unsafe' walking home at night, despite an increase of some 25 per cent in expenditure on policing. More 'officers on the beat' were deployed, but figures for recorded crimes continued to shoot up, with 3.9 million being registered in 1989 as against 2.5 million ten years before. At the same time, the percentage of offences cleared up fell from 41 per cent to 34 per cent. The other scourge was Aids, which was thought initially to concern exclusively homosexuals and drug users. It rapidly became clear that the disease could affect heterosexuals too and the government began explicit advertising campaigns to promote safe sex. The saddest victims of the disease were perhaps the haemophiliacs who had been infected by NHS blood transfusions; only when John Major replaced Margaret Thatcher did the government agree to raise its compensation offer from £34 million to £76 million.

By the end of the 1980s, it was clear that the government was facing difficulties on many fronts. The balance of payments was worsening and the policy of sterling shadowing the deutschmark, while remaining outside the ERM, was proving increasingly untenable. Rises in interest rates were necessary to finance the current account deficit and to maintain the exchange rate, but a recession was already imminent. Chancellor Nigel Lawson resigned in October 1989. In 1987, another blow had fallen with stock markets around the world plunging. In London alone, £90 billion was wiped off share values in two days, pointing out at a stroke to small investors the perils of the stock market. Worse was to come, however. Property values had been rising rapidly ever since the mid-1980s, particularly in the London area. Between 1987 and 1989, house prices rocketed by 117 per cent, compared with some 17 per cent for general inflation. A further hike to the inflationary spiral had been given by the decision, in the 1988 budget, to limit mortgage tax relief to £30,000 for a couple (rather than for an individual) from August of the same year. The scramble to secure a mortgage before the deadline had the inevitable inflationary consequences, even though interest rates by the end of the year reached 13 per cent and were still climbing. The price bubble burst, leaving millions of home-buyers with negative equity, interest at uncomfortably high levels and the vivid impression that property ownership was no more secure than popular capitalism.

In the event, it was none of these factors, but relations with Europe that were the immediate cause of Margaret Thatcher's fall. Her opposition to growing European integration was well-known and had been the subject of much dispute, even when the question of the United Kingdom's rebate from the Community had apparently been settled. The Conservatives' campaign for the European Parliamentary elections in 1989 had been singularly unsuccessful and in December of the same year the Prime Minister was faced with a leadership challenge by backbench MP Sir Anthony Meyer. In October 1990, she was prevailed upon to allow sterling enter the ERM by her new Chancellor John Major, but at an EEC summit in Rome she had again proved aggressively adamant on the question of unity and her report of the meeting to the Commons revealed as much. Deputy Prime Minister Sir

Geoffrey Howe, was moved to action and vigorously attacked the Prime Minister in his resignation speech in the Commons in November 1990. A Conservative leadership election took place, Margaret Thatcher failed to obtain enough votes to win outright at the first ballot and was persuaded by the 'men in grey suits' to resign to avoid further damaging the party and herself. Her place was taken by her own protégé, John Major. The long reign of the 'Iron Lady' was at an end.

Changes in the media were an essential part of the developments of the 1980s. The successful move of the newspaper industry from Fleet Street with its old-fashioned associations and outdated working practices to Wapping, with its new technology and efficiency was a symbolic change in British industrial life and gave a new lease of life to several struggling titles. Television too was to feel the wind of change, as the Conservative government was convinced of the need to encourage new investment and new practices in the industry. The government's first move on coming to power in 1979 was to reject the Annan Committee's proposals for an Open Broadcasting Authority to run the fourth television channel and to award control of the new service to the IBA. Channel Four was to be a different type of television. Its guaranteed income, supplied by the other ITV contractors on a percentage basis, was intended to enable the channel to experiment and cater for minority interests. In this way the possibility of narrowcasting in programming, and even in advertising, seemed to exist for the first time, the more so as the introduction of the new service considerably increased the number of transmission hours and commercial breaks available. The free-enterprise spirit was not forgotten either: the new company was to be a 'publisher broadcaster', commissioning rather than creating its programmes, a substantial proportion of which (in the event nearly a third) were to be purchased from independent producers. Channel 4 went on the air in November 1982 and was available at once to almost the entire British televiewing population. The other move in terrestrial television was the opening of the breakfast time service. TV-am got off to a difficult start, having made the same errors as London Weekend Television some years before, by engaging too many highly-paid big names and attempting to create too high-brow a product. Viewers' initial preference was for the BBC's *Breakfast Time*, which had been launched in January 1983, some two weeks before TV-am started, and which for a time effectively cornered the market. By the summer of 1983, however, TV-am had sacked its stars and was achieving ratings. The specialised audience for this service offered considerable scope for advertisers seeking to reach the market of housewives with young children.

The 80s also witnessed the start of the cable and satellite revolution, which, once more, was favoured by government, but was in fact inevitable in international commercial terms. Satellite broadcasting had been proved to be technically viable by the live transmission of the Olympic Games in Mexico City and of the first moon walk. Equally, the idea of cable was not new: a small number of British homes had received their programmes in this way for years. In 1984, the cable company Rediffusion used its network to transmit programmes originating from Sky Channel, already a part of Rupert Murdoch's News International, for the first time. Initial progress remained slow: of some 135 (local) franchises granted by the Cable Authority by 1990, only 35 were actually operational. Direct Broadcasting by Satellite seemed a more promising option and in 1986 the consortium British Satellite Broadcasting was awarded the contract for three satellite channels. Before its launch, it was preceded by Sky Television, which started broadcasting four programmes nationwide from February 1989. In the event, BSB was effectively taken over by Sky in November 1990, although it was only thanks to the wealth of News Corporation that this service survived its early unprofitable years.

If the 1980s were a period of substantial turmoil in the television world, the same is true for advertising, which enjoyed its own particular boom. Saatchi and Saatchi made its name initially by its work for the Conservatives in the 1979 General Election and soon won other very prestigious accounts like British Airways and Procter & Gamble, acquiring large numbers of agencies worldwide along the way, before its ill-fated attempt to purchase the Midland Bank in 1987. New agencies arose, typically identified by the names of their founders and subsequently, as take-overs multiplied, simply by their initials. Many were highly successful and even more profitable at a time when advertising was a boom industry, whose turnover, according to Peter York, rose from £2 billion in 1980 to £5 billion by 1986. Competition for accounts was fierce, and customers were more than prepared to change agencies in their attempts to find new images and new markets for their products. The 1980s were a frenetic period in advertising and Peter York caricatures the mentality of the time in the following way:

> In the first half of the decade, people were shifting jobs and scurrying from agency to agency and leaving and starting their own agencies at a bewildering rate. A standard procedure was to establish some sort of presence with a medium-to-large agency, quit, launch your own tiny-but-perfect agency with some other disaffected people, promise to offer uncompromising standards of service to your clients, get your picture plus profile in Campaign ... then wait for another medium-to-large agency to buy you out for cash plus car plus share options ... who needed heavy industry? Who needed factories in the Midlands making driveshafts for Austin Rover?[6]

This type of hyperbole was characteristic of the eighties and can be seen in the television advertisements of the period themselves, which frequently sought to portray just such tempting and comforting illusions. On the other hand, it is only fair to point out that the Thatcher years were undoubtedly a time of radical changes in the attitudes of people in general as well as of opinion formers and that the creative talent displayed by agencies and the sheer eclectic variety of television advertisements were at once typical and remarkable.

Nostalgia revisited

Nowhere was the Thatcher Revolution more cogently mirrored in advertising than in the presentation of nostalgia. 1970s ads had had recourse to a relatively distant past as a backward-looking expression of a desire for security in troubled times but the 1980s were to transform this opinion and Margaret Thatcher's recalling of Victorian values was less an appeal to a rose-tinted vision, than a call for initiative and responsibility. The past was no longer 'a foreign country' which offered a refuge from the present but was sought because of its intrinsic, positive values while collective memory or shared experience frequently replaced nostalgia itself. The subject was addressed in a variety of broadly similar ways. Heinz produced a series of advertisements based on the theme of children growing up into unexpected adults. The Electricity Council used the same approach of their product accompanying the citizens at various stages in their lives (with the deliberately ambiguous *Electricity for Life* slogan) and played on positive memories of key moments, childhood discoveries, marriage and childbirth, for example, which were common to most people's experience and were made easier by the presence of electricity. Cadbury's Inspirations (1989) used a similar method in an advert constructed around two old schoolfriends looking at photographs of the good and bad times of their shared youth and thinking of the bond of friendship which was thus sealed between them.

In the 1980s, oldness was no longer a virtue in itself; many adverts featured antique or ancient-looking objects, but these were appreciated and presented primarily for their financial value and intrinsic quality in an age where ostentatious consumption was shown as being the rule. In this respect, it is interesting to note the treatment of tradition by the advertisement for Mr Brain's Faggots from the late 1980s. The commercial contained some of the externals of Victorian or Edwardian realism: the delivery boy with his old-fashioned bicycle, strongly reminiscent of the Hovis advertisements of the previous decade, the empty roads and the benevolent entrepreneur personally supervising his business and being respectfully greeted by his employees. The message *you'll wish you tried them years ago* emphasised that the faggots were a traditional product, but the pack-shot was of the frozen 1980s version and the voice-over put the accent firmly on quality, by referring to the selected ingredients and to the spicy sauce which accompanied them. Most 'nostalgic' advertisements of the 1980s favoured more recent periods than Mr Brain's, using a treatment which sometimes contained a strong element of critical distance. Mercury Telecommunications recreated the old, run-down areas surrounding the river Thames, with a 1950s car, teddy-boy style individual and scrapyard, on black and white film, but only to transform the scene into a new docklands office block. This was a classic example of the then and now theme, with all the positive connotations being situated in the present. Crunchie used an artificially retrospective presentation, centred around an attractive modern model in a variety of deliberately contrived and dated settings, ice skating, playing golf surrounded by figures dressed in 1920s style or enjoying the luxury of a cruise on board a pre-war liner, thus combining the good life of the past and present in a single chocolate bar. British Leyland toyed with the siege mentality of the Dunkirk spirit in a 1981 advertisement showing its cars fighting back against foreign invasion, but the experiment, which preceded the Falklands campaign incidentally, was soon abandoned, probably because of the incompatibility of such old-fashioned associations with the desire to promote, on their own merits, what claimed to be competitive and viable new models.

The principal previous period evoked in the adverts of the 1980s was the 1950s and, more importantly, 1950s America, which made it clear that the association was spiritual and aspirational rather than purely historical. The target audience was not parents but teenagers who were being offered the liberty associated with the purchasing power of their 1950s counterparts, but with none of the constraints. The oneiric and iconic quality of the image was made clear by the fact that the products advertised in this way were often American jeans. Levi's ran a series of advertisements, hinting at the sexual liberation that the revolutionary period of the fifties had offered, and suggesting the new life-style they had proposed, and, by inference, still offered. The most famous of these commercials was perhaps the 1985 laundrette advert, starring Nick Kamen, an Elvis look-alike prepared to strip to his boxer shorts in order to wash his jeans on the spot, having already taken the precaution to place stones in the tub of the washing machine in place of washing powder. The 1980s message of the advertisement went beyond the simple evocation of the past or even of the iconic figure, to illustrate the added convenience of the modern product, which came already stonewashed and, as a previous, graphic advertisement had pointed out, pre-shrunk. Shortly afterwards, Persil gave an example of very similar labour in vain, with a young man being attracted by a shop assistant, and running home to wash his clothes, before returning to find that she already had another suitor. It was appropriate to the comparison of 1980s aspirations with 1950s liberation that the action of the commercial was accompanied by the strains of the song 'why do fools fall in love?' given in voice-over. What is striking is the originality with which the theme of nostalgia was treated and the parodic value which was frequently attached to it at a time when the general trend was to search for positive contemporary values and to promote the United Kingdom as a forward-looking and dynamic community.

Identity and identities

The stereotyping of identities in commercials is typical of the genre which, for reasons of brevity at least, favours a simplistic approach and where representativeness is not necessarily a criterion. The 1980s nevertheless saw a substantial shift away from the restrictive models of previous years, to a situation where various types of individuals were presented, where a certain spirit of independence was accepted, but where the question of belonging, to a social group or to the national community, came to be of particular significance. In this respect, the late eighties contained some novelties. The coloured community started to be more widely seen in commercial advertisements for the first time, even if this remained a timid and 'token' representation,[7] which can be unfavourably compared with the practice in government advertising where a more statistically accurate portrayal was the rule. The reluctance to show coloured people presumably reflected the same commercial logic as that which had kept elderly people out of product advertisements for so long, their supposed absence of spending power. By the 1980s, pensioners also began to appear more frequently in commercials. Grandparents were often used as a comic foil for their knowledgeable and mischievous grandchildren, who, for instance, did not believe their tall stories (Heinz Tomato Soup, 1981) or were anxious to remove as soon as possible all traces of their unwanted affections (Andrex, 1988). Maureen Lipman's interfering mother/grandmother in the British Telecom commercials was equally a comic figure, although not immediately perceived as 'old'. In fact, many retired people had more disposable income and were a repository of spare cash which many financial advertisers were anxious to see invested with them. It was in advertisements for National Savings in particular that pensioners were solicited as consumers. Here, they were accorded the status of 'smart non-tax-payers' and the element of security was reinforced by the picture of them as happy and entirely masters of their destiny. Choices Pensions used an elderly man as a convenient vehicle for a more general message, that it was necessary to think of retirement and that it was never too late to start, showing him highly enthusiastic about the flexibility of the investment offered. The fact remains, though, that 1980s ads strongly intimated that the extended family hardly existed and that pensioners were not in the mainstream of the consumer boom.

The treatment of children in advertisements of the 1980s was somewhat less summary, and amongst the real and idealised visions, the financial and commercial imperatives of the period can be clearly traced. The innocent child still existed, best emphasised by Kellogg's Corn Flakes charming advertisement showing a little girl mastering the art of tying her laces, only for it to become clear that she had put her shoes on the wrong foot, but the street-wise and consuming child was already dominant. The invention of Heinz Beans Street Kids enabled the advertiser to preserve the illusion of innocence, by using an adventurous, but cartoon-based and highly moral scenario, which encouraged children to identify with correct attitudes and to which could be added an up-to-date written message about colours and preservatives. On the other hand, the Weetabix children were more menacingly and uncompromisingly adolescent, with their boots and shaven heads allowing some of the new realities of life to show through. Even Ready Brek succumbed to the temptation of showing children striving to prove their dominance and the same point was amply illustrated by Irn Bru's depiction of an adolescent lifting the pavement in order to sweep away the dirt he had found. Irn Bru's children were in any case stronger than the rest and the name of the product was sufficient warning to customers as to what stereotypes might be expected in its advertisements. The mischievous child of the 1970s was still present. Smarties (1989) showed chocolate buttons wreaking havoc in a school at night and Dairylea, through the comments of a grumpy middle-aged coach driver, suggested the indiscipline to which even the best-behaved of youngsters were prone.

One of the less endearing characteristics of Thatcher's children was a new tendency to demonstrative omniscience and superiority of the kind displayed, for instance, in reminding mothers of the nutritional advice received at school but apparently not followed in the family kitchen (Oxo, 1985). In many cases, the ingenuousness of youth was forgotten and children were shown as growing up too quickly, a necessary part of hastening them along the road towards becoming consumers. Thus Petite typewriters offered the children the opportunity, in the words of the accompanying song, not of playing but of working 'nine to five'. The use of adult voice-overs to accompany acting children was a succinct way of transmitting the message of children prematurely taking on adult roles. Champion Bread employed the voices of Harry Carpenter and Frank Bruno. The Alliance and Leicester Building Society borrowed those of Stephen Fry and Hugh Laurie to accompany the child actors, in a commercial where the adult parallel was much more explicit, with a hospitable invitation to consume alcohol being parodied by the offer of a milk shake. The boys in this advertisement discussed serious matters of mortgages, in exactly the same way as the comedians themselves debated the merits of various financial institutions in other commercials in the same campaign which began in 1987. Moreover, the immediate comic effect served to camouflage the serious point that children grew up quickly. Heinz series of growing children made the process into a guessing game which allowed multiple humorous variations – who would have imagined, for example, that Ian Botham had once dreamed of becoming a ballet dancer – but adulthood arrived soon enough.

Teenagers too found themselves under additional pressure, to conform to the cultural trends of the eighties while trying to see the world on their own terms. The old obsession with physical appearance remained, acne being, for example the object of two different but equally narcissistic advertisements for the antiseptic ointment Clearasil. One was set in a girls' boarding school with spots being shown as a night-time horror, like ghosts, ghouls and other sinister phenomena, the other showed the rivalry of two unlikely sisters, with the ugly duckling overcoming her spots, becoming the legendary swan and capturing the highly eligible boyfriend. Teenage boys could, meanwhile, enhance their own appearance and attractiveness by making abundant use of deodorants, such as new Brut (1988) which surpassed, as the advertisement pointed out, the product previously advertised by the undeniably virile, but ageing, and therefore no longer relevant, Henry Cooper. The teenage years were mostly shown as a very serious period. By the end of the decade relations with the opposite sex were not just the cause of emotional stress, with the ever-present danger of being abandoned by one's boy/girlfriend, but sexual intercourse, implicitly supposed to be the more or less imminent result of such relationships, was the source of more or less serious and recognisable dangers. Adverts for contraceptives, authorised in the light of the Aids scare, emphasised the need for responsible behaviour, but the subject still required a certain delicacy of approach. Durex chose to highlight the risk of unwanted pregnancy and symbolised barrier methods of contraception by physically separating the boy and girl by a wire fence. Mates adopted a light-hearted approach, using the subtitles which were to become a feature of its advertising to revive the time-honoured joke of the embarrassment of the boy asking for condoms in a chemist's shop.

If the dangers of temptation were strongly suggested here, in other fields advertisers were anxious to encourage teenagers to adopt adult ways; consumption was strongly advocated and the financial institutions in particular were keen to promote the wide and even indiscriminate use of their services and credit facilities. All were keen to throw off their conformist reputation and to present to their potential young customers an attractive and novel image. The National Westminster Bank (the *Action Bank*) and the Midland Bank (the *Listening Bank*) were well to the fore in this activity, closely followed by the TSB and the Halifax Building Society. Automatic cash machines were clearly illustrated, wonderful devices which dispensed money at the push of a button, leaving the impression that the funds were available without strings and could be spent forthwith. Halifax's message (1987) was brutally frank: a pretty girl was shown indicating the purchases she wished to make, with the voice-over song *The best things in life are free ... but I want money, that's what I want* making uncompromisingly clear her desire to participate in the consumer boom which was shown to be the prerogative of adults in 1980s advertisements.

The picture of men in 1980s commercials corresponded to a number of identities and revealed a number of activities and interests, some of them new. Man was still only the purchaser of a limited number of products. The comic image of the incompetent, workshy male was still present, a character unable to manage his washing and prone to participating in children's dinner table games when he did not initiate them. The garden held few attractions for him either, Flymo showed him preferring to stay with his feet up in a deckchair. The male as a social animal whose natural environment was the pub was a repeated motif, with various commercials showing the picture of a number of men striding more or less purposefully to their self-appointed destination. This was, however, all part of a mock-serious and even defensive approach to life in which the 'mate' was more important than members of the opposite sex and which was centred around the notion of light hearted pleasure, in beer commercials at least. Various advertisements exploited the milieu to present the sardonically humorous side of man's character: Carling Black Label placed its commentators (Mark and Steve) aside from the main action of the commercials, their exchanged remark *I bet he drinks Carling Black Label* being the prelude to a series of more or less improbable events, like the arrival of a surfer requesting a pint of aftershave or a waterboard employee switching off the rain with the mains supply. Foster's lager used Australian actor Paul Hogan in a similar ironical and vaguely macho way: he was *given some witty scripts in which he was seen observing strange British institutions ... with a wry Australian humour.*[8] In the 1980s the butts of his pleasantries included the pub pianist, fellow Australian Rolf Harris, British seaside resorts and an art gallery, all figures or objects offering a potential for fun or mockery.

There were three rivals to these established stereotypes in the 1980s. The strong and aggressive skilled manual worker or craftsman was a down-to-earth figure in several advertisements and emphasised the positive side of man's physical dominance, and the same image of rugged strength was associated with Rowntree's Yorkie through its truck driver and crane driver. The second new identity was that of the businessman, who had been banished from advertisements since the 1960s because of his remoteness from the concerns of ordinary life, but suddenly staged a comeback, as making money and being efficient suddenly returned to favour. He was not a likeable figure and could never fully become a role model, but his competitiveness and thirst for superiority on the squash court and in the boardroom matched well with the quest for success in professional life which many advertisements proclaimed. He was at least young and physically relatively attractive. The counterpart to this efficient figure, generally known as 'new man' appeared in various guises. He was for Volkswagen, in a memorable advertisement named *Casino* in 1985, a likeable failure, who had *married a sex kitten just as she turned into a cat* and who could accept losing all his (presumably enormous) fortune at the tables, without anything more than resigned good humour. The more individualistic male could also be narcissistic, keen on personal hygiene (Insignia, 1988) and on maintaining his physical shape in a gymnasium (Gillette, 1988). There was also a potentially softer and more domesticated side to his nature: Scottish Amicable showed such a man looking after his children (and, predictably, falling asleep in exhaustion after doing so) and giving a rose to the oldest (and ugliest) secretary in his office. One may wonder, of course, how seriously these diverse images should be taken. Clearly, they were expected by advertisers to appear sufficiently true to life to strike a chord at various real or aspirational levels and it seems evident that the range of male identities proposed indicates that different norms were becoming acceptable. At a time when society and cultural attitudes were changing, identity was no longer a single rigid concept.

Much the same impression can be gleaned from the treatment of women in commercials. The archetypal 'silly woman' was alive and surfaced in various situations, doing the washing of course, in which she remained an undisputed expert, but also stopping for lunch in her office (Philadelphia) and gossiping endlessly and inconsequentially to her long-suffering friend (Kwiksave). Nevertheless, many women in advertisements were shown as moving away from such reductive stereotypes; at the very least there was a new desire to look good and feel good and the wide padded shoulders and attractive perfumes were a standard feature of the presentation. A much more interesting female identity was available in the form of the fully emancipated career woman. In a paper for the Advertising Association, Sue Phipps noted the arrival of the new stereotype, while expressing the view that advertisers were in danger of exchanging one type of (inexact) caricature for another:

> *As well as updating traditional images, the big change in the portrayal of women has come from them frequently being shown at work. However this new aspect of her life doesn't mean she is no longer responsible for the traditional responsibilities. Very few commercials have managed to come to terms with what is perhaps the new stereotype of a career woman. She tends to be either shown as ruthlessly ambitious for the top — more macho than the men although devastatingly attractive along with it, or as some kind of juggling superwoman for whom all the compartments of her life just slot into place. Neither image is of much relevance for the women watching.*[9]

This new stereotype was indeed competitive, not just with other women, although a Vidal Sassoon advertisement put the most literal of interpretations on the idea of 'locker-room culture', but more importantly with men. Adverts sometimes showed specific professional stereotypes, like Bovril's fashion (role) model. The career woman was often seen heading off to business meetings, frequently by air. Virgin Atlantic proclaimed itself 'the business *person's* favourite airline' (my emphasis) and demonstrated the role reversal by allowing a female passenger to glance appreciatively at an elegant air steward, and in fact the travelling was more important than the work itself, which remained ill-defined, *flying off here, meetings there* was the imprecise way the Renault 25 commercial put it. More generally, women were shown as experts in their own right: Heat Electric portrayed a woman adviser discussing arrangements in the family home with a female client and women's famed communicational skills were put to new use by showing them explaining the finer details of savings or money management. The car was an essential part of a woman's life, offering freedom of movement, to match the financial and professional independence she was shown as having already attained and this liberty was a potential point of friction in dealings with men. Occasionally, the would-be dominant woman was treated as a slightly frightening or exaggerated figure: the predatory female had long been a potentially comic figure, and some of the male-orientated advertisements for beer fully exploited the inherent humour of such inverted situations. Financial independence sometimes went too far and was shown shading over into greed (Shape Yoghurt, 1989) while self-assertiveness transformed itself into the anarchic ruthlessness (VW Golf, 1985). It was in the realm of relations between the sexes that the inherent conflicts between competitive identities were most clearly revealed.

The ads of the 'me decade' of the 1980s showed a limited number of perfectly happy loners, sometimes with a touch of the eccentric like the helpful 'brother' in the Miller's Lite commercial, sometimes simply self-sufficient, with only a cat for company. Loneliness nevertheless remained a rare quality in advertisements and in the 80s, with both men and women anxious to establish supremacy, the potential for conflict was considerable. Sometimes, as in Gillette's *the best a man can get* (1988), an international, not exclusively British advert incidentally, male supremacy in all its forms was taken for granted, although it must be remembered that the product aimed to attract the male purchaser. The Levi's jeans advertisements which began in 1988, consistently showed man as physically and therefore emotionally dominant, one of them entitled *Fridge* making the point clearly in the voice over song with the line *when I make love to a woman*. Conversely, other advertisements, notably those for Lloyd's Bank featuring the crusty and backward Leo McKern, presented man as both physically and mentally unworthy of his favoured position which was thus made to appear simply an absurdity. For the woman, the balance between independence, self-assertiveness and loneliness was sometimes hard to strike. An all-woman team produced an advertisement for Camay in 1980 which was uncompromising in this respect: the heroine returned home in her Porsche to find a telephone message that a male friend intended to call her back at 8 p.m.. Her reaction was simply to put the answering machine on again and take to her bath, where she remained when the second call came, smiling at her own cleverness. The female figure in the VW Golf advertisement *Changes* was, if anything, even more single-minded. Having decided to leave her husband, she stormed out of their mews cottage, cast off what were presumably presents she had received, the wedding ring, fur coat and pearls and was about to throw away the car keys when she realised that here was something tangible that she could rely on for the future. As many critics were not slow to point out, this woman's status was, at the very least, enigmatic rather than unequivocally independent and Chanel n°5's commerical *Monument* (1989) gave a fuller development of the ambivalent nature of female identity. It depicted an attractive woman apparently refusing to submit to instructions of an older man who seemed to have enormous wealth and presumably power and influence to match. She also rejected the attentions of an embarrassed but obviously smitten garage attendant before accepting the embrace of a third man who was the real object of her affections. This woman could be interpreted at various levels, the independent career woman, the *femme fatale*, or, for this was a highly ambiguous statement of emancipation, the romantic or submissive woman. The final embrace took place in the shadow of the monument which gave the commercial its name, an isolated pillar of rock with an uncanny resemblance to an erect penis. No doubt the advertiser wished his product to be thought sufficiently versatile to match any or all of these roles.

The frequent use of conflictual situations often led to the adverts displaying a certain emotional coolness, absolutely in keeping with the egoism of the 1980s. There were exceptions, of course; De Beers, predictably enough, put the emphasis on sentiments, while Camay's stridently independent advertisement of 1980 was followed by another in 1983, using the same woman in a bath motif, but finishing with a man arriving and the couple deciding to spend an evening in, rather than at the planned party. The man in 1988 Ford Fiesta advertisement was equally categorical, the car was only the second-best thing in his life. The fact remained, however, that once romance was excluded, as it was in most of the 80s ads, and with casual or predatory sexual relationships deemed unacceptable in the light of the Aids threat, then emotional commitment was difficult to portray. The series of Renault 25 advertisements showed a couple going through a most exciting part of their professional lives, ending with them going into partnership together, but their remarks to one another rarely went beyond the strictly factual or the wife's enigmatically flirtatious reference to herself as *the woman you had breakfast with this morning*. The Gold Blend couple, living in the same apartment block but obviously unattached and attracted to one another, were also surprisingly slow to make any positive amorous declaration, their long awaited first kiss occurring only in 1991. Even infidelity was unsuccessful. Clark's shoes (1988) showed a seducer caught in the act of dining with a new lady and ceremoniously discomfited; Pirelli (1988) reused the old theme of a woman having plotted with her lover to send her husband to his death on a mountain road, only to be thwarted by the wonderful road-holding of his tyres, and thereby unmasked. Bisto (1988) opted for a wholly comic scenario: the unfaithful husband left his wife, not in search of carnal pleasure, but merely to enjoy another woman's gravy. Sentiment, when present in the 1980s, was often shown outside the classic situation of the couple, as illustrated by a Kenco coffee advertisement of 1988. The scene was of a pair of ex-lovers meeting again several years after splitting up. It was clear at once that the woman was happily married, but her momentary sadness for her former sweetheart was quickly eliminated when he produced the photograph of his own wife and family. It would be exaggerated to talk of adverts in the 1980s as consistently showing a time of unstable relationships or of role reversal between men and women, for they contained many examples of married couples with conventionally stereotyped roles. On the other hand, the presence, even of a limited number of different and contradictory identities, gives the strong impression of a society, where individualism was a driving force and where the guidelines of social conduct seemed unclearly drawn.

National identity was also an element which became of importance in the 1980s. For the first time since the didactic 1950s, precise and recognisable, if not actually recognised, places began to play a role in the process of communication and identification between advertiser and customer. In the 1980s, national pride was returning and the notion of a common geographical heritage with emotional overtones was part of this process. Places, both by their beauty and by their inherent familiarity were an important element in this feeling of belonging. Electricity for Life produced a most typical example of the technique in 1988, combining the natural and the technological. The commercial opened with a scene of a mountain in Snowdonia, Elidir Fawr, pointing out that it contained an underground power-station, before moving on to other examples of British engineering prowess, the Lloyds building in London, the Thames barrage, a nuclear power station and finally to a restored canal wharf in Manchester, which was then transformed into L.S. Lowry's painting of the same scene. The communicational method clearly drew some of its force from the complicity achieved by the viewer's desire and ability to identify some of the sights shown, even though the predominance of scenes from England may well have been perceived by some as yet another sign of disregard for other parts of the United Kingdom. Another advertisement, the same year, invited visitors to sample the improbable delights of the Sellafield nuclear reprocessing establishment and pointed out that it was such a popular destination that the visitor centre had had to be enlarged to accommodate them. In the praise of national heritage, even the unsavoury reputation of the plant could be overlooked. Many 80s advertisements depicted leisure activities, which, if not actually practised by the viewer, were nevertheless conceived as somehow familiar and typical and again heightened the sense of complicity. The importance of national identity was reinforced by the simple label *British* which was used without the reticence which it had attracted in the two preceding decades and, more cogently perhaps by the implicit comparison with what was demonstrably not British. Television commercials treated foreigners comically rather than maliciously but almost always stereotypically. The Australian covered his innate lack of refinement by a display of deadpan wit, while the German, however much his cars might be admired, was a ruthless competitor when it came to holiday destinations and one whose native seriousness was unalloyed by positive characteristics. By the end of the 80s the identities which had prevailed for much of the decade were once again called into question, as companies were compelled to face the harsh realities of an imminent recession, but they nevertheless give a clear indication of the types of activities and attitudes which advertisers and other opinion formers were keen to present as typical of a tumultuous decade.

Life-styles

An advertisement for Rennies, first transmitted in 1988, had as its message the busy lives people led and the commercial itself might be judged to have illustrated various facets of the complexities of modern living: coping at the double with domestic life, business, shopping and travel, all of which brought their own particular difficulties and stresses. It is, however, important to point out that the variety of life-styles[10] was a key notion and that behavioural models differed according to social class and/or to income, as well as according to whether a realistic or aspirational point of view was adopted. Age was also a determining factor and one feature of 1980s ads was that they frequently appealed to quite specialised audiences, being therefore of no relevance to the majority of the viewing population at a time when narrowcasting was still not a reality. It was of course true that companies could promote their corporate image, through the quality of their advertisements, even when their target audience was not present.

Many advertisements still dealt with everyday routine purchases such as food and cleaning materials or with public services. Of the top 20 advertisers in 1984, for example, nine were food manufacturers, two were tobacco companies, two were nationalised industries and two more, including Procter & Gamble, the biggest spender of all, produced household cleaning materials. Changes were nevertheless occurring and certain trends could be observed. The amount of retail grocery sales through multiples (principally supermarkets) had risen to 73 per cent in 1983 (as against 27 per cent in 1961) and this had two notable effects in television ads. Although supermarkets still produced their own brands, and occasionally promoted them, stores were anxious to stress the idea of quality, *it asda be perfect* as one commercial proclaimed. As a corollary to this idea even downmarket chains like Kwiksave advertised themselves as places where (quality) branded goods were available. W H Smith and Woolworth adopted the same technique for the promotion of records and CDs and similar methods obtained in discount warehouses' commercials, with Comet, in particular, giving a long list of the different makers whose goods they stocked and the choice they therefore offered to customers, as well as emphasising the flexibility of their opening hours. Consumption was the key notion and many advertisements of the 80s put the accent on conspicuous wealth. Central heating, which had been considered a substantial luxury only a short time before, was depicted, realistically enough, as a standard feature of new homes, but it was heavily promoted both by gas and electricity companies as a necessity of modern living, with the two organisations competing as fiercely in this field as in the field of cooking. In the advertisements of the 1980s though, the home had become more than just a place to live; it was also a repository for items indicating one's good taste or wealth or both. Beyond the huge and well-appointed kitchens and bathrooms which had long been a feature in commercials, decoration and adornment were heavily represented, with tradition and age being allied to quality. The Flavel Emberglow gas fire advertised in 1989, for example, was shown in a large room which also contained a magnificent fireplace, a 'cello, an old and obviously rare book, a pair of ancient spectacles and a cut-glass decanter, the fire itself being 'traditionally cast' to complete the equation between age and quality. Sainsbury's Homebase stores took the idea of accessible abundance one stage further, showing couples entering an empty house which had apparently just been bought and imagining all the items they would need to furnish and equip every part of it.

Such incitement to conspicuous consumption was represented as being normal at a time when, in the image frequently conveyed, there was a lot of money about and when the idea of quality was an understandable selling argument after the privations and general gloom of the 1970s. Despite the improvements in the NHS, private medical care was a frequent element of salary packages and the personal treatment shown as being offered by BUPA, ready access to specialists, comfortable and well-furnished individual rooms, for instance, could be promoted successfully with little exaggeration. Expensive items not only sold without particular difficulty but high cost was actually a positive argument. Gold Blend coffee was 'sophisticated' as were those who drank it and Sainsbury's produced a somewhat tongue-in-cheek version of the same argument for their tomato ketchup, which was 'vintage' in so far as it was made only from one type of Italian tomatoes harvested in a given year, which again justified its premium price. The attitude of self-indulgence was summed up in the 1988 advertisement for the appropriately named after-shave Sybaris: *for the man who appreciates luxury*. Quality foreign goods almost literally 'spoke for themselves', Audi's German slogan 'Vorsprung durch Technik' became famous, with Geoffrey Palmer's superior tones suggesting the brand image as clearly as the details of the life-style the car was associated with, as German couples made their way to their Spanish holiday villas. In 1989 the Sony Trinitron used mime not words to make the same point about quality: *Nothing sounds like Sony, why compromise?*. All aspects of life were dominated by the idea of excellence. Clothes were fashionable and adorned with appropriate and expensive gold or pearl jewellery, while Clark's shoes made an additional point about quality, the softest leather did not creak.

If actual life-styles were different then aspirations varied too. Prudential Insurance in parallel 'his and hers' adverts for its investments produced at the end of the decade an extensive if not substantive list of 1980s wishes and expectations. After the repeated introduction *I want to be*, itself absolutely typical of the 'me decade', the items in the woman's list were sometimes whimsical and humorous, *I want to be a twelve* (a middle-aged woman struggling to get into a new dress), sometimes capricious, *I want to be blonde, I want to be out late* (mouthed by teenage girls), but often perceptive about wishes whether of a trivial or serious nature, *green* (an ecologist), *brown* (sun-tanned), *next* (a bridesmaid), *discovered* (a sculptress), *in by Christmas* (a house-purchaser). The key to a satisfactory life-style was often the correct choice of a home and the adverts showed a bewildering variety, all apparently pleasing their owners, but representing very different social aspirations. Fine, often Georgian, buildings abounded, in the town or the country, while extremely chic modern glass and concrete residences with enormous windows or tastefully renovated older premises were apparently equally in vogue for the most affluent: the Halifax Building Society showed that even a redundant warehouse could provide an attractive city apartment. The desire for owner-occupation on a more modest scale could be satisfied by a modern house on a new development (Wimpey, 1984, and Electric Central Heating Medallion Homes, 1989) and like all homes in advertisements, they were unexpectedly spacious once the camera had passed through the front door. Similar expressions of modest or expansive/expensive life-styles could be found in the choice of holiday or car. Alan Whicker's Barclaycard advertisement conjured up the image of exotic and dangerous remote foreign locations, the lower social classes' more down-to-earth projects were captured by Bold automatic, with the central character apparently just back from a package holiday in Spain, complete with garish flowered shirt, enormous sombrero and toy donkey. The car matched particularly well with real and imagined life-styles and identities and was a particularly carefully targeted product: thus the Seat Ibiza suggested independence, the Ford Fiesta evoked the desire for speed and youthfulness, while the Renault 25 exuded luxury and comfort, an impression reinforced by images of a young boy leaving the vehicle for music or riding lessons.

The 'enterprise culture'

If the 80s were truly the 'me decade' then the strongest source of the egoism was the love of money and what it could bring, the British citizen being at least tacitly encouraged to believe that such prosperity was a national rather than a world-wide phenomenon. Newspapers regularly offered their readers the possibility of winning vast amounts of cash and the very immediacy of these draws and competitions was such that carefully scheduled television advertising was a near essential. Commercials for banks, building societies and insurance companies abounded and this was one of the remarkable transformations in the 1980s, in the wake of a change in the IBA's rules concerning financial advertising and of Stock Exchange deregulation. The clearing banks had first advertised only in 1964 because of a cartel arrangement between them intended to eliminate wasteful competition, but the financial sector was one of the growth areas in advertising in the 1980s. Between 1980 and 1984, TV advertising expenditure more than trebled from some £23 million to £78 million as institutions (banks and building societies) vied with one another to attract young customers in particular. At the other end of the age scale, pensioners or those approaching retirement were wooed by investment opportunities, spurred on by the possibility for most age groups of making their own independent pension arrangements as the government removed the obligation to participate in the state supplementary pension scheme or in employer-run schemes. More in keeping with the enterprise culture of the decade were the various possibilities for starting one's own business which all banks claimed to wish to foster. At the time of the property boom, for most of the population, the search for a mortgage was a major problem and here once more, the financial institutions were keen to offer their services.

Most importantly, the positive portrayal of enterprise was a regular feature of 80s ads. The underlying message of the benefits of business culture was stated very explicitly in an advert for Esso in 1980, soon after Margaret Thatcher took office. Against a simple visual of a tiger, the company's emblem, advancing slowly but steadily up a slope, the male voice-over pointed out that improving business meant improving Britain, that confidence in the country's future meant more investment and that investment created jobs, that the use of new technology required the training of new people and that to climb out of a recession it was necessary to point one's head not downhill but upwards. Esso's planned investment of £600 million was good for the company and good for Britain. This message, apparently loosely based on Abraham Lincoln's inaugural speech, was expressing a philosophy, later hotly contested, that successful business would bring benefits to all according to what became known as the 'trickle-down' theory. The portrayal of successful small businesses, a bridal hire service (Ariel) and a bakery (Natwest), which were then used as a promotional vehicle for other products and services, was one way in which adverts subscribed to the notion, while PG Tips' portrayal of a sales director negotiating hard (over language of tea stickers) confirmed the same impression of the value of enterprise. The sine qua non for business success was, naturally enough, efficiency and modernisation. Often repeated Amstrad advertisements for the PC 2286 emphasised the speed of the new machine compared with its predecessor and the quality of its graphics. British Gas and Radio Rentals stressed the quality of their service, the former demonstrating the care which it lavished on its customers and their heating systems through an extended metaphor presenting the boiler as a patient. The Royal Mail accentuated its versatility both through the depiction of an interview held by video-conference and by the illustration of the manpower and machinery involved in the task of delivering a letter. British Airways showed the public how hard a businessman's life actually could be, as he was presented on an all-night flight from New York, during which he was involved in preparing his report for the next morning on a lap-top computer. Business dealings were not without their down-side, in the ruthlessness and competition which they inspired, but this negative aspect tended typically to be underplayed and restricted to the metaphorical or humorous level. The desire for domination was symbolised by the enormous windows allowing a view not just out but down, while the boardroom intrigues suggested by the British Airways Club Class commercial of 1988 misfired thanks to the quality of service provided by the airline. The same year, the managing director in a Datapost ad gave such peremptory but imprecise instructions to his subordinate that he was dismayed to see a whole office-full of filing cabinets being delivered in time to help him give his morning presentation.

Before the end of the decade, however, the mood in adverts was beginning to change; the actual economic situation in the United Kingdom was such that watching the pennies rather than thoughtless spending seemed a more sensible course of action, the more so as the house price bubble had already burst. The fact was acknowledged by the Woolwich Building Society which, in 1989, presented the buying of a new home as a cross between an obstacle course and a horse race at a time of *galloping interest rates*. In these circumstances, reaction set in, a number of advertisements implicitly attacked the trend towards impersonalisation and the treating of people as automata, while those who had never shared the benefits of the 80s boom were pleased to see a return to greater realism in commercial breaks. As Virginia Matthews concluded:

> *Fat women on council estates are sick of feeling that they have to be young and svelte and twenty-one to use washing up liquid X. On* EastEnders, *they already see characters who look like the next-door neighbours. Now they want ordinariness in the commercial breaks.*[11]

Writing a couple of years before, Barry Day had made a similar point, but the lesson had not been fully learned:

> *The product must be seen as relevant to the way people live which means the communication must start from a common point of reference.*[12]

Some 1980s adverts had undoubtedly erred on the side of hyperbolic aspiration at the expense of reality. There were in fact two trends at work at the end of the 80s. For the average viewer, there was something akin to Schadenfreude at the thought of yuppies getting their just deserts. As Martin Davidson concluded:

> *The 80s brilliantly exploited the link between commerce and a new ethic of self, but it is a link whose heyday is arguably over. There is a sense of come-uppance in the air, as though the price we have to pay for the 80s is now becoming all too clear.*[13]

On the part of advertisers there was a greater sense of economic realism, or a forced awareness of the emptiness of the egoistic vision which had been so loudly proclaimed. In 1988, Natwest ran an advert showing a young man setting up, with the human touch, a successful bakery business. In addition to the prevalent work ethic and the emphasis on a quality product, the boss was shown, with his family and with his workers, lighting the candle on an anniversary cake specially made to celebrate his first year's trading. The sound track was calculated to reinforce the message of collective endeavour, using the apparently original version of Jerry and the Pacemakers' 1960s hit, *You'll never walk alone*, which had been adopted first as the anthem of the supporters of Liverpool Football Club and had subsequently been taken up by many other teams. Audi was credited with having made the most remarkable change in style at the end of the 1980s, with a commercial whose title *Nick of Time* conveyed both the narrative message of the advert, with a man realising his true priorities, driving to a maternity hospital, having picked up his son on the way, where they arrived just as his second child was born, and an ecological theme, for this Audi, like all others, was fitted with a catalytic convertor. The final (female) voice-over stated that the Audi was the natural choice of the heart and the head, and Martin Davidson interpreted the sea-change this advertisement represented in the following hyperbolic terms:

> ... *this is a journey towards repudiating everything we thought consumerism was about. This is advertising participating in its own demise, acknowledging that we buy things for reasons bigger than those of mere consumerism ... there is no doubt that we are being plugged into new values, wonderment, heart and mind coalescing in taking the world into a new generation.*[14]

Communication, continuity and evolution

The 1980s saw further developments in the creativity and technical quality of commercials which had now fully become a recognised genre in their own right. The contrasts within the decade are considerable. Company boss Victor Kiam's personal message (1989) about 'his' Remington microscreen shaver and Fuzzaway cleaning brush, incongruously combined within the same commercial, was to all intents and purposes a throwback to the very early days of TV advertising, apparently transmitted internationally and without the slightest concession to progress. The same year saw another deliberately regressive approach. Lever Brothers launched a new washing powder, Radion, its first liquid/powder variant for over a decade, using the same hard-sell methods that had proved successful when the product had been introduced to the American market. The forceful message of the product's USP, that it cleaned and deodorised, was delivered direct to camera and in commanding tones by a news presenter, with a screen behind him serving to illustrate his words. Writing in *Advertising Works 6*, Brent Gosling admitted the unpopularity of the commercial, *the advertisement has been criticised, not least from within the advertising fraternity. The advertising has been described as harsh, brash, vulgar and offensive and is accused of setting the industry back 30 years*, but went on to claim that there were other criteria. *This communication worked by challenging the housewife. By challenging her confidence in her wash it dares her to try Radion. The loudness of the approach prompts some dislike and recoil but this only serves to strengthen Radion's position as a challenge to be met.*[15] In fact, Radion's effective advert bucked the general trend. The movement in the 1980s, even for everyday products, continued to be away from direct product claims to more modern, 'life-style' commercials, which critics like Sue Phipps preferred:

> *There are of course advertisers who have evolved their stereotyped images to keep pace with the changes in society, and manage therefore to keep close to their consumer ... Both the Persil mum and the Oxo mum have come a long way ... The Oxo mum can hold her own in any forum and there is never any feeling that, by stereotyping her as a housewife, she becomes less convincing ... Unfortunately though it only takes one Radion commercial to give the impression that we are still in the dark ages.*[16]

Other commercials went further along the road of becoming the added value which almost eclipsed the product itself. In the early 1980s, British Rail's slogan had been *the age of the train*, voiced by Jimmy Saville, and later in the decade this was transformed into an expression of corporate endeavour, *we're getting there*. In 1988 and 1989, Saatchi and Saatchi produced two aesthetically memorable advertisements for Intercity which, perhaps understandably, eschewed product claims in favour of the portrayal of a series of enigmatic characters, filmed in sepia tints, relaxing as the journey passed. VW's advertisements for the Golf (*Casino* and *Changes*, 1985) were equally successful in the promotion of the product, without mentioning it intrusively. The life-style and situations portrayed, unreal or remote though they were for most TV viewers, nevertheless struck a chord (*what was striking about the ads was the way in which they talked about the car indirectly, through the person who would drive it*[17]) and represented a classic example of the value of advertising becoming a selling proposition in its own right.

Not all advertisements achieved this of course, but many did rely on the association of brand image with a recognisable and more or less recurrent or developing scenario, through the increasing use of advertising series. In addition to PG Tips, Oxo, Milk Tray and Hamlet, the basic principles behind which dated from previous decades, the 1980s saw two soap opera type serials, for Renault 25 and for Gold Blend coffee, in which the same characters lived through a developing situation. In addition, there were several series, such as those advertising Carling Black Label, Fosters, Castlemaine XXXX, Heineken and the Alliance and Leicester Building Society, which conveyed their message either by humour or recurrent characters or both. By the 1980s, television advertising techniques had become fully developed. The use of an independent voice-over or visuals to communicate details of the message became commonplace, but this was not the end of experiment and evolution. Mates condoms used subtitles to give the text of what characters were thinking as opposed to saying and Rover used a similar procedure in an advert spoken entirely in German, presumably in an attempt to benefit from associations with the favourable, 'quality' image of products from that country. British Airways Club Class allowed the visuals and spoken text to contradict one another to achieve an effect of what would be classed in another context as dramatic irony.

The most interesting communicational feature of the decade, and a sure sign that television commercials had come of age, was the image of advertising feeding on itself as source of intertextuality, in a way which went well beyond simple repetition. Saatchi and Saatchi created an elaborate advertisement for British Airways, with crowds dressed in different colours moving in co-ordinated fashion to produce patterns, the last of which was an eye. Comparisons could no doubt be drawn with the mass images of people united in a common cause who had appeared in the Coca Cola advertisements from 1970 onwards. McCain produced a parody of the typical homecoming scenario, by giving its children, girls included, deep masculine voices as they demanded food, but the two most obvious examples of the technique of intertextuality, what one might call metapublicity, advertising about advertising or advertising perpetuating itself, came in two commercials for Carling Black Label. The first opened with the by now established line, *I bet he drinks Carling Black Label*, which one of the two regular characters addressed to his friend. This time the wager concerned the next man to come through the door. The figure who emerged, to the music of Carmina Burana, turned out to be a surfer, riding the wave which entered the pub, wearing pink bathing shorts, who asked for a *pint of aftershave*. At several years remove, this commercial had taken the images and music of the first Old Spice commercial of the 1970s; the barman's question, whether the surfer wanted *a* straight *glass* (my emphasis), could be taken as a suggestion of homosexuality which Old Spice and other male deodorants had been most anxious to avoid when they were first advertised. The second, and more obvious, pastiche concerned the Levi's stonewashed jeans advertisement of 1985. The following year, Black Label produced its imitation. The scenario was close to the original, with very similar-looking actors, the only difference coming in the punch line. Here, the voices of Mark and Steve, who had been out of shot suddenly made themselves heard. The customary, *I bet ...* was audible, but the reply, *No, he doesn't wash his underpants* gained its significance as it was shown that the two regulars had apparently stripped entirely before starting their washing. This type of parody and direct borrowing from one advertisement from another, often for comic effect, were to be part and parcel of the technique of commercials in the years to come, showing an apparent respect for the competence of the viewer and soliciting his complicity.

Notes

1   Quoted in David McKie (ed), *The Election – A Voters' Guide*, London, Fourth Estate, 1992, page 11.

2   Alan Sked and Chris Cook, *op. cit.*, page 329. The authors categorise Margaret Thatcher as a nineteenth-century Liberal.

3   Patrick Jenkin in the *Guardian* of September 1978, quoted by Sked and Cook, *op. cit.*, page 327.

4   Between 1979 and 1989, the percentage of owner-occupied homes (by mortgage or outright) rose from 52 per cent to 64 per cent, while the figure for council-rented accommodation fell from 34 per cent to 26 per cent.

5   These figures represent the numbers out of work and claiming benefit, the current basis of assessment.

6   Peter York and Charles Jennings, *Peter York's Eighties*, London, BBC, 1993, pages 142 - 143.

7   Writing in *The Listener* of 9th June 1988, Virginia Matthews commented: *The blacks you see in British commercials are hidden behind counters, on the supermarket check-out or they're the cool-Rasta-with-the-ghettoblaster-and-sunglasses-stereotype.*

8   Torin Douglas, *The Complete Guide to Advertising*, London, Papermac, 1986, page 121.

9   Sue Phipps, *A Woman's Place? – The Portrayal of Women in Advertisements*, London, Advertising Association, 1991, pages 17 and 18.

10 This section does not seek to use the term *life-styles* in its philosophical, business or commercial sense, although, as I suggest, many individuals recognised and identified with some at least of the types of activities and attitudes shown in adverts.

11 Virginia Matthews, "Really Useful", *The Listener*, 26th January 1989.

12 Preface to Torin Douglas, *op. cit.*, page 9.

13 Martin Davidson, *op. cit.*, page 93.

14 Martin Davidson, *op. cit.*, pages 92 and 93.

15 Brent Gosling, "The Case for Radion Automatic: A New Brand in the Lever Portfolio", in

Paul Feldwick (ed), *Advertising Works 6*, Henley-on-Thames, NTC, 1991, pages 209 and 221.

16   Sue Phipps, *op. cit.*, page 17.

17   Gavin Macdonald and Anthony Buck, "The Volkswagen Golf 1984-1990", in Chris Baker (ed) *Advertising Works 7*, Henley-on-Thames, NTC, 1993, page 94.

IV

The new realities of the 1990s

As in the 1980s, advertising in the 1990s faced new difficulties and new challenges. The Thatcher era had ended on a note of uncertainty, which prompted a desire for the re-examination of criteria which had been widely accepted for a number of years. The nineties saw a resurgence of the notions of responsibility and service which was fully reflected in the commercials of the decade. At the same time, there was no question of simply 'turning the clock back', new preoccupations like the environment and an ageing population made themselves felt and commercial and government advertisements alike reacted to these fresh demands. The return to power of New Labour in 1997, after the Party's 18 years in opposition, marked a sea change which has had an effect on attitudes within British society, and on the advertisements transmitted. This chapter indicates the substantial developments which have occurred and the opening historical outline stresses not only the political upheavals of the decade, but also the growing preoccupation with television itself at a time of rapid technological innovation. As for the previous chapter, the political and economic events detailed here are a necessary part of the background to both commercial and governmental adverts.

Historical, political, economic and social context

The resignation of Margaret Thatcher brought her Chancellor of the Exchequer John Major to the post of Prime Minister. The new man expressed himself keen to direct a country 'at ease with itself' but the economic difficulties persisted and some of the more radical measures initiated by Margaret Thatcher were still actually to come into effect. The Poll Tax was rapidly and expensively abolished, to be replaced by what was essentially the old rates system reborn. The country was still in deep recession, however, with 3 million unemployed, according to the government's own figures which were widely believed to underestimate the actual total. The Gulf War of 1991 saw substantial British military involvement, but attitudes to this war were different from those of the Falklands conflict: the United Kingdom only played a relatively minor role in an enterprise which was run by the United States and which was, moreover, most widely covered on the international news channel CNN. British troops suffered few immediate casualties, although the longer-term effects of chemical weapons remain to be conclusively determined.

The greater popularity of John Major, compared with both his predecessor and Labour leader Neil Kinnock, proved to be a more decisive factor than the modernising of the Labour party and the April 1992 general election returned the Conservatives for a fourth consecutive term in office, albeit with an overall majority of only 21, which was later to make the government's survival inordinately dependent on minority parties, most crucially the Ulster Unionists. Kinnock resigned from the Labour leadership, to be replaced by John Smith who did much to democratise his party by taking power away from the large trade unions and giving greater importance to individual members, before his premature death in May 1994. His successor was Tony Blair. The nadir in the government's economic fortunes was reached in September 1992, when pressure on the weakest European currencies, the escudo, the peseta, the lira and the pound, led to a panic increase in interest rates and Britain's ignominious withdrawal from the ERM. Chancellor Norman Lamont was dismissed shortly afterwards, to the delight of the popular press which held his monetary policies responsible for the sufferings wrought on the country. In a short time, the pound lost 15 per cent of its value, but this proved to be a blessing in disguise in export markets as the world economy started to improve. The adoption of the European Single Market in 1992 was another factor in the general economic improvement. By early 1995, unemployment was well under 3 million, inflation had dropped to a mere 2 per cent and economic growth over the previous twelve months had reached 3.5 per cent; similarly encouraging economic signs were to be maintained up to and beyond the 1997 election which the Conservatives delayed until the last moment in the desperate hope that the good economic indicators would lead to an upturn in their fortunes. The 'feel-good' factor remained elusive; the problem was, put simply, that the many controversial effects of Thatcherite policies began to be fully realised and the country lost faith in the government and its capacity to improve the situation. The signing of the Maastricht Treaty of 1992 seemed destined to diminish the country's independence, but the root problem at home often came down to money and to the way in which the country was being run. Quangos had taken over many of the functions of elected local government and were dominated by right-wing figures and money was wasted on expensive computer equipment which did not work, like the £48 million spent by the Department of Employment, while John Major's solution to decaying public services was the Citizens' Charter which was unrealistically supposed to improve standards without making funds available.

What made things worse was the realisation of some of the more unpalatable aspects of privatisation; in many cases, shares were thought to have been sold too cheaply and some government ministers who had been involved in privatising industries saw nothing untoward in accepting lucrative offers to sit on the boards of the industries with which they had been involved. The effects of privatised monopolies in the utilities were particularly notorious: while large-scale redundancies among workpeople were announced, directors helped themselves to over-generous pay rises, the most infamous being that granted to the head of British Gas, Cedric Brown, who received a 75 per cent increase in late 1994, to bring his annual salary to £475,000. At the same time, service in these industries was felt to be wanting, the worst example being no doubt that of the water industry, whose rising charges, leaking water mains and inadequate sewerage systems resulted in privations for customers and in Britain having, allegedly, the most polluted beaches in Europe. There were other causes of complaint too. The introduction of market procedures into the health service appeared to create time-consuming bureaucracy at the expense of patient care; by 1994 some 95 per cent of hospital treatment was being supplied by independent trusts, while doctors who had become fund-holders and therefore ran their own budgets, found themselves obliged to carry out more and more burdensome administrative tasks. The government claimed that waiting lists for hospital treatment had fallen from 200,000 in 1987 to under 65,000 in 1994 and that average waiting times had been cut from nine months to five, but this information and the introduction of the Patients' Charter did not allay fears that the figures were being manipulated and that, more fundamentally, the necessary funds were simply not being provided. Cuts in welfare entitlements and in nursing and teaching staff, the dubious operations of the Child Support Agency which pursued absent fathers, the institution of the job seekers' allowance which effectively reduced unemployment benefit and the revelation that some 1.5 million purchasers of the personal pension policies advocated by the government in 1988 had been sold unsuitable products were further sources of criticism and embarrassment. Negative equity was still a substantial problem. House repossessions had reached a peak of over 75,000 in 1991, but by 1994 they were still running at almost 50,000 a year. Moreover, customers were less and less satisfied with the operations of the financial institutions. In December 1991, the Consumers' Association reported that one bank customer in eight had been incorrectly charged, that one in six had had problems with a direct debit or standing order and that almost one in five was dissatisfied with the way the mistakes had been investigated. The figures for 1994 were no better. To complete the government's tale of woe, John Major's 'back to basics' appeal, aimed at a return to acceptable standards in public and private life, backfired spectacularly, with frequent revelations of financial irregularities and sexual impropriety within the Conservative party and the government. Furthermore, the Conservatives were dogged by problems of policy over Europe, with an ever-widening gap between pro-Europeans and sceptics.

The achievements of the Major government have tended to be outweighed by its political weakness. The British economy was in a better state than those of most European countries, especially as, after the dramatic collapse of the Soviet Union and the start of reunification, Germany was slowed by the need to integrate the backward states of the East. Like Margaret Thatcher, John Major took initiatives aimed at improving the situation in Northern Ireland, but the Prime Minister's hands were tied by his dependence on the Ulster Unionists for political survival as the government suffered a series of by-election defeats. 1994 saw the creation of the National Lottery which, despite all the criticisms over its administration by a private consortium and the objection to the enterprise on moral grounds, has been a popular success and has produced vast additional funds for a variety of good causes. The same year also witnessed the long-awaited opening of the Channel Tunnel which has transformed cross-channel traffic and has proved a technological and logistical success, even if the British government's reluctance to provide the high-speed rail links from the tunnel to the capital is in marked contrast with the infrastructure available in France and Belgium. Well before the general election on 1st May 1997, pollsters were predicting that the Conservatives would suffer a crushing defeat and on this occasion their forecasts proved correct. Tony Blair's New Labour swept to a victory the size of which astonished even its supporters (179 seats), leaving the Conservatives without a single seat in Scotland and Wales, surpassing even Attlee's landslide in 1945 and putting at the head of the country the youngest Prime Minister of the century. Expectations for Tony Blair's government were high and certain of the steps promised in the party's manifesto have been taken – the introduction of a minimum wage, action to fight unemployment and improve training, devolution for Scotland and Wales – and with the Good Friday Agreement of 1998, the British government seemed closer than ever to resolving the problem of Ulster.

The 1990s have equally been a period of rapid change in British television. The Broadcasting Act of 1990, which took two years to go through its various parliamentary stages, was intended to deregulate British commercial television and enable it to face the inexorable competition of global media forces. One of first tasks of the new television regulator, the ITC, was to select the companies which would hold the franchises for the regions and for breakfast television from 1993 onwards. The complex and much criticised selection procedure was in two basic stages. Prospective bidders had to satisfy the ITC both that their proposed programmes passed the so-called 'quality threshold' and that their business plans were adequate for the whole 10 year period of the contract; once this hurdle was passed, the concession was to be granted to the highest bidder unless another candidate was deemed to propose programmes of markedly better quality. In the event, this last criterion, added late in the Bill's parliamentary progress as fears arose about the quality of future broadcasting, was never invoked. Severe anomalies existed, however. As Robertson and Nicol had anticipated, prospective franchise holders were not treated equally by *a crazy system in which unopposed franchise holders will succeed by offering a pittance while contestants will pawn their programme-making cash in order to win the right to make programmes they then cannot finance.*[1] These fears were borne out even though all companies had to pay a fixed percentage of so-called 'qualifying revenue' determined by the ITC and based on the population of the region for which they were applying. What was decisive in the event of competition was the additional cash bid and it was here that the absurdities became apparent. Central Television, without a competitor for the Midlands franchise, offered only £2,000, while Yorkshire Television, in a less populous region paid over £37 million to see off its rivals. The case that raised the greatest controversy was that of Thames Television. This London company had achieved a laudable standard of programming, but had caused government displeasure by its independent stance, notably over the killing of three IRA members by the SAS in Gibraltar in 1988 and by the wide coverage it had given to the GLC's anti-abolition campaign. Its replacement by Carlton, whose record has subsequently proved to be undistinguished, was seen as an act of vengeance orchestrated by no less a person than the Prime Minister herself.

The Broadcasting Act showed the importance of television as a factor in British life. When John Major became Prime Minister, responsibility for the media was transferred to the Department of National Heritage; on the arrival of Tony Blair the ministry was re-named the Department for Culture, Media and Sport. The fears expressed in the late 1980s about the ability of independent television to face worldwide competition were soon realised. The 1990 Broadcasting Act had limited mergers between companies, but this measure soon proved unworkable and the ITC authorised take-overs. The situation was regularised by the 1996 Broadcasting Act and the terrestrial programmes available to over 96 per cent of the population are now transmitted by four consortia headed respectively by Carlton, Granada, Scottish Television and Meridian. March 1997 saw the much-delayed and ultimately unexpected launch of Channel Five. The 1990 Broadcasting Act had envisaged the fifth channel, but difficulties over finance and over the obligation on the contractor to retune video-recorders to prevent interference proved substantial obstacles. In the event, Channel Five has achieved a small but increasing share of viewing,[2] captured mostly from ITV, whose audience has declined from over 42 per cent in 1991 to little more than 30 per cent today. The BBC's position has become relatively stable, at just over 40 per cent for BBC 1 and BBC 2 combined and the Corporation's Charter was renewed in 1996 for a further 10 years. The growth of cable and satellite viewing continues apace. By the end of 1998, the number of homes with satellite installations had reached 4.1 million and, according to BARB, the viewing of terrestrial television in these homes has fallen to little more than 60 per cent.[3] The dominance of satellite channels in certain fields, especially Sky in sports transmissions, has given real cause for concern as to the survival of free-to-air services and in accordance with the 1996 Broadcasting Act the Secretary of State for Culture, Media and Sport has been empowered to draw up a list of 'national events' which must be available, if only in the form of edited highlights, without satellite or cable connections. The rapid development of cable services was assured once the interactive possibilities offered by optical fibre cable had attracted several multi-service operators. By July 1998, the number of homes 'passed' by cable, ie having the possibility of connection, had reached over 11 million; more than 32 per cent of these were wired for telephone and 22.5 per cent for television. The fragmentation of the television audience, and the possibility for advertisers to gain access to groups of particular interest, can only be accelerated by the presence of digital television, started on 1st October 1998 by Sky and reckoned in May 1999 to have reached over 600,000 homes.

The fate and role of television advertising becomes particularly significant in this atmosphere of global competition and of programmes initiated from outside the United Kingdom. The previous chapters have attempted to indicate the national character of British advertising and this trend has been maintained in the 1990s, although the use of multinational advertisements has grown and the influence of the international sponsorship of such worldwide events as the Olympic Games and the World Cup can be seen. The decade has also been a period of further substantial technical and creative innovation, while witnessing advertising's growing dependence on its own intertextuality, as ideas of previous decades have been modified and re-used. At the same time, it continues to reflect trends and attitudes in society and within television itself. 1990s commercials are in some ways a reaction to what became regarded as the excesses of the 1980s, but have further developed their own styles and criteria. According to the Advertising Association's figures, spending has continued to increase: the total figure on terrestrial television (for transmission and production costs) rose by 34 per cent in real terms between 1990 and 1998 (despite two years, 1990 and 1991 which witnessed relative decreases) to reach a total of £3,426 million for transmission charges alone, while cable and satellite advertising expenditure has rocketed. In 1992, expenditure was a mere £70.6 million, six years later it had reached £440.7 million.

The caring nineties

Such was the widely used epithet in the early 1990s, by advertisers and commentators alike, to talk of the fundamental shift of opinion which prevailed at the beginning of the decade, a transformation as radical, perhaps, as that which had been observed with the arrival in power of Margaret Thatcher. There was certainly plenty of evidence in the advertisements of the time, to suggest that the egoism of the 1980s had disappeared, even if the term 'caring' is open to a variety of interpretations. One meaning of the expression was the desire to make life comfortable and easy for oneself. The famous and highly praised 'Creature Comforts' advertisements, based on Aardman animations, to promote electricity were a case in point. The emphasis was put on immediate domestic concerns: the facilities electricity brought, how life became more agreeable and more convenient and the reasonable cost of the services in question. The serious desire for consumption of the eighties had gone, and the dichotomy between the message and the means of presentation, with a tortoise named Terry incongruously talking about the pleasures of a shower after his morning workout, was an effective means of communication, using a half ironic tone to suggest good sense and moderation. British Gas adopted a somewhat similar approach in 1991, by employing the character of J. R. Ewing, to illustrate the practical benefits of gas heating; only the more than life-size reputation of such a figure could now justify the opulence shown in his London apartment. Numerous other advertisers emphasised the quality of the service and their desire to help customers, in an attempt to themselves appear more caring than others. The sheer number of such claims ultimately made them appear commonplace and, on closer examination, some of the extra 'service' offered was highly limited. Tesco, Do-it-All and Safeways, at different dates, all made very similar points. Tesco emphasised that its stores offered facilities for mothers with babies, areas for changing, for feeding (with the possibility of warming bottles) and special trolleys. The company also employed extra staff to help with the Christmas rush, while Do-it-All boasted assistants capable of interpreting customers' most incoherent requests for help, and Safeways, adopting the point of view of the child, surprised at seeing so many similarly dressed assistants, stressed its desire to allow customers to shop quickly and efficiently, with the aid of 'queue busters', who could be available at any crisis point.

In 1990, the TSB tried to profit from the inflexibility of its competitors by emphasising its positive side, 'the bank that likes to say yes', and showing rival establishments in inverted black and white to emphasise their 'negative' qualities. Objectively, what the TSB was proposing, longer opening hours one day a week, was hardly a world-shaking improvement, but the notion of the interests of the customer at least being considered was a forceful underlying argument. The tactic was apparently successful, for Natwest countered the following year by indicating that its branches stayed open until 4.30 one day a week. In fact, banks were undoubtedly trying to improve their image and to claim they were responding to customer dissatisfaction. In 1994, Natwest, which had made a determined effort to change its image away from the simple dynamism designed to attract young customers to the *Action Bank*, even set itself the difficult task of persuading customers of the merits of 'reliable' cash machines, at a time when staffing cuts were being announced. Human failings were emphasised by contrasts with automated perfection as a teenager was shown heading for a decisive interview and being frustrated at every stage: by her father's asking her to repay a loan of £10, by a broken heel on her shoe, by bad weather and by her own inability to find the correct address. At a simpler level, the nineties were notable for the heavy promotion of convenience foods, the message for which was nearly always the same, satisfaction without effort, and Sainsbury's also produced helpful recipes for people in a hurry, including ingredients apparently obtainable only at their stores.

The new-found emphasis on customer convenience was instrumental in a determined and successful effort to restore the popularity of the doorstep milk delivery service at a time when more and more people were opting to buy their supplies direct from the supermarket. The creative brief supplied by the National Dairy Council included a number of arguments perfectly attuned with the concerns of the caring nineties, convenience, service, the personal touch and respect for the environment. Ads were to promote the following points:

(*i*) *the lovable, friendly, archetypal milkman — they've forgotten how wonderful he is.*

(*ii*) *He delivers low fat milks.*

(*iii*) *His returnable glass bottles are friendlier to the environment.*

(*iv*) *He's more convenient for weekend extras than carrying heavy, bulky milk home.*[4]

Other advertisers were equally keen to emphasise their desire to put the customer first by the quality of their service. The AA astutely marketed itself as 'the fourth emergency service', a claim which television commercials from 1994 could easily demonstrate as being true by simple visuals. Parcel Force showed its capacity for reliable delivery, whether the circumstances were collecting salmon from a remote Scottish glen or delivering overseas. British Airways toned down its insistence on efficiency in a 1993 commercial for its new Club World travel class; the importance of delivering the businessman 'ready for business' was still present, but the rest of the advertisement emphasised the improved quality of facilities he might enjoy during his flight. In 1990, British Gas was anxious to score points off other privatised or public services. One of its advertisements showed an irate Warren Mitchell, up to his knees in leaking water, unavailingly trying to receive a positive response from his local water company, while praising the questionnaire he had just answered from British Gas, inviting his views on their service. A second commercial, with a similar comic tone as the hero and his wife returned from holiday to find their house had been burgled and even the cooker had been stolen, compared the gas board's promise to deliver any item ordered rapidly with the hero's assumption that the Metropolitan Police's investigation of the crime would be slow and incompetent. Other advertisements stressing the aspect of service and of caring accessibility were the various Rowan Atkinson commercials for Barclaycard, American Express offering worldwide acceptability and insurance in the case of broken purchases or lost traveller's cheques and the Post Office which used a series of animated cartoons to list the surprising range of facilities available at its counters. The commercials emphasised that the Post Office was 'part of everyday life' and stressed convenience and proximity. The point was made in 1990 with a voice-over from Les Dawson in his familiar gossipy housewife role, spreading gratuitous innuendo about the neighbours, and in 1994 by young mothers talking at the swimming pool and by discussions at a car boot sale.

Another part of the caring message was the need to preserve the environment, an idea which was gaining ground in Britain, even if not as rapidly as in many continental countries. The subject had already been present in commercials in the late 1980s, but was more fully developed in the following years, although not always with total seriousness. Environmentally friendly washing powders were promoted and commercials for them were keen to claim, either by the time-honoured demonstration or by a direct and supposedly convincing address to the viewer, that these new products could be as efficient as the others. Where this was not possible, advertisers could at least claim that their new disposable refills were cheaper and produced less waste than the old packaging. Doorstep milk deliveries had similar advantages, highlighted by the milkman's use of a green crate for his bottles, while other advertisements adopted a slightly more tongue-in-cheek argument, proving that excessive seriousness in commercials was and is not necessarily a positive point. The Down-to-Earth range of ecologically-friendly products initially emphasised simply that they were good for the individual, the oceans and the planet, but by 1993 it was felt desirable to adopt a somewhat less didactic approach: the phosphate-free washing powder had been, as the female voice-over stated, 'tested on animals', a somewhat surprising observation in the circumstances, until it was made clear that the 'animals' in question were members of opposing rugby scrums. In 1993, however, Ford was anxious to avoid all frivolity in presenting the sincerity of its intentions, not by referring to the actual characteristics of its cars, but by emphasising, through the use of David Bellamy, its new 'green' image, both by its support for ecological projects and by its sponsorship of the Ford European Conservation Awards.

Altruism was a frequent component of the communication of corporate image in caring 1990s advertisements. Regional television companies continued to offer free air time to Helpline commercials, the objective of which was not to give information, but to appeal for help with various local community service or charitable projects. Sainsbury's, *Animal World* magazine and Littlewood's all made efforts to combine individual action with corporate support. Thus the supermarket was the first to promise regular shoppers vouchers to enable their children's schools to receive free equipment, *Animal World* produced a help ad promising to offer part of its cost price to the Worldwide Fund for Nature and, no doubt with more than half an eye on the National Lottery which was making inroads into its takings while promising benefits for good causes, the betting operator proposed to pay 24 pence to specified charities for every Instant Lotteries card purchased. In this way, so the commercial claimed, there were always winners, namely the beneficiaries of the charities in question.

A small number of companies were able to claim corporate benevolence. BOC took the time in a strikingly beautiful commercial of 1990 to list the wide range of its products and progressive nature of its activities, intensive care systems, optical fibres, microchips and jet turbines, before explaining that the advert showed a lake in Africa (whose location was not precisely indicated) where the company had breathed new life into what had been a dead environment. BP, in 1991, was slightly more specific, illustrating its work in providing solar electricity to distant parts of the earth with the case of a studious boy in a remote African village who could now, thanks to the company's innovation, continue his reading after sunset and emphasising, in an echo of the 'global village', that it was working 'for all our tomorrows'. One of the most remarkable of these illustrations of a change in attitude was provided by the phone company Energis, in 1995. Its commercial, a kind of antidote to 1980s adverts, began, conventionally enough, by stating what was required when a telecommunications network was to be constructed through a rural area: high tech heavy equipment, skilled workers, acres of land (including apparently the site of Stonehenge), high performance materials and billions of pounds (illustrated by scenes of euphoric company bosses leaving the Stock Exchange having just secured a bonanza). Incongruities quickly emerged, however; a Reliant Robin was seen amongst the earthmovers, one of which had a decidedly worried-looking woman driver at the wheel. The punchline was that Energis had found a simpler, cheaper and entirely ecology-friendly solution, by attaching fibre optic cables to existing power lines. The caring advertisements of the 1990s were in stark contrast to much of the previous decade, and reflected a different public mood and expectations, even if the commercials were not entirely innocent or always convincing. Some of the claims hardly stood closer examination, but at least some advertisers were apparently taking new questions into consideration when striving to promote their corporate image or to illustrate the benefits of their products.

Money

Money was to prove just as important an element in adverts in the 1990s as in the 1980s, but the climate had changed, caution was the watchword and, although the decade brought reasonable prosperity to many sections of the population, the enthusiasm for speculative investment had gone and financial institutions had to discover new ways of gaining their customers' confidence. Banks and building societies had been cast as the villains of the piece when the 1980s bubble burst and, for many, the previous techniques of advertising had to change. National Savings could continue as before to use relatively realistic scenarios to appeal to pensioners who had always sought security and a regular income. Of the other institutions, only the Halifax remained consistently upbeat. In 1990, it was still preaching the optimistic message of 'we're in the money' illustrated by a tap-dancing sequence reminiscent of Fred Astaire. Subsequent commercials favoured a collective image. In 1993 it put the accent on the variety of its savings options, PEPs, life insurance, unit trusts and pensions, and showed the happy landings (by parachute) of lucky investors. More generally the emphasis was placed on the personal and responsible approach and on the avoidance of pressurising clients into an unwise step. In 1990, Barclay's conjured up a young adviser to counsel a young man embroiled in tricky negotiations with a predatory landlady, but the emphasis was placed on sound advice about how to deal rationally with the situation, rather than on the introductory gift and the possibility of interest on current accounts. The Barclaycard advertisements stressed additional services (insurance of goods purchased, emergency card replacement and medical assistance) rather than the credit facilities provided, while Natwest put the accent firmly on individual service and on customer choice. A 1991 advertisement featured a pensions' adviser, not the slick, young, dynamic semi-yuppie who might have been expected, but a man of reassuring rotundity whose interests were the down-to-earth pursuits of ten-pin bowling and beer drinking. He was at least more comfortably situated than his counterpart in a 1994 commercial, who had the task of braving the Atlantic waves to visit a couple on the Scilly Isles who were considering investment options. The scenario showed the adviser making 'interesting proposals' but clinching no immediate deal and being prepared to return to discuss matters a second time. Share purchases were, not surprisingly, only rarely mentioned in early 1990s adverts, and again without any suggestion of hard-sell tactics. Natwest pointed out that customers could purchase stocks through their bank, wherever it was situated, and a BT advert of 1991 mentioned that the remaining shares held by the government would soon be available for purchase, but the emphasis was more frequently put on long-term and more secure investments.

Financial advertising was delicate territory in the 1990s. Wherever possible, companies avoided the notion of short-term gain, preferring to stress their expertise and experience in more limited fields or the more general need to be prepared. Scottish Widows and Clerical Medical, in 1991, mentioned their origins in the 1820s, while the latter company's 1997 commercial emphasised that it was *the choice of the professional*. Frequent motifs were that the future was uncertain and that accidents might befall anyone. Allied Dunbar (1997) showed the dangers of redundancy, *the life you don't yet know*, while Royal London (1993) warned viewers to beware because *tomorrow comes too quickly* and Sun Alliance (1995) promised income if one's career was cut short, forcing the point home with the picture of a man in a wheelchair. Investments, pensions and the like were perhaps not the most exciting or even the most immediately intelligible of subjects: advertisers thus had recourse either to humour or to narrative techniques with the details of investments being presented either in voice-over or by screen titles. Virgin PEPs' 1996 commercial played on both these elements: a man, later revealed as Richard Branson, was shown entering a building while being careful to conceal his identity, an image with immediate echoes of shady dealings. The written text indicated that he had already received millions (from the public), but the mood was broken when the message continued that he had enabled them to avoid tax and had taken no charges and no commission for doing so. A 1996 advert for the Stalwart Home Income Plan offered a reassuring solution to one of the trickier problems of the decade, how older people could continue to live in their homes while enjoying an extra monthly income, at a time when more and more members of an increasingly ageing population lived in fear of having to sell their homes to pay for regular nursing treatment or to ensure an adequate income.

The other recurrent aspect in 1990s adverts which differed from those of the 1980s was the simple question of cost. Whereas the former decade had lauded and encouraged spending and luxury, the nineties were shown as a period when all outgoings had to be carefully watched. Direct insurance selling was a case in point. The first advertiser to use television to promote its services had been Direct Line whose initial campaign (and red telephone) dated from 1989 and which had trebled the number of its motor policies by the end of 1992. The nineties saw the rapid growth in advertising for such services, emphasising the common point of cheaper insurance either for all drivers or for certain more or less favoured categories, while stressing the ease of making claims. Direct Line developed its advertising to keep ahead of its rivals. In 1998, it showed a 'couple' discussing an accident which had taken place in the home and which would necessitate building repairs: only later in the commercial did it become clear that the woman was in fact a Direct Line receptionist. The company later extended its business into savings, which again were principally promoted by television. In fact, many categories of businesses were at pains to prove their price competitiveness in the 1990s. The price/quality balance altered as all major supermarkets insisted on price restrictions and Asda supported its claim by reporting that this had been the company's policy since 1973 and included a clip from a commercial of that year to prove its point. Safeway, in 1996, chose to re-emphasise the savings that could be made by purchasing the supermarket's own brand goods, while offering to refund dissatisfied customers as well as providing them with a replacement product. British Telecom, facing strong competition from several other companies in the mobile phone and traditional markets, produced a series of campaigns to illustrate how reasonable its charges were, by promoting its discounts for regularly-called numbers. By the simple expedient of a film projected backwards, BT also emphasised that former customers could return cheaply and easily. Holidays were another area where, according to commercials, substantial savings could be made by contacting the right travel agent, while Esso's price check campaign was widely promoted and apparently successful: the company claimed to have attracted a million extra customers by reducing its prices to supermarket levels. Perhaps most symptomatic of the age were the devices advertised by motor manufacturers to attract buyers. Apart from simple price reductions periodically practised by all companies, some offered additional facilities designed to meet contemporary concerns. Daewoo proposed three years free servicing and AA membership, while Rover offered other possibilities. In 1994 it announced that customers who changed their minds could return a new car within thirty days and be reimbursed and a later ad stated that if the financial circumstances of the 'owner' of a leased car altered, the vehicle could be returned without penalty. All in all, it is revealing to compare attitudes to money in the 1990s, both with the adverts of the 1980s and with the economic realities of the time. The dominant image, favouring caution and security, was in marked contrast with the previous decade, and diverged from the actual financial situation of many British citizens.

New man, new woman, new relationships

The abiding and evolving stereotypes of men and women have always been a rich vein of ideas for advertisers, but the 1990s undoubtedly witnessed a change in attitudes and greater balance between the sexes, and the treatment of the subject attracted attention from outside the world of advertising itself. Bill Frost's article in the Times of 12th November 1997 asked, *Do these ads demean men?* and included a number of examples of male degradation at the hands of women. The article claimed both that products promoted in this way achieved higher sales figures and that the old adage, *get yourself noticed* was still a primary rule in advertising. The counter argument was equally valid: it was a fact that women's professional status was continuing to improve and rigid stereotyping, especially by male advertisers, was liable to be reductive and counter-productive:

> *When the narrow stereotypes are relinquished as ridiculous once and for all, then the way is open for advertisers to depict women in a whole range of roles, not just domesticated or desirable, but free, independent, witty, confident, clever, sociable, playful, intelligent and concerned.*[5]

Nineties ads fluctuated somewhat uneasily between the two extremes, but there is little doubt, firstly that signs of change were clearly visible and secondly that such a delicate subject as sex equality could often only be treated with humour rather than complete seriousness. In the circumstances it is noteworthy that ads featuring children stuck often closely to long-established and increasingly politically incorrect stereotypes and not just in the toys and games field. Fairy Liquid for instance continued to present girls as more efficient at washing up than boys, while the naughty or timid but kind-hearted schoolboy made a reappearance with Quality Street's commercials showing the child offering chocolates to adults, a lollipop lady and a long-suffering neighbour, who had shown him particular favour. An attempt to break the conventional mould was made by Powergen whose 1990 advertisement, with its slogan *the future generation* paralleled scenes of an efficient coal fired power station with images of a schoolgirl carrying out her own successful experiment in electricity generation, in a well-equipped school laboratory.

Male stereotypes in the nineties showed both stability and development, the balance often being determined by the type of product presented. Levi's continued their advertisements along their conventional lines with the image of the dominant and irresistibly attractive male, while Castlemaine XXXX stuck to its macho Australian image. The 1993 advertisement, with its punch-line *the worst case of sunstroke I've ever seen* was one of the more imaginative in the series, sending up the clichés of the sentimental wild-west film by the intimation that such notions as the man tilling the land with a good woman by his side were only conceivable for one whose mental balance was at least temporarily disturbed. The traditional predatory male appeared from time to time, but the 'dubious' nature of the image was carefully maintained by the use of almost caricatural situations. British Airways presented a young man who had abandoned his regular girlfriend to indulge in an amorous weekend in Paris (where else?) with another, when he was discovered and cornered by the two rivals who had now joined forces. *Thought Reader*, one of the Black Label, *I bet he drinks ...* series, worked over the theme of the boss who had just enjoyed a dirty weekend in Brighton (another predictable destination) with his secretary, only for the truth to be revealed when he was out for a quiet drink with his wife. Other advertisements, for toiletries, took the subject of appearance and seduction with surprising seriousness. The narcissism of 'new man' already observed in the 1980s, continued with Radox showing a man relaxing taking his shower and Biactol featured two brothers talking about skin care, while Lynx systeme (1995) showed the damage done to a man's skin by pollution, dirt and late nights and proposed the means for him to fight back. Aftershaves and deodorants took the indulgence into the realms of fantasy and even phantasms. Insensé (1993) presented a man whose fragrance enabled him to attract a woman out of her house and into a beautiful garden, while Paco Rabanne's Excess presented a scene bordering on the erotic; in a shot strongly suggestive of ejaculation, the bottle of deodorant opened spontaneously and sprayed the product as the man admired a dusky beauty on a television screen. Hero aftershave (1991) was equally explicit about male dominance, with rapid images of men being successful at work (bringing in the harvest, hurrying around as a busy doctor and acting bravely as a fireman) and in their amorous intentions which did, however, end in marriage.

The domesticated 'new man' of the 1980s continued to develop in the 90s, gradually being more frequently depicted carrying out a variety of household tasks, but without ever completely freeing himself from his accident-prone or not quite adequate image. A comic treatment of the question was in fact almost inevitable. Persil man of 1990, given the job of looking after the children, paid more attention to his newspaper, which resulted in the children so completely dirtying themselves that washing their clothes became the only possibility. On her return, his wife's reaction to this display of competence was simply to ask 'what washing?' Lenor used a similar device the following year; after the husband had once again apparently triumphed by demonstrating his correct choice of conditioner, admittedly an unlikely turn of events, his wife trumped this ace by a simple, meaningful glance at the sink piled high with unwashed dishes. One has only to think of Geoffrey Palmer's cooking activities for British lamb, dealing with the 'tricky bit' while reading his book, or of the Tetley beer drinker (1993) who stopped the ironing as soon as the transmission of his football match started to realise that the depiction of man's domestic prowess was not to be taken too seriously. Harp's 1993 commercial showing a man fleeing a department store where he had been shopping with his wife to take refuge in the nearest pub might be considered an adequate representation of the typical reluctant male. Sometimes too, man found himself defeated on his own territory. The Milk Tray man discovered in 1993 that he too could be the beneficiary of a present, from a female admirer, which caused him to lose if not face then at least his anonymity. These long-running advertisements were stopped in 1997. As early as 1990, Do-it-All had shown a woman capable of successfully venturing into man's DIY territory, while Shell, in 1991, extracted humour from the comic role reversal of men in a launderette trying to clean car engine parts, while their wives looked on, observing that the improved petrol itself would do all that was necessary.

If 'new man' was not an altogether convincing figure in nineties commercials, then 'new woman' did meet with greater success, although many women were shown condemned to the customary tasks of shopping and washing, or preoccupied with their appearance and especially their hair, as the number of shampoos and treatments advertised continued to mushroom. The motif of self-indulgence was accentuated, generally seriously portrayed although with a tendency to fantasising. Cadbury's Flake showed its latest model, lightly clad, sucking the chocolate bar in a French chateau. Camay associated its new three fragrances with an intimate dinner, an open beach and a ball, while Tia Maria (1993) gave fuller play to the imagination as the central character imagined herself lying in the grass, running down a pyramid of sand, traversing a courtyard full of masked figures, before the liquid in her glass finally revealed a male figure appearing, like James Bond in the opening credits of *Thunderball*, at the far end of a tunnel. The association of the dark liquid with sexual desire and with the impenetrable depths of the subconscious was strongly suggested. The women figures in the advertisements could often be sensual and well aware of their powers of attraction and were still presented as objects of male fantasies, especially in perfume advertisements and in the long-running Bounty 'taste of paradise' series. The

Braun hair styler (1995) at least gave its owner a certain independence, not only could she be assured of elegance, but the machine also allowed her the time to be 'fashionably late' for her planned *rendez-vous*. The predatory woman was, however, still a problematic figure. The landlady in Barclay's 1990 commercial was, from the first, a comic character, as she tried to extract rent from her tenant, while flaunting some rather aged made-up charms. Café Hag's approach was somewhat more subtle: an attractive woman reversed the usual roles by eyeing up a man she had spotted in an Italian café, only to find, when he stood up from behind his newspaper, that he was a priest. The joke was seen on both sides. Boddington beer's *femme fatale* was equally demonstrative and attractive, but again in a role-reversal way: her wiles were shown as being harmless, extending no further than snatching a glass of beer from a passer-by, or enjoying, with only modest sexual innuendo, its creamy head. Only a few advertisers, as we shall see, were prepared to take the game further and into the realms of moral ambiguity.

The growing independence of women was less difficult for advertisers to acknowledge and present; in real life they married later, achieved more at work and had their own incomes. Birds Eye foods were keen to point out that their products were *a taste of freedom*, a term to be taken literally as housewives who used them could have more time for their own pleasures, which, in 1993 for instance, took the form of a round of golf. Rover's 1994 commercial confirmed the impression which had been made in the previous decade, namely that the woman too had her part to play in the purchase of a car. The commercial showed a young woman making her own choice of Rover, driving it home to a rather attractive mews cottage, only to find that her husband (or 'partner', the increasingly preferred neutral term) had selected an identical model as a present for her. The purpose of the commercial was to point out that a full refund was possible if clients (men or women) changed their minds, but at the very least the wisdom of the woman's choice was apparently borne out. Prudential (1991) produced a revealing variation of its 1980s *I want to be* ... ads, by showing a couple whose interests were obviously sufficiently incompatible for a break-up to appear an imminent possibility, a fact evident to the woman but not to the man. The commercial reflected the financial realities and aimed at reminding women that they too had the right to a *personal pension*. The images of the professional woman of the 1980s were again present, but still not entirely convincing. L'Oréal Plenitude returned to the woman on the move of the previous decade, although, as before, apart from the trimmings of car and lap-top computer and the mention of the need to live *with the times*, the exact nature of her activity remained rather vague. Panthène, in 1996, was more precise about its heroine's work as a journalist, and the Bristol and West Building Society produced an unlikely combination of a woman, dressed like a financial adviser, carrying out a plumbing repair, while commenting in voice-over on the different investments the financial institution offered. Quite how this muddled scenario was to be interpreted coherently was left to the viewer's imagination.

The most obvious area of woman's professional competence shown in the commercials was in the field of business, with Ariel showing women running a bakery and tea rooms, to complement the bridal hire service which had been presented some years before. The message remained the same, that excellence was absolutely indispensable and that a proprietress could achieve it, although only with the aid of the right washing powder. In 1991, American Express quoted the Body Shop as an example of a well-run business, directed with attention to detail and imagination. Its female founder was able to express some of her philosophy in the commercial, before the advertising message for the finance company took over. Kenco (1994) also used the image of the woman boss, but in more demonstrative fashion, taking the argument further into the field of the male expectation versus female dominance. The owner of a coffee estate welcomed a man and a woman to his warehouse. When the latter informed him that Kenco would take the best beans for its instant coffee, he suggested that the decision should be cleared with the boss; the riposte *you just have* was a more than adequate rejoinder. Wrangler jeans (1993) chose to treat the question of dominance in a joky, role reversal way, with a powerful woman first ordering potential cowboys to remove their trousers to put on the jeans, nothing less than the uniform of their intended profession, and subsequently having to ford a river, carrying one of the feeble males in her arms. This advertisement was at least tacitly pitched to counter the macho image of jeans promoted by Levi's and the same technique was subsequently taken up by Lees. The theme of the dominant woman in amorous relationships needed, however, to be treated in a different way. Carole Bouquet's Chanel n°5 advertisement of 1993 solved the problem by giving the woman a speaking part and her face towards the camera while only the back of the man's head was seen. The female point of view was further emphasised by Twilight chocolate the same year. At an intimate dinner, the woman was shown expounding her preference in chocolate, *rich, smooth, well-dressed*, while the foolish male preened himself at the use of such flattering terms which he thought applied to him. Only when she reached the epithet *thick*, just as the moment when he almost choked while sipping from his glass, was it apparent that this was the term that best suited him.

Relationships between men and women, particularly intimate relationships needed careful handling, especially within the limited scope of a single commercial. De Beers could unhesitatingly play on the timeless image of their diamonds, but other products needed different tactics. The Gold Blend series got around the difficulty by its serial or soap opera approach, with the long-running love affair of the couple of neighbours continuing into the nineties. Most often, 1990s adverts avoided the pitfalls by adopting, or at least suggesting, a highly moral tone. A new Gold Blend advert played on several stereotypes; the caterer whom a couple were expecting turned out to be a man, although he was only standing in for his sister who was ill, but moral correctness appeared when the girl made it clear to him that the flat was her boyfriend's, not one that they shared, and the that the caterer's amorous attentions were unwelcome. In fact, the treatment of the subject was often very serious. The Ford Mondeo used the slogan, *it brings you to your senses*, a message which applied to the situation being depicted, that of a man driving away leaving a woman in tears, before having second thoughts, turning round and returning, as much as to the car itself. The use of a strong moral framework and the frequent emphasis on marriage enabled advertisers to play on the expectations of the viewer and to attract attention while remaining within the bounds of propriety. Both Abbey Life and Setlers presented, in different ways, the vital moment of a proposal of marriage, the former with the woman taking the initiative and the man offering an almost immediate date after a moment's reflection, the second with an embarrassed man having difficulty posing the question which was obviously expected. Other commercials seemed at first to be more daring, but the impression was not sustained to the end. Mates condoms (1992) showed an attractive woman at a party wanting a man to take her home to bed, as the subtitles at least made clear, only for it to be stated in the dialogue that they were husband and wife. The Peugeot 306 commercial (1997) was in the same vein, with similar emphasis on suggestiveness and female forwardness, but once more within an unexpectedly conventional frame. The *Times* of 14 May 1997 summarised the plot as follows:

> *A guy is washing the car. A woman gets out of bed with someone and watches from the upstairs window. Is he the handyman or maybe the gardener? There's a passionate embrace. The denouement is that they are actually man and wife and the person in the bed was their baby son.*

In these advertisements at least, marriage and parenthood were presented in a positive fashion while the advertiser engaged in a light-hearted and titillating game with the viewer's sense of proprieties.

It would be wrong to suggest that all adverts were equally discreet or so conventionally moral. The range of new services advertised was extended in 1997 to late-night commercials for intimate telephone conversations proposed by the Phone Bar and by Chat and Date, while the interactive Gay Network and the Gay Exchange offered similar contact facilities to homosexuals. The perfume Impulse was more explicit. Its 1996 commercial showed a young motorist's impaired judgement and changing attitude towards a woman who had just collided with his car as he was attracted by her perfume and started mentally undressing her. The following year, a male artists' model became sexually aroused under the amused gaze of a woman student, in a commercial which attracted the horror of some critics, even though the British version of the ad was less explicit than the cut transmitted in other countries. Häagen-Dazs and Fosters collaborated in a daring piece of co-branding in 1992, the first half of which displayed a man and woman in raunchy and suggestive poses, followed by a view of ice cream running down towards the woman's cleavage and being removed by a spoon, all of which was directly based on some of the shots Häagen-Dazs had used for its controversial press and display advertising which aimed at creating *a language for ice cream ... a mood of sensual intimacy between adults.*[6] At this point, on her demand for more, the mood changed, the man spotted a single can of Fosters in the fridge, beneath the ice cream and as she continued to lick her lips in anticipation, the sound of the beer can being opened broke the seductive mood, while the television commentary of a football match intervened, with the succinct message *he's failed to score.* Whether the man's reaction was due to indifference, or to premature ejaculation, as might have been suggested by the noise of the opening can, the stereotypical image of the underperforming male was carefully preserved. If these examples are to be taken seriously, the question of the relations between men and women in the 1990s had become more complicated, although how far advertisements need to respect propriety, and the extent to which they represent a true or aspirational vision of contemporary culture remain unanswered questions.

Heritage

The name of the government department responsible for the media in John Major's administration after 1992 provides a suitable heading under which to consider various aspects of British life in the nineties, although this section covers aspects outside that particular ministry's remit. Tradition had once more become a positive element in the country's self-image and was obviously a part of the technique intended by advertisers to strike a chord with elements in the viewing audience and to attribute to the brands in question the added value of experience and past enjoyment. In 1990, McCann-Erickson produced a commercial for P and O which combined a tinge of exoticism, the music of Debussy's La Mer and a painting strongly reminiscent of the impressionism of Monet or Seurat with the traditional vision of an ocean liner, even though the service advertised was nothing more than a mundane cross-channel ferry. The slogan of this commercial *don't just get across, cruise across* corresponded with the terms used by P and O itself on board its vessels where crossings are habitually referred to as voyages. Shortly afterwards, Smirnoff vodka associated itself with the same positive values of luxury, by showing images focused through a bottle, representing various typical features and characters to be found on pre-war cruise liners. Other products chose the same transparently nostalgic technique; Mr Kipling cakes evoked the fruitfulness of Autumn for their apple tarts, and a traditional Christmas for their mince pies. Farley's baby foods, a long-established brand, used the mid-1930s song, made famous by Noël Coward, *Everything stops for tea*, while Hovis, which had stressed its traditional image in earlier years applied the same techniques when it launched a white loaf in 1991, and saw no need to break the pattern for the further new products which appeared in 1995 and 1997. Similar northern tones served to maintain the message of the Tetley tea folk, who commented on the care and attention born of years of experience which went into blending. All of these adverts took traditional references at face value as essential attributes of the brand image, while a more recent product, Aunt Bessie's Yorkshire Puddings was able to distance itself from the myth, by the equivocal use of the slogan, *funny how some things haven't changed*. Other advertisements strove to profit from the notion of popular memory and of national heritage. Stamps as collectors' items were by now an established part of Post Office business, and some of the widely advertised special issues of the 1990s placed particular emphasis on history and culture. The celebratory stamps for the Queen Mother's 90th birthday (1990) were promoted by a commercial which used archive film footage and other series featured the 200th anniversary of the Ordnance Survey (1991) and the Tudors (1997), who the advertisement showed as interesting chefs in a Chinese restaurant.

Social class is still a strong feature of the self-perception of the British, but was not a question which advertisers, or the population at large, were inclined to treat with undue respect. As Kathy Myers pointed out in 1986:

> The TV commercial featuring a table full of 'upper-class nobs' eating After Eights doesn't mean that the chocolates are targeted at the lesser aristocracy. On the contrary it is a humorous representation of how 'working people' imagine the rich to live.[7]

In fact, the same brand used similar images in the nineties, while likening participants at a dinner party to animals, but Nescafé (1991) was more than gently mocking of the pretensions of a housewife whose leisure pursuit was croquet and who habitually referred to herself by the pronoun 'one'. Anchor cream caricatured the recreational activities supposedly favoured by the upper classes, the Ascot races, the Henley Regatta, opera at Glyndebourne, golf at Gleneagles and, perhaps less justifiably the more proletarian tennis at Wimbledon, before concluding with a parody of yachting at Cowes, where an animal of similar name was to be seen at the helm of a sailing boat.

Commercials of the 1990s give some insight into attitudes towards the leisure activities of the British at the time. The minority and therefore eccentric pursuits of birdwatching, animal photography and Morris dancing were presented in humorous fashion by advertisements for Kit-Kat biscuits and Heineken beer, while the enthusiasm for DIY was reflected both by the number of commercials for specialist superstores and for paints and by the accent that was put on the ease with which good results could be achieved. In shops as in the home, this field was no longer an exclusively male preserve. Fishing, in fact the country's largest participation sport, received a brief mention, while Yellow Pages produced an advertisement based on cricket which unreservedly evoked the old-fashioned atmosphere of the game and its traditions, with authentic pictures of the Grace Gates and Long Room at Lords, accompanied notably by the voice of commentator Brian Johnston. Far and away the most important sporting activity was, however, football, whose importance was boosted by the 1994 World Cup in particular. It was treated as an integral part of national life and appeared in various guises. The playing of the game offered a new black role model in the form of John Barnes, while film clips enlivened several adverts, for Littlewoods Pools and, with more lasting effect, Reebok sportswear which produced a clever montage featuring past and present Manchester United stars. Watching the game could be presented as an archetypal male activity and served for television trailers advertising BSkyB's satellite channels, while Coca Cola, MacDonalds (*the official restaurant of the Premier League*), Carling Black Label (*sponsors of the ... Carling Premiership*) and Persil were among the brands which used the sport as a convenient promotional vehicle. The other major leisure activity shown was holidaymaking, often in exotic foreign parts, although local holiday destinations and attractions were also featured. The recipes for overseas holidays were mainly simple: sun and sea, plush hotels with swimming pools and, in accordance with attitudes at the time, low prices, although some operators offered more. Thomsons emphasised their caring attitude which allowed parents to relax and children to enjoy themselves separately, while Trail Blazers, another company included in American Express advertising, stressed that it could indeed offer out-of-the-way experiences, as well as more mundane options.

The other marked trend of the 1990s was the promotion of the media by television commercials, reflecting a time of ever-growing competition between different sources of news and entertainment. The Murdoch *Sun* owed its rise to popularity to its use of television advertising, which continued through the nineties *No Sun, No Fun* campaign, while other publications were equally keen to promote themselves, often by combining newspaper purchase with additional incentives like cut-price CDs (*Times*, 1993), travel opportunities (*Telegraph*, 1997), Marks and Spencers food vouchers (*Express*, 1996), prize draws or simply cut-prices (the 10p *Times*). The *News of the World* (1994) emphasised its football coverage, while the 'serious' newspapers still stressed the in-depth coverage which their weekend editions could give of a variety of subjects. In 1990, the short-lived British Satellite Broadcasting promoted the range of programmes its subscribers could expect to receive, later BSkyB, with its virtual monopoly in the field and substantial financial influence stressed its various options by advertising one-off events like its first screening of *In Bed with Madonna* (1991) and its on-going exclusive rights to live coverage of Premier League football. Capital Radio also used the rival medium of television to justify its statement that *London's static without it*. The advertisements for *Real Life Drama* magazine (launched in 1993) reflected the ubiquity of popular culture and the trend in television programmes towards voyeuristic reality shows and tabloid talk shows, by promising its readers the tales of *ordinary people in extraordinary circumstances.*

New norms for a new Britain

The 90s saw more than their fair share of new products and the repositioning of old ones. The field of information technology and electronics was particularly well represented with new telephone services, One 2 One, Orange, Vodafone, Onetel and People's Phone all appearing, along with Energis and Cellnet who provided the infrastructure. Advertisers had to show ingenuity to make their products known in a field where competition was particularly strong, One 2 One raised a few eyebrows by using the controversial notion of making contact with the dead, by featuring customers desirous of holding a private conversation with the likes of Elvis Presley and John Lennon. Retail sales of electronics goods were in the hands of existing companies and the emphasis was largely on price and range of equipment, but in the field of computer games Woolworth did at least show imagination, by following the course of a character as he passed along a street avoiding obstacles featured in Nintendo games, with the slogan 'you have to make it to here' appearing at the moment when he reached the Woolworth's shop. Several established products felt the need to change their image: Halfords repeatedly stressed the size of their superstores and range of products stocked, as well as their new venture into the field of one-stop shopping, offering car servicing, the caring nature of which was reinforced by the comparisons between the shop and the waiting room of a maternity hospital. The Milk Tray man was first reduced to more human dimensions before disappearing for good, the manufacturer having decided that a new brand image could not be achieved with a 30-year-old advertising idea. Babycham revamped its image for the third time, this time moving decisively away from romanticism to a 'bigger, bubblier' image, but perhaps the most striking transformation was that of the Midland Bank, which had not only changed its name to HSBC but also used a commercial emphasising new attitudes to life and money. A series of details which would once have seemed exceptional and were now merely commonplace, from a woman priest to an elderly man on an electric mobility scooter and from a black computer programmer to a motorcycle ambulance, served to prove that the institution wished to keep abreast of changes which could be observed everywhere in life and society.

The truly multi-cultural nature of Britain was beginning to make itself felt in commercials. The stereotypical black sportsman or athlete was joined by a growing number of other coloured people going about their normal business and presented, like their white counterparts, as customers in shops or colleagues at the workplace. BT featured an Asian small shopkeeper, a cultural reference par excellence, in its phonecard commercials, thereby illustrating that such ubiquitous establishments also stocked the product, but other adverts were somewhat more active in countering prejudice. Fuji film (1990) showed an Indian woman waiting outside her child's school, with the message of the commercial being simply that good film allowed good pictures to be taken and that these, in the hands of the right journalist could be used to combat racism. The mistaken idea of coloured people as 'foreigners' or 'immigrants' was the implicit message of Homepride in 1996 and 1997, showing respectively an Asian man, with a broad Geordie accent, making a curry and two Chinese girls, very obviously brought up in Scotland, cooking a sweet and sour meal, all using Homepride sauces of course. Malibu in 1993 was arguably more daring: its commercial played on the distinction between a grey northern industrial landscape and the colour and vivacity of the Caribbean. The woman whose silhouette had been featured in the industrial landscape was then shown enjoying a drink with a black man in a bar on a West Indian island. In 1993, Adam Lury wrote: *The media, including advertising is [sic.] not a pane of glass through which we perceive society; it is a creation capable of reinforcing and changing perceptions* and argued that agencies needed to see the commercial advantages in casting black people *as normal people in mainstream advertising*.[8] Nineties product commercials were at least taking substantive steps towards a more representative portrayal of coloured people.

1990s adverts equally reflected some of the more transient trends of the decade. Companies which had sponsored the Olympic Games or other sports competitions were anxious for this generosity to be known to the public. Topical concerns such as clean beaches and the change of status of building societies from mutual associations to stock-market quoted companies, which brought windfall benefits to lucky investors, were mentioned briefly, while the growing desire for healthy eating and the quest for physical fitness were handled with a mixture of seriousness and humour. Jenny Craig products used successful dieters to confirm the effectiveness of the dishes offered, accompanied by predictable before – after demonstrations. Kellogg's Bran Flakes, *a step in the right direction*, declined to labour the point: they showed a father, a newly converted fitness fanatic, eating his healthy breakfast before setting off to run to collect his morning paper, only to change his mind rapidly when tempted by the prospect of using his car to accomplish the task. The collapse of the Soviet Union was a topical motif which enhanced the immediacy of several commercials, for instance for Worthington and Rover (1990) and Barclaycard (1991), the subject being well-adapted to the notions of change, transformation and humour. The approaching third millennium began to feature in advertisements towards the end of the decade, as advertisers sought to show a wider vision which might give significance to their products and to create some sort of lasting message for the historic days to come. In 1996, Lemsips offered the history of the 20th century in 30 seconds, tenuously linking the body copy to the commercial message by the notion of the speed with which the product achieved the desired effect. Attempts to promote the much contested Greenwich Dome and Millennium Experience were made by the extended comparison of the events of the last thousand years with the passing of a single day.

Evolving communicational techniques

In 1997, fears were being expressed that the traditional commercial was doomed to disappear in the face of programme-length 'infomercials', which were first aired on Channel 4 and Granada Sky Broadcasting in November of the same year. The attractions of the format for advertisers were largely financial. Longer, more informative ads could replace repeated shorter commercials, they were cheap to produce (using direct presentation and repetitive hard-sell techniques) and corporate advertising might once more become a viable possibility. Last but not least they could be inserted into relatively inexpensive daytime or late-night slots, as was the case in the United States where, by 1997, the infomercial business was worth some $6 billion. A certain number of other changes had occurred. The use of soap opera or serial type commercials suggested that perceptions of commercials had altered and the blurring of distinctions between programmes and advertisements had already begun. Similarly, in the 1990s, the mention of a freephone number or a web site was introduced as a means of facilitating communication with the viewer, on his own terms. The development of more dedicated channels, by cable, satellite and ultimately by digital technology, could only be a long-term threat to the standard, mass-audience commercial, and, in a less specific way, advertisements aimed at young children and their mothers already dominated morning scheduling. Nevertheless, with the exception of extensive promotion of sports goods on specialist channels, the trend towards narrowcasting in advertising has so far remained relatively limited.

From the technical point of view, the nineties saw further innovations, such as the use of the three-dimensional animated Aardman models in the Electricity Creature Comforts series and the Lurpak butter advertisements. Against this, there were still a number of advertisements employing the most traditional of methods. Daz (1990) returned to the practice of 'housewife endorsements', while Whiskas catfood (1990) resorted once more to an expert witness who just happened to work for a laboratory run by the parent company, Pedigree Petfoods. On the other hand, the possibilities of the combination of dialogue, voice-over and written text began to be fully exploited. There were an increasing number of double advertisements, not just by manufacturers of washing machines endorsing washing powders, but including the promotion of two different products into a single time slot, although often with a hiatus as the commercial moved from one to the other. Thus, the erotic atmosphere created by Häagen-Dazs was shattered when Fosters lager came into the picture and the American Express adverts including other businesses (Body Shop and Trail Blazers, for instance) found the transition difficult to achieve convincingly. Regulations over misleading or unverifiable information led advertisers to make extensive use of written disclaimers, a detail which was particularly important in the case of price watch or price check claims when retailers declared they had *the lowest prices in the area* or made some equivalent boast.

In the desire to be memorable, many advertisements moved further and further away not just from product claims but from the product and its realistic environment. Laughter was one way of achieving notoriety, of course, but products sometimes took other, esoteric routes. In 1993, for instance, Guinness showed its regular actor Rutger Hauer disguised as a scarecrow in what might be supposed to be a field of barley, before transporting the viewer into the realm of dark secrets, the cabin of a long sunken sailing vessel. The same year, Dunlop showed a long series of mysterious and apparently oriental or aboriginal images, cutting back from time to time to the tyres which were being advertised. The commercial achieved high recall ratings, but the link between images and product was difficult to perceive, the more so as the absence of a soundtrack prevented any explicit connection from being made.

Some advertisements, however, adopted a new communicational approach, appealing to the viewer's awareness of the 'rules of the game' and apparently calling commercials themselves into question, or parodying current practice. John Smith's beer commercials claimed to be 'no-nonsense' advertisements and regularly featured a straight-faced comedian, Jack Dee, pointing out that the product could speak for itself and scorning the types of gimmicks which advertisers suggested. The banishing of the incongruous penguins, a standard motif in these adverts, was of course ironic: the animals had made the required impression before being sent from the screen. British Airways (1991) proclaimed its use of an interactive commercial, as a woman in a cinema audience watching an advertisement for weekend breaks recognised her boyfriend on the cinema screen with another woman and called him to account for his perfidious conduct. The interruption did not cut the message of the advertisement: the amorous possibilities of a weekend break in Paris had already been proved and as the scene changed, the commercial continued in the same vein by showing the man catching sight of yet another woman who welcomed his gaze with an encouraging smile. The apparently self-critical stance of nineties commercials was perhaps best illustrated by the Talking Pages commercial of 1991 starring John Cleese and Orange telephone's offering of 1996. In the first, Cleese, in his role as a peasant suitor of a princess, was set the task of obtaining an antique diamond ring in order to win her hand. When he did so, by accident rather than design as he had not used the advertised service to facilitate his task, he was told that the whole affair was a joke as the episode was only a television commercial. In the second case, the advertisement played on the wealth of disclaimers sometimes to be seen on the screen accompanying commercials. In this case, the viewer was informed, Orange was making a *non-introductory offer*, which was *not subject to availability* and the company reserved the right to *introduce more free services without prior notice*. These last two examples serve as adequate indications both of advertising feeding on and parodying itself, and of the indirect and surprising ways found in the nineties to put the message across.

Notes

1 Geoffrey Robertson and Andrew Nicol, *Media Law*, Harmondsworth, Penguin, 1992, page 634.

2 Up to 5.6 per cent for 1998, according to the *Media Pocket Book 1999*.

3 The figures quoted by the *Media Pocket Book 1999*, for homes receiving broadcasts from the Astra Satellite for the week ending 9th May 1999 are as follows: BBC 1 - 20.4 per cent, BBC 2 - 6.6 per cent, ITV (inc. GMTV) - 22.6 per cent, C4 - 6.6 per cent, C5 - 4.3 per cent, Sky - 15.1 per cent, Astra (total) - 32.2 per cent.

4 John Grant, "National Dairy Council – the Milkman Relaunch", in Chris Baker (ed), *op. cit.*, page 11.

5 Danielle Barr, Publicis Advertising Agency, quoted in Sue Phipps, *op. cit.*, page 20.

6 Unattributed article, "Dedicated to Pleasure, Dedicated to Advertising", in Fionnuala Tennyson, *Commercial Break*, London, Advertising Association, 1992, page 31.

7 Kathy Myers, *op. cit.*, page 79.

8 Adam Lury, "Whose Britain?" *Spectrum*, London, ITC, 1993.

V
Government advertising

Advertising by ministries has long been a feature of British life, representing a substantial part of the advertising expenditure of the country in recent years. In 1984, for instance, H M Government was placed fourth in the list of advertisers, behind Unilever, Mars and Procter & Gamble and though that rating was the result of the exceptional circumstances of the mid 80s with several privatisations, overall expenditure continues to place the government among the country's leading advertisers. In 1998, the cost of government advertising time was £7.6 million on cable and satellite television, against £47.7 million for terrestrial channels, which left the Central Office of Information (COI), the executive agency responsible for the majority of government campaigns, in 18th and 19th positions in the respective lists of the country's major advertisers. It is clear that this type of announcement gives special importance to the question of national identity, for the tax-payer is at once paymaster, recipient and beneficiary of the service and the advertising is intended to achieve several ends. It aims to convey information, to create a feeling of identity and empathy by giving a recognisable and acceptable representation of the whole society within which it is transmitted or of that part of the society for which it is intended, and, in the last analysis, it seeks to achieve a culture of solidarity and a sense of purpose. Beyond this, it may strive to change not only the superficial attitudes but also in the longer term the behaviour of the citizen/consumer. For this type of advertising, care and attention in the communication with the population is essential, in order to maintain the impression of unity.

The task facing government advertising is not easy. On the one hand, genuinely informative announcements, giving details of new regulations, services or benefits, may serve a useful role and seem uncontroversial, but the line between information and manipulation is a thin one and the authorities may be suspected both of trying to gain political advantage for the government over opposition parties and even of indulging in propaganda, in their attempts to influence the hearts and minds of the citizens. The process may become a high-risk strategy, the more so as setting the right tone and communicating with what is potentially the whole of the viewing population at any given time, without causing offence, can be an uncertain exercise. For product advertisements which do not seem relevant to them, the reaction of the majority of the population is likely to be indifference, but in the case of government advertising, voices are always liable to be raised if one or more sections of the community see themselves as unfairly represented or more simply if the advertising is believed to be inappropriate or not cost effective. The difficulty lies with the eclectic and changing nature of the viewing public and their habits. It is becoming harder for advertisers to reach families viewing together with the growing numbers of second and even third television sets, the use of VCRs and the multiplicity of channels available. Government advertisements are placed with a view to reaching the audience deemed most appropriate for the message, but transmission times must also conform to scheduling regulations. Beyond this, as Michael Brodie, Director of Advertising at the COI wrote in 1993, there is always the great imponderable of the actual public reaction:

> *All this may sound very innovative and well thought through, but how does it work in practice? The real world isn't like the theoretical one. For a start, there is one totally unforecastable element – the public.*[1]

The failures tend to attract comment more readily than the successes, especially when the advertisements have a potentially party political content. In August 1994, for instance, Matthew Taylor, Liberal Democrat MP and spokesman on the People's Charter gave a catalogue of the costly failures of government advertising:

> *£540,000 spent on the Charterline, a now discontinued phone line on the Citizens' Charter which received an average of just 25 calls a day at an average cost of £68 ... a £6.2 million campaign – Helping the Earth Begins at Home – aimed at promoting energy efficiency to reduce global warming produced just 12,080 telephone responses and 19,250 coupon replies – at an average cost of £197 ... a £2.7 million Department of Health campaign to promote a Travelsafe code that explained the risk of contracting HIV abroad produced 11,453 coupon replies, Mr Taylor said, at a cost of £234 each.*[2]

Other examples are equally well-known. In 1984 – 1986, a series of poster and television adverts were produced highlighting the ravages of heroin, with the strap-line 'skin hair by heroin' and a standard before – after approach. This technique proved misguided, because of the misunderstanding of the attitude of many drug users, for whom standard life-style criteria did not apply: *some addicts admitted that at the time of first opoid use they wanted to become addicted in order to share the life-style of addicts.*[3] The case also illustrated the difficulty of communicating with particular groups within society. In 1986, the contested campaign promoting Family Credit, a benefit devised to replace the equally contentious Family Income Supplement, was another notable failure which incurred the wrath of the National Audit Office which chastised the whole project for poor planning, poor targets and poor results. The 'Enterprise Initiative' or 'blue whoosh' campaign of the late 1980s was an embarrassment for exactly the opposite reasons, namely that the response was so massive that the funds available at the DTI were exhausted even before the campaign itself, lasting only six weeks, was terminated. These difficulties highlight both the importance of research and planning and the problems which arise in government advertising which is not centrally controlled but depends largely on variable departmental budgets and needs. The COI's Annual Review for 1990 – 1991 showed a clear appreciation of the particular communicational difficulties faced by government campaigns:

If the government is going to tell people the things they need to know, if it's going to try to change their views and perhaps change their behaviour, then we need to know what they already know, we need to know what their assumptions and preconceptions are, we need to know — literally and metaphorically — what language they use. Hence the need for the early stages of research.[4]

By their nature, too, the subjects treated by government advertising tend to be serious, matters of life and death or at least of major financial import, while their treatment may involve emotional appeals and a measure of intrusion into individual lives which ordinary product-based or even corporate commercials would hesitate to impose. The hybrid nature of the television medium may also be an obstacle in this regard. Government advertisements are placed within 'natural breaks' in the same way as ordinary commercials, which may cause problems of scheduling to avoid unfortunate juxtapositions,[5] and the two types of messages may become confused or contradict one another, since the attitude expected from the viewer is different. The rules of the game for consumer goods are well understood: the commercial aims at promoting awareness or knowledge of an article, may encourage a positive appreciation of brand image and the quality of advertising can also reflect favourably on its sponsor. At the same time the accent is placed on consumption, with the viewer being offered the choice, at least tacitly, between the product on offer and other comparable goods. In government announcements, specific services may be the subject of the advertising, or the message may be one of enhancing awareness of the needs of others or of one's own rights, but often such a definable aim is not apparent and the end result is less obvious or the desired effect is more gradual. Government advertisements cannot hide behind the illusion of a product to sell, citizenship is not of itself an item to be consumed and yet the message needs to be as convincing as for consumer products. This chapter will analyse the way in which government advertising has tried and still strives to achieve its difficult objectives, by illustrating recurrent advertising concerning what might be classed as more or less non-controversial 'citizenship' issues. This will be followed by an examination of politically contentious issues and before the argument moves on to consider more closely the communicational techniques employed to persuade the public to accept the government's ideas on the nature of identity and of citizenship. The final section will be devoted to a particular attempt at putting some of the principles of political communication into effect in the troubled situation of Ulster. A brief outline of the history and development of government television advertising would first seem desirable.

Historical outline

The body principally concerned in this field is the Central Office of Information, which was born in 1946 out of the wartime Ministry of Information, which had, after a shaky start, become an effective means of communication between government and people. The peacetime COI was conceived as a centralised organisation to be responsible for coordinating all government-sponsored publicity and served to promote the image of the United Kingdom abroad as well as transmitting information for home consumption, through promotional films, publications, events and, a relatively minor aspect in immediate post-war years, advertising. Until 1984, the COI directly managed the publicity budgets of most government departments; since then it has worked on a commission basis and was, until 1996, with a few exceptions such as the Health Education Authority, National Savings, the nationalised industries and the Scottish and Northern Ireland Offices, the organisation through which government bodies were required to organise their campaigns. Government ministries can now act independently of the COI, a fact which has led it to pay greater attention to cost effectiveness and has also brought drastic reductions in staffing levels, from 1283 in April 1979 to little more than 300 full-time employees today. The advertising division of the COI has been relatively untouched by these changes, as in the 1990s some 85 per cent of creative advertising work has been undertaken, on tender, by commercial agencies on the COI roster, a list drawn up on the recommendation of the independent Advisory Committee on Advertising.[6] Media buying is equally undertaken by private enterprises.

The COI's output for television in the early stages was in the form of public service announcement 'fillers', used by the BBC and subsequently the ITV mainly for continuity purposes. The first commercial as such was for Army recruitment in 1956, a 60-second ad which was broadcast over a 12 week period at a total cost of some £161,000 (including around £5,000 for production). In 1973, in response to the report of the Select Committee on Nationalised Industries, which advocated the allocation of peak-time for public service announcements on health and safety measures, the ITV companies pointed out that, in the calendar year 1972, over the whole network, some 22,000 fillers had been broadcast, with an airtime value of some £2 million. The latest figures, for 1998, indicate that fillers are still widely used, with the number of free transmission slots obtained from all channels, including the BBC, reaching 230,000. Over the years, advertising has come to be the COI's major enterprise, representing rather more than 60 per cent of home expenditure in the late 1980s and still some 50 per cent today, about half of which goes on television, although actual spending is highly volatile and influenced by exceptional factors like the timing of general elections as well as by departmental budgets. The figures given below from the COI's own reports indicate that advertising income over the period 1992-1998 has varied markedly, and should further be compared with the much greater activity in the late 1980s. Income for 1992-1993 was in fact only 49.1 per cent that of 1989-1990.

COI Annual Advertising Income (at cash prices, £m)

1992 - 1993	1993-1994	1994-1995	1995-1996	1996-1997	1997-1998
47,057	63,157	55,196	63,663	69,396	59,039

Moreover, some advertising campaigns are regular and ongoing, like the commercials against drinking and driving or the current promotion of the Labour government's New Deal, which will benefit from a budget worth £18 million over the three years up to the end of 2001, while others represent one-off reactions to various factors. The table below, taking as an example the year 1993, indicates the variety of subjects covered by COI television campaigns, as well as revealing several of the buying conditions and criteria attached:[7]

Campaign	Period	Areas	Target audience	Comments
Car crime	1.1 - 31.3.93	network, exc Scottish, Ulster, Grampian	adults	no children
Condoms	1.1 - 31.3.93	network, C4/SC4, BSkyB, UK Gold, Sky Sport	adults 16 - 34 adults	post 21.00, post 22.30, no children[8]
Energy efficiency	1.1 - 28.2.93	network (exc Ulster), C4, SC4, GMTV, satellite	ABC1 adults	
Smoke alarms	1.1 - 22.1.93 3.2 - 21.2.93	network, exc Scottish, Ulster, Grampian	adults	post 19.30
Inland Revenue	12.1 - 26.3.93	C4 / SC4	adults	
Territorial Army	1.2 - 28.2.93	network, C4 / SC4, satellite	16 - 34 men	
Rear Seat Belts	2.2 - 23.2.93	network (exc Ulster) C4/SC4, GMTV, satellite	adults	post 19.30 no children, no wildlife/circus, no satire
Child Support	15.2 - 18.4.93	network (exc Ulster) C4/SC4, satellite, GMTV	adults housewives with children	no air time post 24.00 end breaks only
Organ Donors	1.3 - 31.3.93	network, (exc Scottish, Ulster, Grampian), C4/SC4, satellite	16 - 34 adults	avoid kids and light entertainment
Cycle Helmets	25.3 - 4.4.93	network, C4 / SC4, satellite	children 10+	older kids' programmes
Child Road Safety	26.4 - 16.5.93	network (exc Ulster) C4/SC4, GMTV, satellite	all adults 16 - 34 adults	
Car Crime	1.5 - 31.8.93	England, Wales, C4/SC4, BSKYB,	adults	upweight May drip June - August
Family Credit	8.5 - 2.7.93	network (exc Ulster) C4/SC4, GMTV, satellite	adults	upweight daytime
British Telecom	24.5 - 14.7.93	network (exc Ulster) C4/SC4, GMTV, satellite	ABC1 adults	
Drink Drive	29.6 - 29.8.93	network (exc Ulster) C4/SC4, GMTV, satellite	16 - 34 men	post 19.30 restriction
Electoral Register	13.9- 3.10.93	network (exc Ulster, Scotland), C4, BSkyB, UK Gold, cable	16 - 24 adults	
Child Road Safety	14.9 - 4.10.93	network (exc Ulster), C4, BSkyB, UK Gold	adults 16 - 34 adults	no kids
Territorial Army	1.10 - 7.11.93	network, BSkyB	16 - 34 men	spot buying
Energy Efficiency	10.10 - 17.11.93	network (exc Ulster) C4/SC4, BSkyB, UK Gold, Discovery	ABC1 adults	
Regular Army	12.11 - 25.11.93	Ulster only	16 - 34 men	
Drink Drive	7.12 - 31.12.93	network (exc Ulster), C4, BSkyB, UK Gold	16 - 34 men	post 21.00 restriction

Despite its changing role, the COI still has substantial bargaining power. Although exact figures are not available, it is believed that the Office is able to keep agency commissions on adverts to around 10 per cent and the 1997 – 1998 *Annual Report and Accounts* claimed that the cost of media television buying was £22 million, whereas the value of the air time obtained was rather over £31 million.

Citizenship

Much government advertising does not raise questions of principle or even of policy and consists in informative and instructive commercials which appeal to the common sense and the self-interest of the viewer, to the extent sometimes of appearing to emphasise what should be self-evident. This is not to demean the significance of the messages in establishing effective communication between the authorities and the people, nor should it be forgotten that many of the adverts serve as timely reminders in the case of momentary lapses of concentration. They frequently also appeal to a sense of civic responsibility or altruism which takes these commercials well along the path of influencing not just immediate behaviour but also underlying attitudes and of giving a clearer idea of what 'Britishness' is or at least should be.

(a) Preventing crime and domestic accidents

One of the most obvious fields for 'self-interest' advertising is crime prevention. The common argument involved is that of loss of the goods themselves, or of secondary damage or inconvenience, such as no-claims bonuses, distress and wasted time. As always, for government campaigns, it is important to consider the range of target groups for which the commercial is intended. Progressively, the subject of theft has taken on a greater seriousness and the potential dangers in every situation have been exposed. The first lesson to be learned was that thieves could strike at any time and anywhere and that nothing was safe from their clutches. While many of the adverts of the 1970s and 1980s showed the vulnerability of the unsecured home to simple burglaries, or the ease with which unscrupulous conmen could gain access, especially when the householder was elderly or gullible, in the 1990s, the targeting generally became more specific and up-to-date, reflecting new dangers. The walk-in thief at the workplace, or the professional (foreign) crook at the airport were evoked to point out the risks that could be run in unexpected situations, while further emphasis was placed on the types of goods which criminals might wish to get their hands on. The particular danger in the 90s was shown as being the theft of credit cards but in other fields, the accent also changed. While the fear over motor vehicles in the 1970s had been the taking of older models by joyriders, with the associated risk of loss of no-claims bonus, the stolen cars in the 1990s were shown as more tempting to the professional crook, either for their fitted equipment like radios or telephones, or because of the inviting presence of personal belongings and valuables left for the taking. The 1990s also repeated the earlier call to cyclists to take special care over their machines. Everywhere, the need for vigilance was stressed. Such basic messages as lock your car when you leave it, put valuables out of sight, fit better door and window locks and use them were repeated warnings, while the role of the police crime prevention officer was stressed in the 1980s.

As criminals were shown as becoming more ruthless, the means to deter and thwart them became more sophisticated; the use of deadlocks, handbrake locks and alarms was recommended for cars, while the marking of valuables with invisible pens or the stamping of bicycles with the postcode was presented as a valuable aid to the recovery of stolen goods. The 1970s advice to leave on a downstairs light if you were out in the evening, gave way to the mention of more elaborate timer devices which were shown in 1990s ads surprising the intruder as he prepared his break-in. Similarly, the warnings to older people to put the chain on the door and ask for identity documents from any visitor, just like the advice to tourists to keep their passports and traveller's cheques separate and to note the numbers, were shown as being common-sense and, above all, effective precautions. The accent was put on deterring the criminal and making him look elsewhere. By the 1980s, the Neighbourhood Watch scheme was portrayed as another means of dissuading the criminal. In fact, the message of the adverts worked at both the individual and the collective level, and became increasingly serious. While the 1970s had featured caricatured crooks, dressed up like Fagin or easily identified thanks to masks and a large bag helpfully labelled SWAG, and while at the end of the 80s commercials employed the use of the voice of magician/comedian Paul Daniels and a visual demonstration to reinforce the ease with which cars could vanish, the condemnation of criminals became more and more categorical. In 1984, they were depicted as magpies, not just stealing valuables but wreaking destruction in the home, by 1993, car thieves were likened to hyenas, preying on the defenceless and showing no compassion towards their victims. The accent was also put on the sadism of a thief who rang up his victim in the middle of the night to announce that his car had been stolen or again on the unbridled greed of criminals participating in a stealathlon and able to gain control of a lady's whole bank account by the simple expedient of obtaining her credit card. The fear of crime was, according to the COI, real and growing,[9] and the reaction had to be both individual and collective. The ease with which some crimes could be committed was stressed once more, and everyone should take greater care over routine precautions, but, more than this, the problem was soluble if the community worked together to combat the menace. One 'Crimestoppers' advertisement appealed to the public spirit of every citizen, by depicting ordinary people, wearing police helmets, deterring a set of drunken youths bent on molesting two girls waiting at a bus station. The voice-over message was unequivocal: Britain was a country where, with public support law and order could be rapidly restored:

> *If everyone was prepared to report incidents they'd seen, you'd be surprised at the effect it would have on crime ... You won't even be asked your name.*

The advertisements of the early 1990s reinforced the message of social cohesion by using children to remind the viewers of the different options open to them, while the need to be mindful of the welfare of weaker members of the community like the elderly was a frequent motif.

Another field for collective and individual responsibility was that of the domestic accident. The spate of personal accidents and fires around 5 November had long been a concern of the British authorities, who had tried to encourage participation at organised and supervised bonfire parties, but in the late eighties a more concentrated effort was made to warn of the hazards, with commercials centring on the injuries children were likely to sustain which could even include severe visual impairment, and putting the responsibility for their well-being very firmly on their parents. In fact, youngsters were shown as being more generally vulnerable, with commercials of 1992 and 1996 pointing to the dangers of liquids being placed within their reach inside unidentified containers, which resulted in thousands of cases needing hospital treatment. Similarly, parents were advised of the need to reflect and to be careful in the selection of toys and in supervising the way children played with them. Thoughtlessness and carelessness were shown as being the causes of a variety of accidents, and the consequences of such mistakes were made abundantly clear. The dangers of fire caused by portable heaters (1993) were expressed adequately in the title of the commercial *Time Bomb* while the risks associated with inextinguished cigarettes were graphically illustrated by the slogan *don't die for a smoke* (1992). The 1995 advertisements warning about carbon monoxide gave as their principal message the information that heating systems needed to be checked regularly, that the danger sometimes came out of the blue and that children might be better informed or more alert than their elders and should be heeded. Once more, individual and collective responsibility was evoked. It was up to everyone to ensure that routine precautions were taken before going to bed (extinguishing cigarettes, pulling out electrical plugs, guarding the fire and closing all doors), *turn off before you turn in*, while parents were reminded that inadequate ventilation *can kill your family*. The garden was also a place of particular risk, with the commercials of 1991 giving a catalogue of the errors likely to be committed by *Mr Neanderthal – the missing link between the garden and the Casualty Department*, from falling over cables or off insecure step ladders, to risking eye damage by using a lawn-edge trimmer without goggles, not forgetting the final trick of cutting the cable of the lawnmower.

(b) Health preoccupations

Health questions have been a regular feature of government warnings. The problems evoked are numerous, skin cancer, eye damage, cot death, whooping cough, Aids and drug taking, not to mention the risks of smoking, although in this latter case the government's stance has always been ambiguous. Television commercials for tobacco products were only finally stopped by EEC directives, while poster advertising even for cigarettes continues. At the same time, campaigns have been waged to discourage smoking, either by the soft approach, accentuating the social disadvantages with smokers being less likely to attract the opposite sex because *it's like kissing an old ashtray* or, more radically, by accentuating the real argument, the health risks. The campaign in the 1990s with John Cleese comparing the ashes from a cigarette with those from a funeral urn was a particular example of the new, harsher technique. Many of the arguments given about health come into the category of sensible precautions: having one's eyes tested regularly, avoiding dangerous exposure to the sun and the need to be careful in the use of medicines, to respect prescription doses and to administer products safely. In the latter case, the important sub-text was that the citizens' duty was to avoid calling on the overstretched on health services to carry out routine tasks but to take responsibility for themselves. Various potentially serious medical problems were raised. Whooping cough, an almost forgotten but dangerous disease, could be prevented by immunisation and the need to persuade parents to have their children vaccinated against a variety of almost eliminated infections became a major concern of the 1980s and 1990s. Cot death was another subject requiring careful handling. Even if the number of victims was small, around one a day according to the commercial, the effect of these inexplicable fatalities was traumatic. The advice given to mothers was that of best practice, concerning smoking, how to put the baby down and how to keep him warm, but the tone adopted was inevitably gentle. It was necessary, above all, to warn new mothers without arousing dreadful memories in those who had lost their child in this tragic way.

The questions of drugs and Aids were delicate. Much was made, in the nineties, of the effects of solvent inhaling, often seen as a substitute for drugs among poorer youngsters but with equally catastrophic results. The 1992 campaign emphasised once more parental responsibilities in identifying signs of abuse and the simple written message, accompanied by gruesome sound effects, was seen as a means both of informing and shocking, without resorting to the high-risk strategy of showing details of the practice and thereby glorifying or facilitating it. After the failure of the heroin campaign mentioned above, anti-drugs commercials emphasised the progressive nature of the problem, its social consequences and often fatal outcome. In this case, the appeal had to be made to particular social groups, users and their friends, rather than to parents and to the wider community, and an accurate portrayal of behaviour and attitudes was essential.

The dominant health question of the 1980s and 1990s was the problem of Aids. The disease had been discovered in the early eighties and associated directly with homosexuals and intravenous drug users. The realisation that hetrosexual intercourse could transmit the virus led to an approach in faster campaigns which was direct and explicit, *bang bang you're dead*, but it was clear that information concerning the true risks was an essential part of the prevention process. Eighties commercials tended therefore to be 'scientific', with hospital specialists stating the simple medical facts, or 'cataclysmic', using the symbolism of natural or man-made phenomena, such as tombstones or the birth of an iceberg. The message of avoiding the social exclusion of victims was handled largely by voluntary organisations, for example, through the National Aids Helpline, while 1990s government commercials emphasised that a single act of intercourse, homosexual or heterosexual, was sufficient to transmit the disease. One advert featured the testimony of a 28-year-old heterosexual who had contracted HIV within the familiar context of a brief sexual fling while on holiday. It was also stressed that wearing a condom was an adequate preventive measure. The subject was still considered delicate. Although the government had authorised the advertising of branded contraceptives in an attempt to encourage their use, official announcements concentrated their efforts on making the practice an unexceptional matter. Two advertisements of 1992-1993 approached the problem in different ways, the first, which could only be transmitted after 21.00 showed a certain Mrs Dawson who worked on the production line in a factory and made and saw thousands of sheaths every day. Her counterpart, whose commercial was only authorised after 22.30 was a Mr Brewster, an old-age pensioner who recounted his experiences with Geronimo, the condom which he donned when making love in his youth, but which required washing and cleaning after every act of intercourse. The inference was that modern condoms were both simple and pleasurable to use, and a small price to pay for 'safe sex', but the whole anti-Aids campaign was a classic example of government adverts moving from the stage of information to the objective of changing behaviour patterns and of the need to handle a potentially intrusive, yet vitally important, subject with delicacy.

(c) Sensible precautions

The growing trend towards ever more exotic foreign holiday destinations or towards independent rather than package-deal trips was conceived as bringing further dangers about which British tourists needed to be informed for their own good. The emphasis was placed on the risks and inconveniences run and on the need to behave responsibly both before and during one's stay. The dangers depicted included accident or illness necessitating health insurance, theft and the complications it could bring and, last but not least, the potentially far-reaching consequences of law-breaking in foreign countries. The message in the late 80s was 'get it right before you go', an argument which applied to all aspects of foreign travel and indicated the strongly informative nature of the commercials which, like many other government campaigns, were combined with the provision of a booklet obtainable from suitable outlets, in this case travel agents and post offices. To reinforce the point, the advertisements themselves were graphic and uncompromising: the effects of a road accident for which they were blameless on a young, happy but uninsured couple, an older husband and wife faced with taking all the necessary steps after the loss of their valuables, a process which was likely to occupy them throughout their week's holiday and, most striking of all, the effects of law-breaking. The rowdy behaviour of the 'lager lout' was not mentioned, but the limits of the powers and duties of British consuls were clearly indicated. Advertisements further pointed out that foreign countries' legislation was not the same as that of the United Kingdom, in the case of dress regulations for instance, and that the law of the land had to be respected. In 1992, the danger of unintentional drug-smuggling was explicitly evoked. The scenario was familiar enough, with a young man meeting a girl in a club and agreeing to transport an article for her, only to be caught by the customs in a foreign country, imprisoned, subjected to various indignities, but, worse still, running the risk even of capital punishment, *in some countries they give you life, in others they'll take your life*. The message was stark, but the accent was substantially similar that of the other commercials concerning holidays which stressed the individual's need to act sensibly and to take the necessary steps for his own comfort and even survival.

The longest-running subject of government advertisements, almost from the beginning of television, has been the question of road safety, in its many ramifications from simple information about roadsigns or new regulations, through to the horrors of high-speed crashes and the abiding dangers of drinking and driving. The advertising techniques have undeniably developed, in line with product commercials, away from explicit messages towards more narrative- or dialogue-based techniques, but the underlying motifs of providing information, and encouraging care, anticipation and attention to the needs and difficulties of others remain constant features. The early government commercials put particular emphasis on education. Such novelties as pelican crossings, zig-zag lines near pedestrian crossings, box junctions and even 'continental' road signs were explained in commercials as well as in other media and in the Highway Code. When radial-ply tyres first appeared, the public needed to be warned of the danger of mixing them with cross-plies and here again the advertising technique remained predominantly didactic and demonstrative. Perhaps the most striking changes concerned the opening of motorways, with their specific warning signs, and as late as 1986, commercials were still being produced, targeting no doubt occasional motorists, indicating that, for instance, the hard shoulder was not at all the place for casual stops. This theme was developed in 1993 by a commercial that further detailed the dangers for the unwary. A woman driver had broken down, very sensibly not tried to effect repairs and notified the emergency services in the approved manner. She nevertheless committed the cardinal error of remaining in her car with her children, forgetting that 10 per cent of all fatal motorway accidents occurred on the hard shoulder. Generally, road safety messages often seemed to be making quite elementary points and the early ones were presented in a pedagogical and almost moralistic tone. The need to be careful in snow and fog, to keep one's distance and to use the necessary lights all seemed self-evident, but were nevertheless mentioned, while the dangers of badly loaded caravans and ill-adjusted headlights were also emphasised. The 1970s saw the appearance of the 'ambler gambler', a risk-taker who was simply an accident waiting to happen by virtue of his desire always to be quicker and more daring than his fellow motorists and who was finally shown getting his comic come-uppance at the hands of another amber gambler, dressed in similar fashion, driving an identical car equally badly. The superior tone of the message did not stop there, however; a commercial in 1986 pointed out the dangers of aggressive driving to passengers, fragile shopping and unwary pedestrians, but the voice-over message was uncompromisingly self-righteous *fierce braking is the sign of a bad driver*.

The campaign encouraging the wearing of seat belts was one of the most memorable of the early attempts by the government to influence behaviour at the wheel. Public resistance was considerable, often on the grounds of individual liberty or the hypothetical danger of slowing escape from a car after an accident; the problem was not solved until technology developed sufficiently to make belts easier to put on and take off and until the government finally bowed to the inevitable and made their wearing compulsory. In the seventies, however, it appeared that many motorists were only prepared to use their belts for long-distance trips during which high-speed motoring might be the rule. In 1974, the clunk-click commercials featuring Jimmy Saville sought to persuade motorists of dangers nearer to home, by pointing out that most accidents occurred locally, many of them at low speeds, and that the consequences could be horrific; the testimony of unfortunate victims, with their disfigured faces, was used to demonstrate the consequences. By the 1990s, rear seat belts were the bone of contention and here again the government had recourse to two types of presentation, factual details concerning the numbers of accidents and a graphic mock-up demonstration showing what could happen to unsecured children even in a low-speed crash: head injuries, being crushed by adults or flying through the windscreen. Here, not surprisingly, the responsibility of drivers in general and parents in particular was invoked. Other commercials stressed the need for sensible precautions and for drivers and their vehicles to be in a fit state to take to the road. Tyres, viewers were repeatedly told, required to be checked regularly for pressure, tread and uneven wear, while the drivers themselves should ensure that their sight met the required standards. To complete the list of advice, the particular danger of driver fatigue was stressed, with common sense advice on stops and on fresh air being given. The risk was graphically illustrated by one advertisement, addressed to the professional commercial traveller, featuring a representative who consistently failed to heed warnings and ended up not late for his appointment, but in a fatal collision.

Certain commercials were directed to specific groups, with a view to encouraging awareness and reasonable conduct. Thus, instructions for children on how to cross the road and what not to do in the street were hammered home by the use of cartoon figures, like Beatrix Potter's characters Mrs Fluffy Tail, Willy Weasel and Policeman Badger, as well as by the Green Cross Code demonstrated by a batman-like figure. The first commercials featuring this character proved misleading, as children were apparently inclined to wait at the roadside expecting the actual green-cross man to come and help them: later commercials therefore added the line *I won't be there when you cross the road.* Similarly, it was thought more effective for older pedestrians to be advised by other elderly people about how to cross safely, as they could convey more convincingly the uncertainties and dangers which were felt. Motor cyclists were another particularly vulnerable group and campaigns regularly put the emphasis both on training to learn good riding practice and on the advisability of being properly equipped with a helmet which was the correct size, undamaged and conformed to the BSI requirements. Once more, these road users tended to represent a relatively uniform age group and the voice-over used in the advertisement was that of an older man, pronouncing the didactic message of the need to learn the skills *to be a real rider.*

(d) Thinking of others

Most road safety commercials sought to influence both attitude and behaviour and the arguments revolved around the notions of thinking for oneself, thinking for others and expecting the unexpected. Thus the 'dummy' who in 1994 presented both right and wrong ways of doing things was capable of the crassest blunders, never looking out for cyclists, turning and reversing into them without warning and even knocking them down by the well-timed opening of his car door. In a second advertisement, he corrected his mistakes by helping his child to cross the road in exemplary fashion, in accordance with the Green Cross Code. Motorists were reminded of the difficulties faced by elderly people trying to cross the road, hampered by their poor hearing and failing sight, and therefore dependent on the motorists' understanding of their difficulties and anticipation of their likely actions. Even minor errors were shown as having potentially fatal consequences, like parking at junctions which cut visibility, but the commonest faults were not anticipating what others might do, such as the children running towards an ice-cream van, or more fundamentally simply driving too fast. As the message of the nineties read, the solution was to *kill your speed – not a child* and the commercial indicated that a car travelling at 20mph only had a 5 per cent chance of killing any child it collided with, while even at the normal speed limit of 30 mph it had a 50 per cent chance of doing so. The commercials made no attempt to minimise the serious consequences of accidents, either physical or mental, or to hide the fact that lives were permanently ruined by such events. Although the commercials were frequently directed at one particular target group, the cumulative effect was that, in one capacity or another, the whole community was affected by road safety questions. One category of anti-social behaviour stood out above all others, namely drinking and driving, which was and is regularly condemned in commercials, especially around the Christmas and New Year periods, but also at other strategic moments in the year. The directness of the message is justified by the fact that, even allowing for the fact that British law is more lenient than that of many other countries, motorists driving with more than a certain blood-alcohol level are committing a criminal act, whether or not they are involved in accidents. The fact of being caught and charged has been, significantly, only a minor feature of the commercials' messages, which have concentrated on the idea of social responsibility and the dire consequences on the lives of victims. By the late 1980s, advertisements were concentrating on the notion that *drinking and driving wrecks lives* and the point was made in a variety of emotional ways, from the poignancy of the junior school class with one empty desk, through the indignation of the fireman who had just removed a dead woman from her car, only to find her baby afterwards, to the grief of a mother visiting her child in hospital, knowing full well that she would never recover. In these circumstances, the courage of the victims was illustrated, but so was the irretrievable transformation of their lives. The technique of the advertisements was and is to demonstrate in a plausible way[10] the disastrous effects of such criminal action and to encourage a climate of thinking in which such behaviour is no longer acceptable.

It would be wrong, however, to take too negative a view of the messages of government advertising; the desire to establish social norms and to encourage socially-beneficial actions has been an equally recurrent and persistent feature. The growing crime rate and the fragmentation of families meant that keeping an eye out for what was happening in one's neighbourhood was to be encouraged as an act of solidarity, rather than being considered a mere unwanted intrusion into the affairs of others. The creation of Neighbourhood Watch schemes, whose effectiveness was lauded by commercials, was part of the process, but the notion that anything suspicious should be reported to the authorities was the message of several commercials. The messages *don't wait till it's too late* or *don't leave it to someone else* emphasised the necessary sense of individual responsibility for the common good and could be applied to a variety of situations. As early as the 1970s, through an animated cartoon, holidaymakers were encouraged to warn the coastguard of boats in difficulties and informed that the service could be contacted through the usual 999 number. The importance of contacting the fire brigade in case of emergencies was also stressed, but the majority of commercials emphasised that contacting the police was an essential part of preventing crime: crooks were no longer immediately recognisable by their appearance, but suspicious behaviour should be notified immediately and it was made clear both that the authorities accepted that mistakes might be made and that contacting the police in case of doubt was simply part of *being a good neighbour*. Social responsibility extended into other fields and ensuring the cleanliness of the streets became a periodic cause of concern. The Keep Britain Tidy Campaign, launched in the 1950s is still running today and much of its publicity passes through poster advertising rather than through television. Nevertheless, there have been exceptions. A 1989 commercial entitled *Clanger* used the simple expedient of litter making a noise as it was dropped, surreptitiously hidden or simply left behind, to remind people of all classes and social groups that a consistent effort at tidiness was necessary. In this commercial, the litter lout was always shown attracting the disapproving gazes of his fellow citizens and no group or individual was free from censure. By the 1990s, the attack had turned to the problems of dogs soiling pavements. Owners were urged to *scoop the poop*, in order to ensure the convenience of their fellow citizens, but the most striking advertisement was no doubt that depicting a middle-aged man leaving his home, greeting his neighbours in customary fashion before proceeding to crouch and defecate in the gutter like a dog, an action which, not surprisingly, caused dismay on the faces of the passers-by. The message of this uncompromisingly scatological commercial was no doubt to point to the contradiction of otherwise respectable people allowing their pets to contaminate the environment in this way.

(e) Positive action

The important role to be played by parents was a perennial feature of government advertisements. In addition to the specific concerns with the new and recurring dangers indicated above, it was made clear that it was they who were primarily responsible not just for the welfare of their families, but also for their development into good citizens of the future. The common-sense advice that children should not talk to/accept lifts or presents from strangers was a repeated theme addressed both to children and to the parents whose role was to communicate the warning in a manner that was at once clear and undramatic. In the 1990s, school bullying was on the increase and once more the role of parents (and teachers) in helping to counter this antisocial behaviour was stressed. Commercials addressed to children advised them to tell an adult they could trust, in order to be spared further unpleasantness, and so that the bullies themselves could be helped. Parental responsibility for less satisfactory aspects of their children's behaviour was also emphasised directly. The choice of an air rifle as a present was not directly condemned, but it was made clear that the sensible approach was to realise that it was not a toy to be aimed indiscriminately, but that its use required both care and, ideally, training through a gun club. Parents were also encouraged to think of the specific needs of boys and girls. In a 1970s commercial that might have seemed in advance of its time,[11] they were reminded that a girl's ambition should not stop at getting married and having a family, but that she should also think of her longer-term future by ensuring that she had the necessary skills and education to get beyond the dead-end or unskilled job that would otherwise await her when her children left home. With boys, the potential problem was that of slipping into vandalism and crime through a lack of parental control and interest. The question *do you know where your lad's going tonight?* was intended, in a commercial shot to the words of the song *it's a crazy world we're living in* simply to make parents aware that youngsters could not be relied upon to look after themselves and that they could easily slip into bad ways.

Commercials made much play of the positive side of citizenship in a large number of advertisements encouraging blood and organ donorship. The National Blood Transfusion Service always needed new supplies, but the Aids scare made people less willing to volunteer and efforts had to be made to encourage the practice in a number of ways. The fact that blood could be given easily and conveniently *whenever you can* was an important part of the message, as was the fact that all classes and groups within society were welcome and the positive feeling of doing good for the community was enhanced by pictures of bright and well-decorated rooms with their contingent of attractive and smiling nurses. The underlying notion was the appeal to people's better nature by their willingness simply to help others with the gift of life. Sometimes more specific messages were included, the new local rate telephone number of the Blood Transfusion Service needed to be communicated and the uses to which the donated blood was actually put also figured in commercials. The standard objections, *I would if I knew how, I need all of mine* and *I've never given before* were all shown as inadequate in the face of the simple statement of social responsibility that *giving blood saves lives*. Organ donorship, a more delicate matter, of course, was also regularly promoted and used essentially the same arguments of helping others, although care had to be taken to emphasise the need for intending donors to register and carry their cards and to advise their nearest and dearest of the decision they had made.

Some government commercials then went beyond the simple approach of encouraging people to look after themselves and their own interests and took them into domains where a sense of responsibility for others and the values of positive citizenship were emphasised. Many government advertisements have an informative quality and provide details of which the public should be reminded: advice to first-time voters on the need to be on the electoral roll is an important part of their training as citizens while indications of educational or career opportunities in the public service are another legitimate subject of viewer awareness. Periodic advertisements for recruitment in the nursing and teaching professions, as well as in the police and armed services have therefore remained a feature of government advertising and it is understandable that such commercials should portray the future careers in the most positive of lights. There has also been specific emphasis on the volunteer services like the Territorial Army and the Special Constabulary, where the announcements have stressed the material benefits and interest of the work and the professional standards required, as well as the idea of commitment to helping one's country or fellow citizens in time of need. In all these fields, attempts have been made to recruit members from the ethnic minorities and a memorable advertisement placed by the Metropolitan Police in 1990 used a text loosely based on Rudyard Kipling's famous poem *If* and featured a black actor. This does not mean, however, that government advertising is without either dangers or critics. In retrospect, many of the commercials produced in the early days not only seem old fashioned in their approach and unnecessarily dogmatic or moralising in their technique, which is perhaps inevitable, but also tend to concern themselves with matters which are either too trivial to merit comment or which seem to represent excessive intrusion into individuals' lives. In other words, the 'nanny state' is not just a creation of the late 1990s. Back in the 1970s, it was thought necessary, for example, to remind people that unlagged water pipes were likely to freeze and burst in winter, that eating too many sweets was bad for your teeth and that children needed to be careful about playing on the ice of frozen ponds. If it is easy, with hindsight, to point to the apparent superfluity of many such announcements, it is harder to say how current government campaigns will be judged in the future.

Serving the nation or serving the politicians ?

Increasing concern has been felt in more recent years about the relationship between government advertising, party political advantage and even propaganda. The term 'public service advertising' was habitually attached to information formulated by the government, but in the Thatcher years in particular, the question of the 'propriety' of campaigns became a contentious issue, especially as advertising for political purposes was still forbidden. This section seeks to examine the announcements of the 1980s in rather more detail, before indicating and briefly discussing the initiatives taken by the Blair administration since May 1997.

Before the arrival in power of the Conservatives in 1979, there had only been minor skirmishes over advertising between the political parties themselves and between them, the COI and the ITA/IBA. In 1971, the Heath administration planned to place commercials inviting the public to go to the Post Office and obtain leaflets about Common Market entry; this move was vetoed by the ITA, and the IBA acted similarly four years later when the Wilson government proposed the same facilities during the EEC referendum campaign. Plans to publicise the 'fair rents' envisaged by the 1972 Housing Finance Act were also forbidden. The generally accepted convention was, firstly, that no promotion of government measures was to be allowed until any Bill had passed into law and, secondly, that political advantage should not be sought by the government itself, but the matter remained delicate. The ITA's 1971 decision was based on a precise interpretation of the 1954 Television Act, for which Counsel's advice was sought:

> *Thus the Authority, relying on Counsel's Opinion for its interpretation of the wording of the [1954 Television] Act, accepted advertisements from the government of the day when that government was exercising its executive function in carrying out the law as enacted by parliament, or when exercising the prerogative of the Crown, but not when promoting the merits of government policy or attempting to attract public support. Governments might buy advertising time to explain to the public how family allowances or social security benefits might be claimed, for example, but not why they had or had not been increased.*[12]

This situation was to change radically under the Thatcher government, whose recourse to advertising came to be seen as going beyond the simple task of informing the public about legislation. Various objections to government practice were raised: the quantity and cost of advertising, the fields in which it was used, the length of the Conservatives' tenure of power and the contradiction between central government's use of the medium and the prohibition on local authorities from doing the same. The last two points need only brief explanation. The campaign waged in 1984 and 1985 by the GLC under Ken Livingstone, to prevent its abolition, was sufficiently successful for the government to take sweeping measures, under the Local Government Act of 1986, to limit local authority publicity.[13] The Conservatives' control over the levers of power was such that, in 1985, the Cabinet Office's note *Central Government Conventions on Publicity and Advertising* envisaged allowing the government to explain controversial matters provided the recipients' interests were directly affected, the former restriction on the need for prior legislation having disappeared, although, in practice, the change had no effect on the production of television commercials.

The main arguments, however, concerned the amount of government advertising especially in controversial fields, notably employment, social security benefits and privatisations. The increases in spending in other areas were relatively modest, and the more extensive use of television was undoubtedly a major factor in the rises recorded. The key figure was Lord Young, *the man who sold advertising to Whitehall*. According to Margaret Scammell,[14] as head of the Manpower Services Commission he raised advertising expenditure from £2 million to £4.3 million in little more than a year and went on to promote vast increases at both the Department of Employment and the Department of Trade and Industry, where spending rose from £1.8 million in 1986-87 to £31.3 million in 1988-89.[15] The DTI's campaigns included the rapidly oversubscribed Enterprise Initiative scheme which offered companies professional advice on how to improve their businesses and the promotions of the European Single Market in 1992, with advertisements featuring, amongst others, Richard Branson and Alan Sugar, declaring how important the opening of European business was to them. Fears were aroused in some quarters by the DTI's more and more political stance and Mark Jones' remarks in 1988 were less prophetic than descriptive:

> *The DTI's ethos of advertising is becoming more blatantly political. If this spreads to other departments, like the Department of Employment, it could affect how unemployment is portrayed by the government.*[16]

Unemployment had in fact become a major political issue and the government's Action for Jobs campaign of 1986 to 1988 sought to bring down the figures, not only by providing employment opportunities, but also by scaring off the register people who were already working, undeclared, in the black economy. Despite the success of both these strategies, or perhaps even because of it, the government was accused of promoting its own political interests by advertising contentious measures, at a politically expedient time (shortly before the 1987 election). Family Credit, like its predecessor the Family Income Supplement (FIS), was designed to encourage the return to work, by providing additional resources to low-income families. As such, the measure was not free from controversy and the initial advertising, at a cost of £3 million in press and television promotion, was a flop, leading the COI to transfer the account to a different agency. The new benefit publicised by a new multi-media campaign, achieved higher take-up rates than the FIS, perhaps because instead of emphasising the amount of the benefit and what it might buy, the commercials concentrated on the 'testimonial' technique and illustrated the types of families who could benefit.

The disputes concerning employment and social security were as nothing, however, compared with the controversy aroused by the privatisation campaigns, the bill for which reached well over £100 million between 1984 and 1987.[17] The process was crucial to the government both politically and economically and no effort was spared to ensure its success. Costs were increased by advertising both at the pre-privatisation stage, to give a favourable impression of the viability of the company and the likelihood of it becoming a thriving private-sector operator, and once the sale had been completed, as well as during the share-offer period itself. Several of the sell-offs were of relatively minor importance in the government's desire to create a share-owning democracy and the stock market crash of 1987 substantially dampened enthusiasm, but the major 'popular' privatisations of British Telecom, British Airways and British Gas achieved all that the government had hoped, and more. Advertisements encouraging participation in privatisation were akin to ordinary commercial marketing, impressing prospective purchasers by the quality of the product on offer, as well as convincing them of the validity of an underlying political and economic concept. The BT flotation attracted some 2.3m shareholders, many of them first-time share-buyers while the BA offer was oversubscribed 35 times and the initial trading price of 119p gave a more than adequate profit to the institutional and individual investors who had part-paid their stock at 65p. The ultimate success was, however, British Gas, whose 'Tell Sid' campaign was the archetypal example of popular marketing, with 'Sid', a character who never appeared, being rapidly understood as a metaphor for the British people as a whole.

> The phrase, 'If you See Sid, tell him' quickly passed into the vernacular, and was clearly understood in research to communicate that everybody should pass relevant information about the share offer to friends, family and acquaintances generally.[18]

The essential strategy was to convince the public that the flotation was for everybody and that no-one could afford to neglect the opportunity. As Alison Turner of Young and Rubicam explained:

> The strategy we developed [...] was to encourage participation in 'The People's Share Offer'. We aimed to create a feeling of excitement consonant with a great national event, and to develop beyond this, a feeling that everyone would want to participate; people would be missing out on a unique opportunity if they did not participate... To announce the share offer, and stimulate interest in it, the advertising used the analogy of the Jubilee beacons, and communicated that everyone, everywhere was invited to join in this national event.[19]

Privatisations were to be one of the main legacies of the Thatcher years and raised important questions about the use of government advertising to change public attitudes. Apart from the boost that the sale of shares gave to the stock market and the general association of the process with the enterprise culture of the 1980s, it is interesting to consider the state's role in changing popular mentalities and in a certain redefinition of the rights and duties of the citizen, who was encouraged to participate in what was tantamount to an act of national solidarity, by acquiring his own share of the national heritage. By the mid 90s, doubts were being expressed both about the prices paid for shares and about the viability and even morality of the whole venture. It is true also that opposition parties remained hostile to the notion of privatisation, which was one of the major arguments invoked to suggest that the government was overstepping the mark by pushing through policies which failed to achieve widespread public support. The case is not altogether conclusive, however. Privatisation had been part of the Conservative election manifestos and any party in government has the right, if not the duty, to implement the programme it has promised to the people. The bone of contention about privatisations was in the end, not that people were paying individually for what they already owned collectively, but that the government, by its powerful position and by extensive advertising for which the taxpayer picked up the bill, was going beyond and abusing democratic processes by influencing behaviour in a partisan way.

The arrival in power of the Labour party under Tony Blair, with a massive parliamentary majority necessarily brought an upheaval in the field of government advertising, the more so as the number of campaigns in early 1997 was limited in accordance with convention concerning pre-election periods. It is too early to evaluate objectively the success or even the reforming intentions of the new administration, but the government advertisements broadcast since the election victory present the picture both of change and of continuity and indicate a difference of approach from John Major's administration. As Mark Jones had aptly remarked almost 10 years before, a change of government would inevitably mean a change of tack: *If Labour were elected, they'd spend even more money on government advertising than the Tories, albeit on different aspects of reform.*[20] It is also possible to detect a more open approach to communication with the greater availability of information via the web site of the COI. Such questions as service recruitment and safety have continued to be handled as before: the latest fire warnings concern the dangers from chip pans (an echo of the 1980s), while other new commercials on an old theme were launched to reinforce garden safety, although the campaign as a whole was sponsored by Greenbrook Electrics as well as retailers Do-it-All and B and Q, which was an innovation. The recent campaign from the DVLA, designed to combat road tax evasion, like that to discourage TV licence dodging, is no more than the normal business of government. 1999 has seen commercials to encourage nursing training and to persuade those who had left the profession to return. The Financial Services Agency launched a campaign in 1997 to help those who had suffered from pension mis-selling at the end of the 1980s, which may be regarded as marginally controversial, while 1999 has seen the first commercial for many years encouraging recruitment to teaching pointing out the valuable work done by the profession in developing and stimulating young minds, which would seem to correspond closely with Tony Blair's statement that his priorities in government would be *education, education and education.* There has also been a campaign encouraging environmental awareness, under the general logo of *Do your bit* and covering transport, energy, waste and water questions. Similarly, a campaign was produced to combat the millennium bug while the launch of the Euro on 1 January 1999 was preceded by another series of adverts designed to increase awareness within the business community. To avoid accusations of bias and propaganda the neutral slogan *perfect planning prevents pathetic performance* was chosen. Most of these issues might reasonably be seen as of general rather than party-political importance, and the public service nature of the campaigns has been carefully maintained. The New Deal and the New Deal for Lone Parents campaigns are, however, clearly identified as Labour policies designed to resolve national difficulties and the success of the projects remains questioned, despite the favourable figures quoted by the ministries concerned. Here once more, we see the desire of government to implement its policies and to encourage their general acceptance, both on the part of employers and employees, and to promote changes of both attitude and behaviour amongst the citizens. In these cases too, the question may be asked, to what extent the Blair administration, like its predecessors in the 1980s and 1990s, is using the machinery of government advertising to go beyond the simple stage of informing the public and trying to change hopes and aspirations and to redefine citizenship in a way which will further its own party political objectives.

Communication and persuasion

The primary requirement for government advertising to be successful is for it to find the correct tone which is capable both of unifying the viewing public and of making it feel concerned by the information which is being presented. The difficulty of trying to appeal to the whole of a population is a substantial one indeed, although, as we have seen, certain commercials are orientated towards certain groups and the choice of channels and transmission times makes a degree of targeting possible. Sometimes, too, campaigns have developed separate advertisements grouped around a single theme, like fire safety or the dangers of carbon monoxide poisoning, but portraying people of varied social and age groups, thereby giving a greater degree of individual impact. The common aim remains the provision of accurate and convincing information, associated, most often with the feeling that the actions favourably described represent a correct response to questions of public interest or of public duty.

Within these general parameters, the establishment of a feeling of common purpose, or of connivance or complicity, is important, as are various techniques which make the announcements striking or memorable, effects which are most often achieved by shock/surprise, humour and the sense of belonging. It is also true that the techniques of government adverts have evolved, just like those of product commercials, and that various devices may be used at differing times to achieve similar effects. The importance of slogans and catch phrases was realised from the start, and, like their commercial equivalents, public service announcements initially relied heavily on voice-overs, especially with the more 'authoritative' male tones and, as we have seen, the pedagogical, didactic and even moralistic tenor of the adverts was apparent. Sometimes this was inevitable of course, and for technical reasons it was often preferable to use animation or simple illustration to make the points of the argument, rather than running the risk of producing less than realistic detail or even of glorifying error. For questions such as the correct way to wire electric plugs, or what motorway warning signs looked like, there was no better method than a clear illustration of the items or processes concerned. Cartoon characters were ideally adapted for commercials aimed at children, and had the added advantages that authenticity could be dispensed with, while dangerous consequences could still be demonstrated. The Green Cross man became a familiar figure, while the use of two different commercials, one a cartoon and one not, allowed the advertisements on how to react to bullying to be appropriate both for younger and older audiences. Three main technical developments in government adverts nevertheless stand out: the growing professionalism of the announcements as agencies became more and more heavily involved, the steady increase in dialogue commercials and the more and more widespread use of television adverts as a first contact, which would then lead to telephone calls and/or to the distribution of information leaflets and brochures.

An essential feature of the communication was to be the impression of realism, created by the use of settings which were both contemporary and familiar, if not actually recognisable. This is not of itself surprising: public service announcements seek to promote reactions to events in the here and now and it is important for scenes and characters to look and to sound real and plausible. If we take as a principle that nothing in a television commercial is left to chance, then it is clear that within the context of British society, with its class-awareness, the choice of accent, the registers of language, the model of car and the residential area are all clear pointers to the types of characters presented, and it is essential for the various pieces of coded information to be consistent with one another. In the case of Family Credit, for instance, the life-styles of the families shown had to correspond to the expectations of those likely to be recipients of the benefit.[21] The portrayal of society as a whole also has to be more generally representative, with an appropriate percentage, for instance, of women and of ethnic minorities, for everyone has to feel that the message involves and concerns them. A recent Territorial Army advertisement is a case in point: of the four characters shown, one is a woman and one is black, but they can all work together as a team. In another notable 1990s advert encouraging adoption, the coloured population was deliberately targeted; almost all the adults shown as coming forward to offer a home to a child were of Afro-Caribbean or Asian origin, reflecting the high percentage of children in these groups in need of adoptive parents.

Humour and shock have been perceived as effective devices to attract viewers' attention and to reinforce the mnemonic impact. Humour is a means of dedramatising the situation, of reducing tension and of overcoming taboos, all of which can have the effect of making the message more palatable. The role of Mrs Dawson and Mr Brewster in making condoms into a part of everyday life has already been mentioned, and the subject was deemed too sensitive for a simple factual presentation. Several advertisements invited viewers to laugh at the folly of others, the amber gambler, the holidaymaker unable to see that the dinghy sailor who so amused him was in imminent danger of drowning and the gallant knight galloping to save a damsel in distress who fell off his badly placed ladder as he tried to save her. In the latter case, the scenario was so obviously contrived as to be humorous even before the accident occurred. The Keep Britain Tidy commercial, *Clanger*, used the standard comic device of the tables being turned as a respectable businessman, having critically observed a boy who had failed to place his litter in a bin, was then caught leaving his own newspaper behind. Humour is, however, often little more than a veneer, to be seen through, in order for the message to be more effective. The mother who left a child's fire engine at the top of the stairs, for the grandmother to fall over and find herself in traction in hospital and who bought another child a *dead cheap* toy which almost blinded her was a comic figure, but only in so far as her lack of awareness was caricatural and intended to arouse in the viewer a sense of superiority at having identified the dangers. Similarly, the pedestrian who was road tested for safety was comic because of the extended pedestrian/car metaphor in the voice-over commentary but only until he met with an accident which again necessitated hospital treatment.

The humour itself sometimes went to the limits of acceptability, however, and the scatological scene of the man fouling the pavement or the gallows humour of John Cleese's anti-smoking commercial are well into the register of shock, rather than ordinary comedy. The weapon is to be handled with care, of course. Any suggestion of levity is likely to be counterproductive and we may wonder at the portrayal of the criminals George and Lil in the 1970s anti-burglary commercials. They were shown as caricature thieves going off for an evening's work robbing other people, only to return home to find that they themselves had been victims of a break-in. The biter-bit scenario was was comic, but it may be asked whether the effect was not to make a serious subject seem less critical. An awareness of the dangers of trivialisation showed through in the road safety campaign of 1994, where the central figure, the dummy, was first shown committing a series of elementary errors of road safety, but then mended his ways to become *not such a dummy after all*. The use of shock tactics sometimes runs the same risks of excess. Once again, they have been a common feature of government announcements, from the severely injured patients in the 1970s seat belts campaigns to the physically and psychologically damaged victims of drinking and driving or other grave road accidents. The acoustically accurate sounds of children damaging their health, perhaps permanently, by inhaling solvents, or again the dramatic picture of a drugged youngster drowning after falling from a bridge were equally uncompromising, and the immediate effect on watching such commercials can only be one of pain and horror. Such brutal details are a feature of the realism peculiar to British government adverts and seem to correspond to popular expectation. Whether, in the longer term, such portrayals of pain and suffering will not come to be as numbing to the senses as the more explicit of news bulletins covering third-world disasters is a moot point to which it is impossible, for the moment, to give an answer.

The inculcation of a sense of identity or of belonging to a common culture is arguably a less controversial but equally effective communicational tactic in government commercials. The technique often employed is that of inclusiveness, a key notion for the sale of shares during privatisations, but also important to make all sections of the community feel concerned and ready to help in the case of the search for blood donors. More recently, advertising for the New Deal has adopted a similar approach, showing various recognisable areas of the country with their inhabitants and typical accents or, more powerfully, pictures of masses of people all heading towards the same destination. The message of the commercials, with employers speaking out about their desire to give employees a chance is another part of the inclusive principle. Another variant of the same device is the identification with the characters presented in the spots. This can be achieved by showing recognisable types within a familiar situation, but more frequently the contact is strengthened by confession or testimony, sometimes by voice-over but more effectively through words spoken directly to camera. In their different ways, the anti-Aids commercials, the Family Credit campaign, the New Deal and Cot Deaths announcements have adopted this recognisably authentic and direct technique.

Similarly, familiar faces or identifiable intertextual or cultural references are another element of common interest and of the sense of belonging and has arguably a more direct impact in public service announcements than in product commercials, since there is no danger of a clash between the personality and brand image. Thus the viewer might have recognised, in the 1970s, the warm and gentle tones of Deryck Guyler explaining pelican crossings or the figure of Shaw Taylor, the presenter of ITV's crime prevention programme *Police Five*, advocating the secret use of postcode marking to ensure the return of stolen goods. More recently, commercials loosely based on television's *Mastermind* and charity Telethon were likely to strike a chord in the popular mind and therefore become more memorable. There is no substitute for a clearly or logically presented message, but the various techniques mentioned here have undoubtedly helped to make government commercials more effective. Public service announcements frequently have their functional (or factual) side, which gives them an objectivity and the ring of truth. Appeals to the psychological and emotional registers and the use of sociological and symbolic references are additional techniques which may allow the commercials to move viewers beyond the stage of recognising the truth or validity of the arguments, to the point where the commercials start to have a direct influence on behaviour. If one accepts that the objectives of government advertising are to inform the people and to persuade them to combat the faults within society itself, then there is also a need for individual and collective actions to be seen as part of the same process of redefining the role of the citizen. The change in the anti-crime slogans between the 1980s and the 1990s is significant in this respect; while in earlier years the message was antagonistic, *don't let them get away with it*, it was later transformed into the more persuasive and inclusive expression of citizenship, *together we'll crack it*.

Advertising for peace – an example of political communication

In 1988, the British Government, in the form of the Northern Ireland Office (NIO), decided to try a new communicational approach to the problems of terrorist violence in the Province, a series of television advertisements, produced by the agency McCann-Erickson (Belfast) and screened on Ulster Television and to a lesser extent on Channel 4. The campaign lasted until the arrival in power of the Labour party in May 1997 and its 17 commercials have remained largely unknown in mainland Britain. It nevertheless represented a novel attempt to solve a long-standing political problem, which, after various initiatives in the 1970s and early 1980s, culminating in the Anglo-Irish Agreement of 1985 was still as troublesome as ever: in 1988 there were 737 shootings and 257 bombings. Attitudes on both sides of the sectarian divide had hardened, political initiatives had fallen by the wayside and the British government felt the need to try a new technique which might find a longer-term solution to the problems, which could build on slow advances and which, perhaps above all, would bypass both local politicians and paramilitary groups and involve the 'people' in a sense and in a way which had not been done before.

The technique of using advertising to ameliorate or alleviate the situation in Ulster was not a complete novelty; it had been attempted in the 1970s at the time of the launch of the Confidential Telephone, but the differences between the old and new techniques of communication were clearly marked. McCann-Erickson was a highly respected advertising agency, noted for its contribution to various government campaigns in Northern Ireland, as well as holding a number of major commercial accounts, such as Coca Cola, Del Monte, Esso and Nestlé. The advantage of this indirect approach to creative questions, with the material at arm's length, as it were, from the commanding government authority, was evident. However, *Advertising for Peace* was a genuine government campaign which adopted a long-term and gradualist approach, aiming not merely at changing immediate behaviour and reactions, but ultimately, and much more ambitiously, at transforming mentalities and reconstructing society. It also took place at a time when the British government was trying to promote the idea of the Province as an area where normality was returning, prevented only by paramilitary (and especially republican) violence.

The campaign itself traversed four broad phases[22] and was necessarily adapted to suit changes in public mood and in the security situation. The initial intention, simply put, was to encourage the use of the Confidential Telephone, which had begun in 1972 but which, in 1988, became a more organised facility, allowing callers from anywhere in the Province to use the same telephone number, which replaced the local numbers hitherto available for the purpose. Andy Wood, Head of the Northern Ireland Information Service, detailed the original brief supplied to McCann-Erickson as follows:

> The initial brief was 'give us a product, a service which will enable people in Northern Ireland, the people who are suffering directly and indirectly as a result of paramilitary activity ... to report suspicious activity'.[23]

By 1993, although the number of telephone calls had increased and although a greater quantity of information was becoming available to the authorities, the level of violence within Northern Ireland showed little perceptible decrease and the campaign moved over to a more offensive stage, pointing in brutal fashion to the horrors of violence, accentuating the criminality of such actions and the painful consequences, not just for the terrorists themselves, but also for their families. When the IRA and loyalist paramilitary cease-fires were announced in August and September 1994, the tone and tenor of the advertisements changed abruptly, away from the picture of destructive terrorism to the evocation of a highly optimistic normality (clearly a movement from one of the NIO's long-established arguments to the other, its diametrical opposite). It is well-known now that this cease-fire was not by any stretch of the imagination a total cessation of violence and that the euphemistically called 'punishment beatings' (in reality kneecapping, elbowcapping and other forms of extreme brutality) continued as the paramilitary groups sought to maintain and even extend control over their own particular areas. The IRA bombing of Canary Wharf in February 1996 signalled the end of the cease-fire, swept away the optimism and placed the NIO in quandary over the advertisements it should transmit. The initial reaction of the authorities was relatively measured, the optimistic advertisement *Boys* was still screened, but with an amended final shot emphasising the compatibility of different traditions, before the decision was reached to rebroadcast two of the most explicit of the violent advertisements *I wanna be like you* and *Lady* and to devise a new one, depicting the gulf of horror opening up once again before the inhabitants of the Province. To reinforce its message, the NIO opted for a new advertisement, *Timebomb*, featuring a child, having apparently toyed with the idea of a commercial including controversial and expensive archive footage of Nazi sympathisers burning down churches.

The adverts themselves were subject to the normal codes concerning commercial television, notably in respect of transmission times, especially with regard to the 9 p.m. watershed, but also employed many of the common characteristics of commercial and government advertising: the appeal to both the rational and the emotional registers, the studied use of visual and verbal techniques and the widespread recourse to repetition, suggestion and slogan. At the same time, in order to appeal to the socio-economic groups which were particularly targeted, aspects of popular and television culture, linguistic idiom and specific kinds of intertextual references were included. The importance of creating a valid impression of reality was of particular significance within the suspicious context of Ulster. Finally, of course, there was an appeal to such basic emotions as the desire for the well-being of family and friends, the innocence of youth, the need for human solidarity and the sense of belonging to a specific and identifiable community in which one might reasonably have a sense of pride.

The 'realism' of the advertisements was achieved in a variety of ways. The settings were, for the most part, recognisably similar to those within the Province. In *A Future*, for instance, while the pictures of boarded-up houses and graffiti appeared authentic enough, the documentary character of the footage was reinforced by the use of actual archive material showing explosions or real bomb damage. Many of the events depicted were real but it should not be forgotten that what was being given was not news, current affairs or history, but a representation of events. The characters themselves within the commercials did not speak directly: their 'thoughts' were heard in voice over, their 'ideas' were translated into or transmitted by song, they might look directly at the camera in an apparent attempt to convince, the accents seemed to be authentic, but all this was no more than a portrayal of reality.

Many of the advertisements were based on the principle of dramatisation, both 'showing and telling', ie not only portraying but explicitly stating the specific message. More than that, the situation faced by an individual was shown as being representative of that faced by others, and more importantly, the individual's reaction to events would affect, so the message of the adverts ran, the fate not only of himself and his family, but the whole community. Awareness and education were to become self-education, which would then promote the securing of common social and community values. Within this context, the common experiences of the people became a uniting factor, and all aspects of this shared inheritance were useful to the advertiser's purpose. Television culture and awareness of the mechanisms (sound and vision) of advertising were part of this equation, music and film were others. Music has the advantage of its mnemonic effect, but also acts as an emotional stimulus, with the additional advantage of being polysemic and of evoking several feelings at once. Apart from the familiar *Danny Boy* (the Londonderry Air) and extracts from the

Byrds' *Turn, Turn, Turn*, based on verses from Ecclesiastes which was a major popular success in 1967, *Advertising for Peace* also adopted the words and music of two other artists closely associated with the movement for peace and reconciliation in Northern Ireland, the American Harry Chapin who regularly performed in the Province until his death in 1981 and, most notably, Ulster's own Van Morrison, whose recordings of *Brown-Eyed Girl* (1973), *Have I Told You Lately?* (1989) and *Days Like This* (1995) accompanied the advertisements screened during the paramilitary cease-fires. Borrowings from other elements of popular culture helped to reinforce the effect of the campaign: the melodramatic qualities of some of the advertisements were not so far removed from those of such highly successful mass audience movies as *The Godfather* or again *Flashdance*, the music from which, *Lady, Lady*, accompanied the advertisement of the same name.

Identification goes further than this, of course. The language, clothes and interests of the characters depicted were both familiar to those living in the Province and typical of the socio-economic groups to which the characters supposedly belonged, the voice-overs were mostly given in recognisably local accents, which reinforced the impression of adherence to place and strengthened the concept of a shared cultural experience. It was in this way that the absurdity of prejudice and the counter-productiveness of conflict could be hinted at most clearly. If the toddlers in *Citizens* could coexist peacefully, if children in *Northern Irish Humour* could share common jokes, then why, so the viewer was expected to ask himself, could adults not be more tolerant with their neighbours.

The whole Advertising for Peace campaign was, as I have suggested, fraught with imponderables. There was no sure way of knowing whether the campaigns were having the desired effect. As a part of their promotional effort, McCann-Erickson, along with a handsomely presented set of the advertisements, provided figures and details of the apparent reactions to the campaign, presenting the whole enterprise in a most favourable light. They run as follows:[24]

Name of advertisement(s)	Launch date	Reaction
A Future	Jan 1988	result: 51 per cent increase in calls
Silence	1990	result: 22.4 per cent increase in calls
Jigsaw, Bleak, Eye-shutter	1991 - 1992	result: 477 per cent increase in calls, 81 per cent of all adults favourable to the police, 8 per cent unfavourable
Lady, I wanna be like you, Car wash	July 1993	result: the all-time peak response, 729 per cent higher than 1988; public approval at 71 per cent, disapproval at 5 per cent
Next	Nov 1993	research result: 64 per cent all-adult favourability to the Confidential Telephone, only 3 per cent unfavourable
Time to Stop	Spring 1994	result: 88 per cent of all adults view Confidential Telephone as important to Northern Ireland. First cease-fire declared 31st August
Time to Build	post cease-fires, Oct 1994	research result: 86 per cent all-adult favourability, 3 per cent of adults unfavourable
Citizens	April 1995	research result: 82 per cent all-adult favourability, 6 per cent of adults unfavourable
Boys, Yours and Mine, Stars, Humour	June 1995	research result: 82.5 per cent believe these ads will make a difference to Northern Ireland overall "Bright Side" research result: 86 per cent favourability, 75 per cent of adults believe they encourage people to accept each other's differences

From the technical point of view, the agency itself can be justifiably proud of what it called its "psychological creativity". It won awards for two of the advertisements, *Lady* and *Timebomb*, indicating recognition of the technical and professional standard of the products proposed and, in this respect at least, the advertisements remained faithful to the words of McCann-Erickson's own logo, they did represent a kind of *truth well told*, even though the exact meaning of *truth* is open to conjecture.

The fact remains that the task of educating and transforming the Northern Irish population as a whole was always going to be extremely difficult to achieve. The mutual mistrust between the communities is a well-nigh insuperable obstacle, while it is equally difficult to persuade the nationalist population of the good faith of any enterprise emanating from the British government. The long history of prejudice, half truths and manipulation had led to a long-established fear of 'dirty tricks'.[25] The role and portrayal of the police was another problematic factor: despite claims to the contrary, the Royal Ulster Constabulary was far from convincing the nationalist population of its impartiality, which immediately cast into doubt the success of any campaign advocating greater cooperation with the defence forces. 'Truth' is therefore a relative, not an absolute commodity and it could be argued that the NIO and McCann-Erickson were more interested in 'telling' than in 'truth'. The attitude of the British population and the British government has also been equivocal. The campaign was the creation of the Thatcher and Major administrations and the initiative, like most of these governments' interventions in the Province, was cloaked in a veil of secrecy: reliable indications of costs were not available and the campaign received remarkably little press coverage in Great Britain. It was therefore, in national terms, a low-profile if not a low-risk strategy. The change of government in May 1997 was to herald a radical shift in approach, putting an end to the campaign. The process in advertising leading from awareness to action may take a considerable time and it seems clear that *Advertising for Peace* had, over the nine years of its existence, achieved all the positive results it was ever likely to attain, most importantly, without causing any obvious adverse reactions. If one views the campaign as a stage in the gradual process of transformation of attitudes within the Province, then it is possible to conclude that the advertising series had a number of beneficial results in both the short and the long term and may well have contributed to the calling of both paramilitary cease-fires. One major question nevertheless remains to be considered, namely the legitimacy of such a technique, in the transmission by a government agency, of an overtly political communication intended to change the attitudes of the people. What is not in question is the 'humanitarian' element of the campaign, for few can contest the desire to reduce the extent of terrorist violence nor the correctness of the chosen method but beyond this lies the more questionable concept of a government's right to try to manipulate its citizens' long-term behaviour and attitudes by a portrayal of events which some would consider as inaccurate, others as propaganda. The NIO's approach was never fully transparent and Andy Wood's remarks on this subject were less than conclusive. On *The Late Show*, he stressed the 'authenticity' of the scenes portrayed, emphasised that the advertisements had passed what he called 'the journalistic test' but conspicuously failed to address the aspect of manipulation which is central to the case of *Advertising for Peace* and indeed to the question of government advertising in general.

The Northern Ireland campaign is a different example from the majority of government adverts, but it nevertheless reveals the extent to which commercials can be used to combat the dangers assailing society. The subjects treated vary from the deadly serious to the almost trivial, but the overall message remains largely similar: the citizen should be reminded of the risks, informed of the possible remedies and encouraged to react in a way which is not only for his individual benefit, but which will help to achieve the common good.

Notes

1   Michael Brodie, "Time for a Change", *Spectrum*, London, ITC, Spring 1993, page 15.

2   Nicolas Timmins and Stephen Goodwin, "Government advertising 'wastes millions'", *The Independent*, 2 August 1994, page 6.

3   *The Howard Journal*, February 1986, quoted by Martin Davidson, *op. cit.*, page 159.

4   COI, *Review of the Year 1990 - 1991*, page 10.

5   The potential conflict of interests prevents anti Drinking and Driving advertisements from appearing within the same commercial breaks as commercials for alcoholic drinks, for instance.

6   *The ACA is an independent group of senior media and marketing executives, appointed by the Chancellor of the Duchy of Lancaster, to advise on the nomination of suitable advertising agencies for government work and related matters*, standard note added to COI press releases.

7   Source: correspondence from the COI dated November 1993.

8   There were two separate commercials, one authorised for transmission after 21.00, the other after 22.30.

9   *Crime is increasing ... Crime is believed to be rising because society is becoming more materialistic, less cohesive, less law-abiding, etc., and because discipline and deterrence are too lenient. Men are concerned about the threat of crime to property, especially their car, and the reaction of [their] wife to burglary of their home. Women are concerned about personal attack outside or inside the home, and the violation of their home.* COI Management Survey entitled *Crime Prevention 1989/1990 Campaign*, January 1990, page 3.

10 The December 1998 campaign showed footage taken by the police at the sites of real accidents, a different example each evening. Channel 4 transmitted just before Christmas a series of programmes entitled *Smashed* on alcohol abuse. The first one was devoted to drinking and driving.

11 In fact, COI cinema advertisements had been covering the theme of job opportunities for a number of years.

12 Jeremy Potter, *op. cit.*, page 197.

13 *A local authority shall not publish any material which in whole or in part, appears to be designed to affect, or can reasonably be regarded as likely to affect, public support for a) a political party or b) a body, cause or campaign identified with, or likely to be regarded as identified with a political party.* Local Government Bill 1986, Part Two, quoted by Kathy Myers, *op. cit.*, page 117.

14 Margaret Scammell, *Designer Politics*, Basingstoke, Macmillan, 1995, pages 212 - 213.

15 Lord Young resigned from the DTI in July 1989.

16 Mark Jones, "Department of Propaganda," *The Listener*, 5 May 1988.

17 The main privatisations were as follows: BP (1979 - 87), British Aerospace (1981 - 85), British Telecom (1984 - 93), British Gas (1986 - 90), British Airways (1987), British Steel (1988), and the water and electricity companies in England and Wales (1989 - 91).

18 Alison Turner, "British Gas Flotation: How Advertising Helped Extend Popular Share Ownership", in Paul Feldwick, (ed) *Advertising Works 5*, London, Cassell, 1990, page 317.

19 *ibid.*, page 316.

20 Mark Jones, *op. cit.*.

21 The campaign featured, for example, a holiday on a British beach, a single-parent family and various spectators at a children's football match.

22 The different stages, and the advertisements included in each, are as follows:
   I.   Confidential Telephone : phase 1 (1988 - 1991):
         A Future (1988), *Silence* (1990), *Jigsaw* (1991), *Bleak* (1991), *Eye Shutter* (1991)
   II.   Confidential Telephone : phase 2 (1993):
         Lady, I wanna be like you, Car Wash, Next, Time to Stop
   III. The Time for Reconstruction (1994)
         Time to Build
         Time for the Bright Side (1995)
         Citizens, Boys, Yours and Mine, Stars, Humour
   IV.   Timebomb (1997)
         Lady, I wanna be like you, New Boys, Timebomb.

23 Remarks made on BBC 2's *The Late Show* in 1995.

24 Some at least of these statistics seem to have been generally accepted, and were partially reprinted, for example, in the broadly nationalist *Irish News*.

25 Documented, for example, in a series of articles published by the *Irish News* under the generic title of the *Dirty War*.

VI
Institutions and Quangos

Not all advertisements fit neatly into the categories of 'product' ads or government announcements. Many commercials are only of local interest and circulation, others appear on an occasional or irregular basis, but are nevertheless part of British television culture and are accepted features on commercial channels. This chapter will examine some of the more widely known of such advertisements, which are or were familiar to the viewing public and which attempt(ed) to make a contact which is other than the strictly commercial, but finds its roots in a sense of community and of belonging to a common and immediately recognisable culture, be it national or local. The final part of this section will be devoted to Party Political or Party Election Broadcasts, which represent a different form of communication, but which reflect in their own way individual and national aspirations.

Television and the National Lottery

Television has long been anxious to promote its own self-image and to establish itself as a central feature of national culture and identity. The 1990s have seen harder times for existing channels, and both the ITC and the BBC have felt it necessary to ensure themselves of public support and recognition, albeit in different fields. Changes to the question of regulation and doubts about continued funding were particular questions which inspired the two organisations to transmit their own announcements on their own services, although the methods they adopted were fundamentally divergent. Following the 1990 Broadcasting Act, the ITC was at pains, in what has become an ongoing campaign of information and apparent transparency, to inform viewers of its duties and responsibilities. Apart from making its Codes and Reports more widely available and thus making the public aware of their rights and of how to make complaints, the ITC began its own magazine, *Spectrum*, available on request. A television commercial was produced to inform viewers of the existence of the Commission, to explain the meaning of its name and to emphasise its role and function. The position in which the BBC found itself was more critical. In the 1980s, the idea of privatising some or all of its services had been mooted and the opposition of the Thatcher government to an organisation which it judged politically biased, threatened the independence of the BBC and even its continued existence. The situation changed somewhat in the 1990s, the Charter and the licence fee were renewed, but the

Corporation was keen to prove that it was keeping its promises to viewers and found itself under pressure to justify its expenditure, especially in the light of additional investment and the commercial joint ventures it had planned for satellite and digital channels. Advertising its own products (publishing, educational materials, audio and video cassettes) on television was something the BBC had done for a long time, either by short messages at the end of programmes or by more substantial announcements in 'promotional time', but it clearly felt that a special effort had to be made to explain and justify the continuance of the licence fee. Over the Christmas period 1998, a series of advertisements entitled *Future Generations* (or *small people* on the BBC's internet site) were screened at fixed times, the object being to appeal for future support by reminding viewers of different ages of the Corporation's varied children's programmes in the past and thereby by appealing to elements of common television heritage. The Corporation's new slogan, *you make it what it is*, was intended to reinforce the need for involvement and co-operation while emphasising the scope of the opportunities on offer.

The *Future Generations* commercials (whose scheduling was announced in advance and which were therefore close to programmes or short documentaries in concept) unashamedly played on the predictable registers of nostalgia and childhood memories to excite public sympathy and support. Numerous clips and settings from children's programmes from the 1950s onwards served as a backdrop to a young schoolboy, dressed in the type of uniform typical of the early days of television, strolling along the meandering paths of collective memory while speaking his hard-headed, late 1990s message of financial constraints. From Bill and Ben through to the Telly Tubbies, the range of children's programmes, educational, entertaining, magical, dramatic ... were called up to allow viewers to relive their childhoods, and to impress upon them how important it was for today's children and future generations of small people to have the same opportunities for entertainment, amusement and learning as they had enjoyed. In terms of communication, the large number of programmes featured allowed everyone to identify at least some of the examples, thereby sustaining interest throughout the multiple screenings of basically similar announcements all transmitting the same message. If the newly-created ITC had tried to develop its own identity and image of openness, the long-established Corporation unashamedly relied on the emotional appeal of the desire to ensure the best for one's children, along with the fond memories of a past but abiding television heritage to put over a message combining quality and nostalgia.

In addition to its responsibility for the media and other aspects of culture and leisure, the Department of National Heritage acquired the additional duties of running the National Lottery which was instituted by the Major government in November 1994 and rapidly captured the public imagination. In the first six months of operations, sales of tickets and scratch cards had totalled £1,876 million, there had been 396 winners of £100,000 or more and some £1/2 billion had been raised for so-called 'good causes'. Heritage Secretary Stephen Dorrell adopted the type of hyperbole to be followed by his successor Virginia Bottomley when he declared:

This is just the beginning. The runaway success of the National Lottery will mean that over the coming years communities will be provided with new and enhanced facilities, for the use, benefit and enjoyment of everyone.[1]

By September 1995, £1 billion had been raised, a month later the minister was able to point to the fact that 75 per cent of households were playing and, in February 1997, it was announced that the funds raised for social and community projects had risen to £3 billion. Not everyone was happy with arrangements, however; charities claimed that the donations they received were being hit by the Lottery, some religious groups objected to the principle of the state encouraging gambling, many thought the huge prizes occasionally won were excessive and the operator, Camelot, and its directors were accused of immoderate personal gain, a charge which the Conservative government was keen to deny. The incoming Labour administration rapidly put in place a number of measures, culminating in a restructuring of the enterprise into what the White Paper of July 1997 called the People's Lottery and making plans for the appointment of a non-profit-making operator after 2001. Pressure was successfully applied to make Camelot limit both its profits and the bonuses received by directors.

Despite these substantial difficulties, the Lottery was and is a major financial success and advertising and promotions (including television) were a significant factor in the smooth and profitable launch of the enterprise. The attractions of the Lottery were of several kinds: the chance of winning, the creation of a weekly television programme, which achieved very high audience figures for BBC 1,[2] and the belief that ticket sales would also help a variety of deserving causes. Television adverts chose to stress two main points, the possibility of winning (*it could be you*) and the idea of the Lottery as a national game, more loosely associated with the notions of identity and heritage. They were only part of a high-profile integrated campaign, the aim of which had to be to ensure that, as nearly as possible, the whole British population should be aware of the start of the new game and how to play, an objective which was fully attained. The shooting stars, pointing finger and slogan used in the initial commercial were to become a regular feature but the most important first advert went out of its way to emphasise the 'cosmic' significance of the event, with a view of the earth then of the British Isles from outer space, followed by recognisable scenes succinctly suggesting the far-flung and attractive corners of the United Kingdom, its ancient history, its maritime and industrial past and present and the recreations and inventiveness of its citizens, in a manner reminiscent of that already employed by the Electricity Council in its pre-privatisation campaign. When the scene finally cut to a home, the commercial strove to highlight the family image, the atmosphere of benevolence suggested by the hand in the sky and the picture of well-being, while the size of the likely first jackpot, £2 million, was added by voice-over. Later advertisements focused on the chances of winning for other groups in society. From the very beginning, the appeal of the Lottery proved irresistible and for many viewers, watching the live Saturday night draw became an essential element of the week's viewing, while commercials have continued to maintain its high profile.

Charities

The arrival of the National Lottery was only one of the challenges facing British charities in the 1990s. In 1989, the IBA announced a radical change in policy, by allowing them to advertise in order to raise funds, a move which heightened the television profile of the organisations themselves, while reflecting the belief in individual benevolence and in voluntary action dear to the heart of Margaret Thatcher. As is the case with many other nations, the British like to see themselves as generous givers, ready to help the needy at home and abroad, and the IBA's decision seemed likely to bring substantial benefits. Advertisements had been transmitted before, of course; the first charity actually to advertise on television was the Marie Curie Cancer Fund and in the 1980s both the Samaritans and Lynx, the pressure group opposing the fur trade, had produced commercials for British television, reminding the public of their existence and mission, in uncompromising fashion, but without specifically requesting funds. Nevertheless, as some charities found to their cost, the problems with television advertising were considerable. Many agencies agreed to work without remuneration, but air time was an expensive commodity and although, initially, many of the needs could be met through so-called 'promotional time', that is to say the minutes that companies had left after programmes themselves and paid advertisements had been accommodated, this source of free access to the airwaves soon dried up in the face of rising demand. Moreover, television companies were becoming profit-orientated in the 1990s, and the public's much vaunted generosity was not without limits as what Bob Geldof called *compassion fatigue* set in, when faced with ever-growing requests for donations for projects at home and abroad. British television companies, modelling themselves on the example of the United States, where typical stations were highly selective in the granting of free air time, which they saw only as a bait to attract paid advertising, became less and less generous, and the dropping in 1995 of the biennial Telethon, which had raised no less than £24 million for children's and disabled persons' charities in 1990, was a clear sign of changing attitudes. The recession and compassion fatigue were blamed for the decision, which according to the *Times* was welcomed by many ITV companies and advertisers.

It is true that the number of charities, and the growing calls on public generosity, put extra pressure on the market. In December 1991, according to the *Daily Express* there were some 180,000 charities, with a new one born every thirty minutes, and even with total donations reaching £18 billion annually, the average Briton was much less generous than he thought, giving only £1.28 a week, compared with £1.97 the previous year, a figure which was only half what the average American was prepared to offer. In simple monetary terms, many early commercials resulted in losses for the organisations responsible: the RSPCA's DRTV (direct response television) campaign in December 1989, aimed at combating cruelty to animals in general and the thoughtless giving of pets at Christmas in particular, raised, according to the Society's director of public relations, only £4,000 in donations, compared with a spend on air time of £100,000. This is, however, not the whole story. Commercials (often individual or limited in number, but part of integrated multi-media initiatives) may contribute to the longer term promotion of a cause or of ideas, which is hard to quantify and may bear fruit only over a number of years. A part of the task of charity adverts is to remind the public of their moral duty by presenting uncomfortable facts which may be easily overlooked or forgotten. Progress towards adequate short-term returns was slow, but that did not stop the flow of commercials. In 1992, according to a survey produced by Millward Brown and summarised in *Marketing Week* of 26 November 1993, the top 21 charities received only 61 pence in donations for every pound spent on advertising, while in the last three months of the year, spending was £9.8 million, as much as that of Tesco.

Where early television advertisements did succeed was in their creative and memorable qualities. The British Design and Art Direction Book for 1991 included advertisements for no less than four British charities or charity associations, all domestic. The Terrence Higgins Trust (an Aids charity, named after the first Briton to die of the disease) produced *Hopping Pecker*, an explicit colour advert advocating the use of condoms, with the emphasis on freedom and pleasure, which, consciously or not, complemented government commercials which favoured a more serious factual approach. There was no appeal for funds, but the written text made the offer of information to be obtained by a simple telephone call. The collective campaign against child abuse, filmed in black and white and with a harrowing female voice-over message, evoked the surprisingly frequent molesting of children, (*every night in Britain alone, 300 children below the age of 6 are subjected to sexual abuse by their fathers, close relatives, or so-called friends*) and appealed to viewers' sense of public duty to pledge funds to combat the scourge. The housing charities Shelter and Crisis used graphic presentations of the conditions in which the homeless lived (whole families accommodated in rooms the size of prison cells or individuals simply sleeping rough in the dead of winter) to remind viewers of circumstances which should not be tolerated in a civilised society and to call for donations.

It has become progressively necessary for charities to develop and to position themselves thoughtfully, in the hope of attracting support. The Christmas/New Year period is admirably suited to impacting with a wider, well-disposed audience, but the timing, placing and the conception of commercials have all required to be re-examined. For cost reasons, there has been a steady move away from terrestrial channels to more specialised and much less expensive satellite and cable services. In 1995, according to BARB, over 14 per cent of adult impacts were on satellite television, as against 26 per cent on ITV and 56 per cent on Channel 4, the latter having long been the preferred station in view of its more closely defined audience and the existence of programmes such as *Countdown*, specifically aimed at older people with substantial disposable income. It was notable, for example, that donors tended to be influenced by a sense of affinity, a fact which charities were not slow in taking into account when fixing the scheduling of commercials. Daz Valladares commented generally:

> *More than three-quarters of us – older people, probably because of a sense of fellow feeling, give to old people. Church-going Catholics and Methodists give to denominated charities. Pet-lovers support animal charities.*[3]

Cathy Bond later added the specific illustration, *Help-the-Aged finds that Asian-focused channels are proving lucrative for its Third World DRTV appeals.*[4]

Increasingly, major charities have become aware that the notion of 'brand image' could also apply to them and that the approach in commercials should be adapted to what they wished to achieve. The contrasted styles and objectives of cheap, direct response advertising, soliciting an immediate act of generosity through poignant images, on the one hand, and of more sophisticated and careful long-term multi-media campaigns intended to promote a cause, on the other, have come to be regarded as an essential part of thinking, although few charities have a strong enough profile to dispense entirely with DRTV. The regular Oxfam £2 a month appeals (begun in 1996) illustrate the point. The photography and colour used in the third-world scenes is both beautiful and effective, the voice-over message emphasises the key notions that donations will help the victims of drought and poverty to help themselves and that the positive results will be permanent. However, a target figure for gifts is set, significantly, not just a one-off donation but a regular commitment over a period of time. This latter solution is a way of realising the immediate effect of DRTV while instilling the longer-term habit of giving, which is what charities most wish to achieve. Indirect or additional promotion has also been helpful and the association of good causes with other advertising campaigns, exemplified by the promotion of the NSPCC by the Yorkshire Building Society and HP sauce's promise to pay the same organisation 1p for every promotional bottle sold (in 1994 and 1996 respectively) is a case in point. The image of a charity, as conveyed for example by the NSPCC's Happy Kids logo, has proved a convenient way both for sponsoring companies to attract public favour by indicating their involvement and generosity over welfare matters, and to provide the causes themselves with free advertising and a guaranteed supply of funds.

Charity advertising is a field in which it is essential to find the correct psychological approach for the occasion. A one-off emergency appeal for the Third World and sustained or regular campaigns to aid the under-privileged at home cannot necessarily be conducted in the same way. Appeals by the Salvation Army, the NSPCC and charities for the homeless are a regular feature of Christmas viewing, but the balance has to be struck between the portrayal of need and the impression that donors are helping people to help themselves. The Salvation Army's Christmas appeals are a typical example. Reminding the public of the sordid conditions and needs of those who sleep rough is relatively easy, especially with black and white images and limited lighting, but the impression needs to be given of possible self-improvement and, in this particular case, it must be demonstrated that what is a religious organisation is acting in a purely humanitarian way and not imposing its own ideas on the people it serves. The Army's reputation is a considerable asset in the process of persuasion. Thus the 1995 Bleak Midwinter campaign contained a number of key elements intended both to awaken the viewers' memories and to recall some of the traditions of the Army, in order to convey and reinforce the request for funds. The advertiser was immediately announced by a shot of its badge and by the playing, by brass band of course, of a familiar Christmas carol. The actual charitable work, the well-known 'soup run', was shown, but the commercial insisted that the immediate relief of suffering and the comforting of 'those who accept it' was only the first step in a process which would restore them to normal conditions of life. The direct appeal for funds, fixed at £15, rounded off the message of the commercial. The task facing charities is, however, not an easy one. The '£15 ghetto' (or £20 or £30 ghetto for that matter) is potentially limiting and changes in public mood must be respected. Donors like to feel involved in the work in which they participate: writing in 1996, Mark Nohr indicated what he called the four *'Golden I's'* – *four creative principles which are working in fundraising direct marketing – Involvement, Interaction, Instant Gratification and Intimacy.*[5] This phenomenon no doubt explains why commercials inviting donors to 'adopt' a third-world child have become an increasingly common feature at a time when the general lack of generosity calls into question the favourable image the British have of themselves.

Persuasion is easier in some cases than in others, although commercials aimed at helping children and sick or old people, at home or abroad, are likely to achieve a more positive response than those for the able-bodied. The Save the Children Fund's April 1991 appeal was a striking success at a time when famines in Africa had lost their immediate impact and when a flood in Bangladesh and the plight of Kurdish refugees in Iraq were already hitting the headlines. The campaign, 'Skip Lunch. Save a Life,' carried the simple voice-over message that the price of a lunch could buy someone food for a month or pay their medical costs for a year. The initial spend on television (for air time and production costs) was fixed at £18,000, but the additional coverage given in news bulletins and free screening of adverts on BBC and ITV,[6] along with celebrity appearance from the charity's patron, the Princess Royal, helped to achieve a massive response. Writing in *Advertising Works 7*, Julie Davey claimed:

> *A single week of advertising activity in April 1991 generated a revenue of £5.5 million … It did so by avoiding the numerous pitfalls of a huge and complex issue and by providing a simple 'rate of exchange' mechanism which encouraged participation. It did so by linking two worlds which are apparently poles apart via a common concern – food. It captured the imagination of the media and the hearts (and stomachs) of the public, engaging them in a collective effort to combat famine.*[7]

Six months later the same charity launched another emergency appeal, also featuring the Princess Royal, but achieved a response rate[8] of only 1.8:1, proof enough that the success of commercials was not guaranteed, even if their presence on the television screens was now an accepted fact.

The notion of a caring community, acting in solidarity to defend its members is one of the underlying principles of the Helplines which have long been a feature of television advertising. The two versions of this phenomenon, the so-called Community Helplines and the various Telephone Helplines, have fundamentally different functions, although both are in essence voluntary organisations. The former act in a manner similar to charities by soliciting help from members of the viewing public for various social and welfare projects, but they are essentially local in scope, as the term 'community' suggests, most often bearing the name of the town(s), district(s) or area(s) in which they operate. Limiting funding means that advertisements themselves are normally simple affairs, like many other purely local commercials, and consist either of a member of the organisation talking directly to camera, or of a voice-over commentary accompanying still photos of work being done, gardening, decorating, transporting disabled people etc, for which the public's assistance is requested. Telephone Helplines function differently: their aim is to provide assistance, advice and support rather than request it, the initial contact being made, as the name of the organisation suggests, by telephone. Once more the advertisements are relatively simple and their placement depends on the good offices of the television companies involved, but the types of assistance offered are very varied. The work of Telephone Helplines can be readily integrated into a more general strategy of passing welfare messages and advice on social questions. It is well-known that the plots of soap operas sometimes raise issues of immediate public interest and the mentioning of Helpline numbers can be a useful extension of the process. Sometimes too, the existence of Helplines is directly quoted to reinforce government advertising on citizenship and welfare matters. The 1990s have seen numerous examples of this process. The number of the National Aids Helpline was given at the end of the government's testimonial-style Aids advertisements between 1990 and 1992 and, more recently, two further Helpline messages were carried over the Christmas period 1998 by Channel 4, which had set up its own telephone service. The first followed an episode of *Brookside* in which a 'drug rape' had taken place, while the second was placed just after programmes in the series *Smashed* dealing with the effects of alcohol in various aspects of daily life. These examples are further proof of the blurring of the distinctions between programmes and commercials and of the ways in which the emotional power of television can be harnessed to appeal to a sense of national and communal duty.[9]

Local and national

Collective commercials form a part of the network of information and promotion available to the viewing public, reflecting and influencing cultural and social trends and appealing sometimes to limited sections of the community. Individual holiday or leisure destinations are, for instance, advertised either locally or in the case of widely known attractions, like Alton Towers or Whipsnade Zoo, nationally.

On other occasions, the advertising by organisations such as local or national tourist boards features the activities available in a whole area and promotes the idea of a distinctive local identity, although, for cost reasons, television is often a relatively minor part of such campaigns and is intended to create initial interest which can then be followed up by other means. One of the more successful campaigns of the 1980s, that for Torbay in South Devon, was a typical example. The resort was aware that the taking of holidays in Britain was in decline, (with intended stays in England down in 1982 to 22 per cent as against 28 per cent three years before) while its own satisfaction rating was high among those who did visit the area, many of whom were regular visitors. The television message was simple: the 10-second commercial displayed the resurrected title of the area, *The English Riviera*, complete with palm tree to give the appropriate exotic associations, along with the names of the towns of Torquay, Paignton and Brixham and the details of the address from which brochures could be obtained. In the period from December 1982 to March 1983, the commercial was shown over a three week period in the London, Midlands and South regions and the following year the Midlands and the Yorkshire were targeted at a cost of some £32,000. Results were substantial: for 1982 - 1983, the Tourist Board recorded an increase of 27 per cent in advertising response and the following year a rise of 37 per cent.

Television served in the 1980s as part of collective campaigns to encourage permanent resettlement of industry and population in response to the changing economic situation and to new lifestyle expectations. In 1981, the London Docklands Development Corporation was created and set about the task of regenerating some 8 square miles of former docks, most of which were vacant and/or derelict. Because of the target audience, high priority in the campaign was given to the London area for television (500 men TVRs, mainly through the mid-break of *News at Ten* every weekday for four weeks) and to the quality press. The intention of the campaigns in 1982 - 1983 was first to create awareness of the area and excitement about the regeneration project, while later phases (television only) were to concentrate on the specific benefits of the area and on development opportunities. The common line throughout was *Why move to the middle of nowhere when you can move to the middle of London* and the television commercials all featured crows, thereby stressing the important argument of proximity, 'as the crow flies ...'. The impact was substantial and television advertising was a significant phase in what has become the successful regeneration of an unlikely area. This type of collective advertising designed to attract industry or population has become a trend in itself. The new town of Milton Keynes launched a similar project in 1990, promoting a different if less specific identity. As a 'greenfields' development site, the area had been one of the targets of the London Docklands' adverse publicity (*50 miles [80 kilometres] from London*), but, understandably, the new town's development corporation saw advantages in this distance when it came to produce its own advertising. The commercial emphasised the living conditions in the new environment, presenting, through the eyes and from the point of view of a boy sitting in a car, the contrasts between the city and the semi-rural environment: *a bush, a bin, a brick, a bus, a skip, a block, a crane, a brick, a queue, a rush, etc.*, compared in his thoughts with *a cloud, a tree, a field, a cow, a flower, a horse, a bike, a kite, a game, a shop*, all duly illustrated and leading ultimately to *I wish I lived here*, accompanied by the title Milton Keynes. The latest area to promote itself in this way is Swindon, where children's aspirations and actual job opportunities, *the home of the Honda Civic* are combined. If nothing else, these sets of advertisements indicate the promotional opportunities offered by change of emphasis and point of view, while illustrating the variety of expectations to be found within different communities at different times.

Beyond local or individual pride, collective advertising often accentuates national consciousness and the feeling of patriotism and belonging. The word 'British' or 'English' has been a periodic feature of campaigns for such diverse produce as meat, cheese and apples. The British lamb promotion had begun in the 1980s with a series of commercials featuring the typecast Geoffrey Palmer, but in 1997, the marketers of British meat became more aggressive, notably as the BSE scare began to die down and the possibility of encouraging the consumption of home produce became a plausible operation once more. British lamb and, more controversially, British beef were now portrayed as *the food of love*, in a classic attempt to use the technique of positive association. Personalities as varied as Thora Hurd, Denis Healey and Edward Heath have served to endorse different British cheeses. In 1989 and 1990, the newly created Cox Promotion Committee equally sought to play the national/patriotic card, with their slogan *Real English Cox's taste English to the core*, read in the rich voice-over tones of Michael Hordern and combining with the portrayal of supposedly typically English pursuits, boys playing conkers, a girl riding a horse, to the familiar accompaniment of Australian Percy Grainger's 'English Country Garden'. Finally, the Dairy Council's attempts to slow or reverse the fall in doorstep milk deliveries owed something to the appeal to national tradition as well as to more recent ecological and convenience arguments. The service was promoted as a supposedly typical feature of British life, with the smiling, whistling milkman, the almost silent milk float and the clink of bottles being a reminder to some of a tradition going back to the 19th century, or at least to the Second World War, when milk was one of the few plentiful foods and was believed to have been delivered whatever the dangers and difficulties.

In 1994, the Sea Fish Industry Authority tried a new approach to the questions of communication and customer complicity, with an advert of three and a half minutes, almost short documentary length, which explained that there was a new commercial which might be seen by some 70 per cent of the population as it was to be shown on Channel 4, GMTV and satellite channels, and went on to explain the objectives of the promotion and the research that had gone into its conception. The announcement, fronted initially by the chairman of the Sea Fish Industry Authority, the appropriately named Barry Skipper, showed scenes of boats returning to port and unloading their catches, followed by illustrations of the filming of the commercials themselves. The viewer was reminded that fish had not been advertised for some time which had reduced consumption, but the presenter went on to explain that the original intention, to emphasise the health benefits and taste of fish had been dropped in favour of what research had shown to be a more promising avenue, the variety and different ways of cooking the product. This promotion was to be achieved by setting up a series of 'conversations' prompted by the repeated question, *what's your idea of a nice fish dish?* Having shown the viewer the mechanisms that were to operate during the campaign which was to last five weeks, the chairman of the Authority handed over to one of the commercials, with the words, *here is our new thirty-second commercial. I hope you like it.* The novelty of this approach was considerable, the effort to involve and engage viewers in the whole advertising process and convince them of the value of the campaign, even before the commercials were screened, was evident, but it is equally clear that the implied appeals to Britain's maritime heritage, to the beauty of its coastal scenery and to the efficiency of its fishermen further strengthened the message. Such an advertisement could only be collective and showed the way in which heritage and shared experience could be a central plank in the argument given.

Political broadcasts

Party Political Broadcasts and Party Election Broadcasts (PPBs and PEBs) have been part of the British political scene since the early 1950s and, as such, are a recognised feature of British life. Despite the public's indifference to such blandishments which seems to grow as the professionalism of the campaigns themselves increases, they give an idea of some of the real and imagined concerns and attitudes of the population. The situation in the UK nevertheless has one major advantage for the sceptical public, namely that advertising for political causes is forbidden and thus that the number of broadcasts which any political party can transmit is determined by the number of seats it is contesting, and not by its capacity to buy air time. There are, at present, no total limits on advertising spending and the percentage of expenditure on television, as opposed to other media, is variable. Technically speaking there is a difference between Party Political Broadcasts which are intended to be part of a long-term explanation of policies and the Party Election Broadcasts which take place during the actual period of campaigning at local or national level, although, in practice, the differences are often slight. Until 1983, broadcasts were scheduled simultaneously across all the existing channels; since then the viewer has been able to obtain some respite by switching between stations, even if election coverage remains a major element of news and current affairs broadcasting. The latest review of procedures governing PPBs dates from June 1999, when, after consultation, the BBC and the ITV decided to limit broadcasts outside election periods to key events such as the Budget, the Queen's Speech and party conferences. A detailed example of the new allocations has been drawn up and is intended to last until 2004.

Both the morality and the nature of such promotions has long been called into question. The idea of publicising a political ideology or at least its direct political manifestations, as one would breakfast cereals or washing powders, was anathema to some, and for many years before the 1987 election, the Labour party's stance was generally hostile, adding a more specific dislike to what was already established as a general aversion to advertising. Kathy Myers sums up the point of view thus:

Advertising is the PR profession for capitalism, justifying rampant consumerism, diverting resources away from the economic infrastructure and reinforcing the values which perpetuate inequality and economic exploitation. In short, advertising is part of capitalism's self-justification system, its ideology.[10]

It was a mark for some of Labour's desire to modernise, to others an indication that it was abandoning its fundamental principles, when professionally planned advertising returned during Neil Kinnock's first bid to become Prime Minister. Other less radical but equally vociferous critics observe in recent campaigns a trend towards American-style presidential elections, with policy matters being neglected in favour of the projection of personalities and the well-chosen sound-bite. What is undeniable is that the techniques have been both varied and evolving, and that the PPBs of the 1950s now seem, if anything, even less plausible and even more contrived than the product commercials of the same period. Brian McNair,[11] quoting different sources and basing his remarks on American examples, classifies broadcasts as 'primitive' (when the rehearsed or artificial quality is evident), 'talking heads', 'negative', 'production' or 'concept' ads, in which the big idea(s) of the campaign become(s) paramount, and finally *'cinéma vérité'*. Within these parameters, witness ads, using vox pop, personal testimonials or the neutral reporter technique are further variants. It is fair to add that British politicians are now much more skilful in their exploitation of the medium and that narrative commercials, with more or less explicit messages have become increasingly frequent. The field of political advertising is frought with uncertainty: a planned broadcast may have to be changed almost overnight both to accommodate chance events and to counter opponents' claims and, in any case, the television commercials are part of a larger integrated multi-media strategy.

The first Party Political Broadcast, featuring Harold Macmillan, dating from 1953 and presented by MP William Deedes, was certainly in the 'primitive' category, as the Minister of Housing and his junior, Ernest Marples, presented their broadcast from the home of a fortunate and duly impressed family in Norfolk. The tone of the message was moralistic, as Macmillan declared that every citizen's duty was to help to achieve a financially strong Britain by aiding the export drive, which was a sure way of achieving better standards for all. It contained what might have been considered, had the term been invented, the first sound-bite, when he observed, *a house, you know, when it comes down to it, it means home*, obviously striking a chord with what was a matter of major public concern.[12] The first move towards a more innovative approach occurred during the 1959 General Election. The Conservatives, who by now had hired an advertising agency to run their campaign, stuck with traditional methods, with their first broadcast consisting of an 'unscripted' but amicable conversation between members of the Cabinet, in the well-appointed library of the Prime Minister's home. Labour, on the other hand, chose to try to generate excitement by using a news format of linked PEBs 'from Labour's Radio and TV Operations Room in London', introduced by the then Anthony Wedgwood Benn and featuring various Labour politicians, notably the leader Hugh Gaitskell, with another MP Woodrow Wyatt asking the questions. This technique was undeniably more lively than what the Tories were offering and the vox pop was, for the first time, negative, as the failures of the incumbent government were exploited. What is interesting about Labour's broadcasts is the presence of Wedgwood Benn, who was to play a key role in the victorious campaign of 1964, and the fact that an innovative and imaginative series of broadcasts had no substantial impact on the result of the election, in which the Conservatives were returned with an increased majority. It is true that Prime Minister Harold Macmillan was no mean television performer, but this was only the first of many examples in which the party that 'won the campaign' 'lost the election', thereby raising what have become fundamental and continuing doubts about the impact of such advertising.

1960s Party Political Broadcasts were largely dominated by Harold Wilson, who became leader of the Labour Party in 1963. In the election of 1964 he was faced with the less than telegenic Alec Douglas Home and in 1966 by the relatively inexperienced and somewhat awkward Edward Heath. By now, the importance of television as a medium influencing voting patterns was established. On election night 1964, the BBC had scheduled an episode of the popular sitcom *Steptoe and Son* at 8 p.m., but Labour objected, fearing that its supporters might prefer to stay at home and watch the programme, rather than journey to the polls. Finally, it was agreed to screen the programme an hour later and use it as a lead-in to the planned results service, a change which Wilson estimated would be worth a dozen seats to his party. In the event, Labour's majority was just four. With his carefully cultivated image of the ordinary man, complete with Yorkshire accent and pipe, Wilson took personal responsibility for Labour's PEBs as well as for current affairs programmes as commentators Butler and King emphasise in their remarks concerning the 1966 election.

> *Producing his own scripts, speaking from behind an imposing desk, the Prime Minister's primary concern in both his broadcasts seemed to be to promote his 'family doctor image'. Soft in voice, sober in dress and serious in mien he appeared the personification of respectability and responsibility. Partisanship was muted; his two broadcasts contained 42 mentions of 'Britain', 39 of 'government' and none whatever of 'Labour'.*[13]

In the end, Wilson's predilection for television exposure was to be part of his undoing. It was the Prime Minister himself who, in November 1967, announced the dire news of devaluation to the British population, including the infamous observation that 'the pound in your pocket has not been devalued', a comment which aroused the mockery of political friend and foe alike.[14]

The PEBs in 1970 tried to break away from the conventional 'talking head' or question-and-answer model and sought to raise issues which politicians thought were the public's main concern, notably the key question of the cost of living. For one of its broadcasts, Labour produced an imitation of the popular series *University Challenge*, chaired by Bernard Donoughue, who was blandly described as a Senior

Lecturer at London University although he was already advising the Prime Minister's office on polling data, and featuring two teams, new voters and the rest. Both agreed that people were better off in 1970 than in 1964, but were not aware that the rise in living standards was by 20 per cent. The Conservatives concentrated on the issue of prices and wages and their most notable broadcast was based on the format of ITV's *News at Ten*, containing news items condemning Labour's record, complete with mock commercial breaks, one of which showed a pound note being snipped away by a pair of scissors. Another imitation commercial in this 'shopping basket election' included a dissatisfied working-class housewife who had decided to try a new brand, the Conservatives, instead of Labour. 1970 was notable for the unexpectedness of the final result, although commentators have sought causes other than advertising for the late swing which led to Labour's defeat. In February 1974, it was Labour who played the domestic card, with Shirley Williams presenting the shopping bag and Denis Healey making the implausible promise to do everything, if elected, to keep down the cost of living. Edward Heath, embroiled in the miners' strike and the three-day week, sought to play on the patriotic theme of 'who runs the country?', but, as the results showed, the Tories had misjudged the public mood. The campaigns of 1974 were generally undistinguished and lacked the imagination of 1970, at a time when the results of both elections were always going to be close. It seems reasonable to say that the pervading pessimism was reflected in the broadcasts themselves and in the response to them. PEBs, like politics itself had to await 1979 before making a decisive move forward.

More accurately, the key date was 1978, when Saatchi and Saatchi were appointed to run the Conservatives' election campaign for the first time and adopted a more immediate and cogent communicational style. Their first PPB graphically illustrated the theme of Britain going backwards by projecting film footage featuring commuters and Stephenson's rocket in reverse. Their famous *Labour Isn't Working* poster had much greater impact and was held largely responsible for James Callaghan's decision to postpone the election until 1979, when, in the aftermath of a winter of strikes in the public service, the government was a sitting target for negative advertising. The Conservatives' broadcasts exploited the apparently apocryphal comment 'what crisis?', attributed by the right-wing press to the Prime Minister himself, and went on to point out that Labour's policies penalised ambition and skill, through a mock lawcourt scene, that Britain had suffered more than other countries from the economic recession and that British workers found themselves much worse off than their continental counterparts, a motif always calculated to pique national pride and produce strong reactions. Attacks on the Labour government's record were relatively easy to produce, at the end of what had been almost a decade of privations. A potential problem was with the image of the Conservative leader, Margaret Thatcher herself, who was still remembered by some as the Milk Snatcher who, when Education Secretary, had restricted free school milk, or more simply for her shrill, home-counties voice and predilection for silly hats. Another reason for Callaghan's delaying of the election till 1979 had been the additional opportunities it gave for Mrs Thatcher to produce some fatal gaffe, but in the event, she came over in her PEBs as a softly spoken, rational and concerned woman, appealing to what came subsequently to be known as 'middle England' and sharing the reasonable aspirations of ordinary people. The Conservative victory was a triumph for the party, a triumph for its leader and vindicated the type of grass roots, basic campaign organised by Saatchi and Saatchi. As Margaret Scammell observes:

> *What appeared new about the Saatchis was the rather candid attempt to operate at the level of gut feelings in a more systematic way, using survey methods to this end. They brought a clear understanding that voters needed to be wooed on their own emotional territory, and not preached to, 'educated' or argued with.*[15]

Perhaps too, as James Callaghan himself later observed, people were just ready for a change, a factor which reappeared with renewed force in 1997.

The result of the 1983 election was a foregone conclusion: the Falklands factor weighed heavily, while the opposition was split. Michael Foot's unimpressive leadership of the Labour party and the incongruity of the SDP and Liberals fighting together as the Alliance combined to make the Conservatives invincible and to give them the largest victory in terms of parliamentary seats since 1945. The campaign itself had little effect on the result. Changes did at last begin to appear in Labour in the mid-1980s. The GLC's anti-abolition campaign, ultimately congruously orchestrated by the 'Hard Left', started to make the party aware of both the power of and the need for advertising in the attempt to influence opinion. It was no longer inconceivable, as former Labour head of advertising Nick Grant put it, for marketing principles to be applied to the domain of opinion forming:

> *Selling a philosophy, because it is intangible, is much more complex than selling a product. All we are endorsing about advertising is the narrow, highly methodical technique. We are not endorsing the style, the form or any particular way of advertising a product. We're trying to extract and benefit from the scientific techniques of marketing and apply it to a different world.*[16]

Neil Kinnock began his work of reforming the party and appointed Peter Mandelson as its first Campaign and Communications Director. Meanwhile, the Conservatives, who had appreciated the advantages of long-term coordinated planning, produced, as early as 1986, well in advance of any possible election, a memorable PPB in which each party was represented by a motor car. The Conservative's blue car purred along the open motorway of progress, while Labour's red vehicle was shown as often expensively broken down and unable to cope with the added burden of trailing along a caravan of union bosses, while trying to counteract another red car, symbolising extremist tendencies, pulling in the opposite direction. As for the Alliance, their Reliant was equipped with two steering wheels and two drivers, which allowed it to try to go in two directions at once. The 1987 election was notable for Labour's spectacularly presidential presentation of Neil Kinnock, while the Alliance employed the communicational skills of John Cleese to ridicule the extremism in both the other parties. The Conservatives showed Margaret Thatcher in most visionary mood, basking in the glory of the company of world leaders and announcing her intention to roll back the frontiers of socialism. In the event, Labour's most highly media-oriented, stage-managed and coherent campaign made little impression as the government had once again mobilised the voters' sense of pride and/or self-interest. As the *Guardian* of 15 June 1987 reported:

> The BBC TV/Gallup election survey revealed an electorate whose mind had been firmly set. Fully 81 per cent of respondents claimed to have decided their vote before the campaign began, a higher percentage than for any election since 1966.

The late 1980s saw signs of change with the emergence and rise of other parties and indeed of different issues. The Green Party campaigned actively against the 1992 Single Market by literally showing as faceless men, the major industrialists and bureaucrats, who were to run Europe. The 1992 General Election was notable for the portrayal of the Labour and Tory leaders. Neil Kinnock was much less prominent than in 1987, mainly because his party realised that he was an electoral liability, a man who had abandoned his principles but still aroused antagonism. On the other hand, Prime Minister John Major was the Tories' strong point. Arguably the most memorable advert of the whole campaign was a PEB which has come to be called simply *The Journey*, directed by John Schlesinger, which, with more cinéma than vérité, took the leader back to his roots in Brixton, presented him mixing with ordinary people before taking him on to Lambeth where he had been a councillor and finally to Westminster. Much of the commercial was filmed in the Prime Ministerial car and, along the way, Major was able to point out where he had lived, after a moment of contrived suspense wondering if the house was still standing, to stress his humble origins and to emphasise how his experiences had convinced him of the value of Conservative principles. This broadcast reflected the changes in attitudes and aspirations which the 1980s had brought and was admirably pitched to appeal to what was called 'Essex man', who ultimately held the key to the election. If newly-prosperous voters in the south of England, whose origins were similar to those of the Prime Minister, could be persuaded to stay loyal to the Conservatives, then the battle was won, and this turned out to be the case. Labour's bombshell, a narrative advert known as *Jennifer's Ear*, based on a real case concerning the fate of two little girls, both diagnosed with a painful ear complaint, turned out to be controversial. Despite the absence of a voice track, a device which ostensibly allowed voters to draw their own conclusions, the intended message was transparent enough: one girl was able to jump the queue for an operation because her parents could pay for private treatment, while the other had to suffer ever more painfully until her turn at last came round. The storm broke when the full truth of the story was denied by the child's mother, a Conservative voter, after her father had revealed the details to the Labour party which he supported. The media hype which followed effectively reduced the impact of Labour's potentially well-judged attack on NHS waiting lists which were a potential source of embarrassment to the government.

By 1997, the situation was again different. The Labour party had a new and popular leader in Tony Blair, while the Tories were mired in sleaze and controversy and apparently unable to create amongst the general public the 'feel good' factor which the country's economic performance might have justified. A PPB by Labour, featuring the comedy team of Fry and Laurie, lambasted tax dodges for the rich and the lucrative boardroom positions offered by privatised monopolies to former government ministers and undoubtedly caught the public mood. The Liberal Democrats and SNP flexed their growing muscles and clearly felt that for them the time of major advance had come. Saatchis' most effective contribution for the Conservatives, a poster of Tony Blair adorned with demon eyes[17] launched in August 1996, was banned by the Advertising Standards Authority following Labour's complaints and, although the 'eyes' motif figured in a PEB, the loss of the poster substantially weakened the Tories' campaign. The replacement 'red tear' posters and commercials, showing a housewife and more significantly a lion weeping as bad news of Labour Britain broke, caused confusion among electors and was a conspicuous failure. Even before polling day, the Conservatives seemed to have accepted defeat: John Major himself vetoed another controversial Saatchi proposal, a picture of a plastic mouth with a pair of eyes inside and the slogan *What LIES behind the smile?* and refused to sanction a £1 million last-minute press blitz. Much of the election battle was fought using posters, the cost of which represented some 83 per cent of the Conservatives' budget and 78 per cent of Labour's. Unlike newspapers, radio and television, which could be ignored, they were seen by all and the brevity of the messages accorded well with the propensity towards sound-bite politics. The Liberals, on a much more limited spend, parodied the main parties and their futile arguments, by a Punch and Judy scene featuring Messrs Blair and Major, but also emphasised the positive reputation and competence of their leader Paddy Ashdown. Labour's television broadcasts were perhaps the most exciting part of what analysts universally dubbed an uninspiring campaign. The Tories used no fewer than three 'talking head' pleas by John Major, while Labour's tasks of highlighting the personality of their new leader and of pointing to the Conservatives as being indifferent to public concerns and as having been in power too long were straightforward ones, for such arguments were readily accepted. Labour's so-called 'bulldog' broadcast was a particular success. The animal itself was, of course, carefully chosen to symbolise the whole nation (including traditional, Tory-voting elements) and to evoke images of courage and power. The parallel editing, with the animal becoming increasingly restive as bad news of the Tory years was repeated, before breaking free, heightened the effectiveness.

The value of political advertising has never been conclusively established. In 1997, the huge expenditure made no difference to the result, as, once again, voters' minds were made up well in advance. The PEBs and PPBs of what is now almost the last 50 years are nevertheless a fascinating subject. They represent, of course, not the public's view of Britain, but the politicians' ideas of the nation's concerns and supposed values, but they reflect, in their own way, developments in national interests and self-perception.

Notes

1   Department of National Heritage press release DNH 073/95, dated 15 May 1995.

2   In 1996 and 1997, editions of *The National Lottery Live* were respectively 10th and 15th in the list of the programmes attracting the largest audiences.

3   Daz Valladares, "Charities find relief in targeted advertising", *Marketing Week*, 27th November 1992, page 14.

4   Cathy Bond, "Breaking from conventions", *Marketing*, 13 March 1997, page 40.

5   Mark Nohr, "The state of donation", *Direct Response*, May 1996, page 53.

6   Worth an estimated £480,000 if purchased at normal commercial rates.

7   Julie Davey, "Skip Lunch. Save a Life", in Chris Baker (ed), *op. cit.*, page 414.

8   The response rate compares donations with expenditure. The average rate for the Save the Children Fund is around 3:1, but press advertising for the *Skip Lunch* campaign achieved a return of 10:1.

9   The 1999 *Children's Promise* Millennium Final Hour Appeal, sponsored by Marks and Spencer and featuring the "*man in the golden suit*" was another example of hybridisation. The 5-minute broadcasts were regularly programmed by the BBC in peak-time.

10 Kathy Myers, *op. cit.*, page 85.

11 Brian McNair, *An Introduction to Political Communication*, London, Routledge, 1999, pages 105-106.

12 It was only in 1953 that the Conservatives fulfilled their manifesto promise to build 300,000 homes a year.

13 D E Butler and Anthony King, *The British General Election of 1966*, London, Macmillan, 1966, pages 135 - 136.

14 The memoirs of Barbara Castle and Tony Benn refer to the performance respectively as *complacent* and *his absurd broadcast saying the pound in your pocket won't be devalued*. Ben Pimlott's recent biography claims that Wilson never uttered the notorious words *the pound in your pocket*.

15 Margaret Scammell, *op. cit.*, pages 87 - 88.

16 Quoted by Kathy Myers, *op. cit.*, page 122.

17 The idea for this poster apparently came from an interview in the *New Statesman* of 9th August 1996 with left-wing MP Clare Short, who dubbed the party's communications specialists, "*the people who live in the dark*, before going on to claim that *the obsession with the media and with focus groups is making us look as if we want power at any price and we don't stand for anything. I think they [the people who live in the dark] are making the wrong judgement and that they endanger our victory.*

VII
Advertising culture

This chapter adopts a change of approach by proposing to examine commercials in a different way, namely not for their representation of British society, but rather as a manifestation of what might be called 'British television advertising culture', that is to say as the specific and typical constituents of the spectacle which commercials offer to the British viewer. It is true that British advertising is influenced by and exhibits numerous international if not universal techniques and concepts, from myths and symbolism through to semiology, synaesthesia and the general appeal to human emotions, but this is not our primary concern here. The aim is to study, in more systematic fashion, some of the characteristic features of advertising which have been evoked in previous sections, in attempting to identify how the particular medley of disparate elements combined in commercials can be seen as a recognisable and anthropologically distinctive British television phenomenon. The chapter will open with a brief discussion of the notion of 'television culture', before moving on to discuss the elements of advertising culture itself.

Television culture

That adverts are an integral part of the spectacle offered by television is now undisputed, the argument is only half-jokingly presented that the commercials are better than the programmes and the term 'television culture' is relatively widely accepted. In the earlier days of the medium, much thought was given to its potential for good and evil, and for some, televised 'mass culture' had strongly pejorative associations, being considered as responsible for the demise of more traditional culture.[1] A more general acceptance of television as an instrument of 'popular culture' has now arisen, with rather less negative connotations:

> ...the popular is what the many like and do; the popular is that which is outside the sphere of 'high culture'; popular equates with 'mass', implying manipulation and passive consumption; and the popular might be that which is done by and for those who do it, rooted in the creative impulses of the people.[2]

Much of television obviously no longer offers the kind of improving 'high culture' favoured in the Reithean BBC or even in the first days of commercial television, and ITV, with its advertisements, has always appealed to a larger and less selective audience, but the distinctions between types of 'culture' are less and less rigid and the hybridisation of genres is visible within programmes themselves and also in the interaction between them and the commercials which surround them. It has long been realised that television is a complicated medium and that viewer response to commercials is conditioned by viewer reaction to programmes and vice versa. This fact was recently acknowledged by no less an authority than Richard Hoggart:

> Mass culture has a very short breath, it has to be successive, to move on always and relentlessly. It can rarely stay with any subject, even if that subject is, on more careful view, very important and in need of longer attention. Hence the addiction to jerky, short-breathed trivia; 'word bites' to match television's 'sound bites'. Television advertisements must assume a very short attention span. Airtime is costly so the message must be punched home quickly. It would be interesting to know how far this relentless process feeds into and affects general programming.[3]

This observation at least suggests that advertising can be regarded as a recognisable element of mass or popular television culture and forms part of the creative aspirations and common audiovisual heritage or collective experience of the British.

Memorability and value

The question of what makes an advertisement memorable once more evokes the communicational dilemma already touched upon, namely to what extent should adverts seek to entertain and to what degree does such a process help or hinder the communication of the key information. Attitudes to commercials are very different and may depend on the kind of message involved (social, commercial, governmental, for instance) and on whether one adopts the standpoint of the general public, or if one prefers to side with the creative or marketing professional. That adverts are a source of common concern and interest seems unquestionable, for television commercials are a field about which the public at large feels it is entitled to have an opinion. The tendency amongst viewers is to esteem most highly the adverts which they enjoy, frequently because of their humour or originality, or again for their topicality or for the presence of certain recognisable personalities. The capacity to recall commercials either spontaneously or with prompting is regularly monitored by such features as Adwatch in *Marketing* magazine as well as by the advertisers themselves, but popular memory of adverts is sometimes fallible. The Cinzano adverts featuring Joan Collins and Leonard Rossiter, for instance, are well-remembered by a generation of viewers for their humour and predictable outcome, although many, when asked the name of the product, mistakenly reply Campari or Martini.

Advertisements also arouse wider interest in the media. BSkyB made them the source of a game show called *Commercial Break* and both Rory McGrath and Jasper Carrott have produced programmes (and cassettes) containing real advertisements and parodies, interestingly enough, from the point of view of the general cultural argument, comparing British productions, usually favourably, with the offerings available in other countries. Periodically, collections of 'best commercials' are produced, but not without arousing controversy by the omission of certain well-loved examples. Media correspondent Andrew Culf, writing in the *Guardian* of 19th April 1996, after the production by the Institute of Practitioners in Advertising (IPA) of 'the definitive list of the top 100 television commercials of all time', lamented the omission of such favourites as the PG Chimps, Yellow Pages' J. R. Hartley and the Gold Blend couple, while no fewer than six Volkswagen adverts (including one from 1963) were included. The ITC's now defunct *Spectrum* magazine boasted a regular feature, inviting figures from the production and television worlds to present their favourites. Jane Hewland, in the Summer 1994 edition encapsulated the idea of adverts as a cultural product when she wrote:

> *We must have viewed over 2,000 commercials from around the world to make the series [Commercial Break]. British commercials stood out head and shoulders above the rest for their inventiveness, their humour and their production standards.*[4]

In the same series, David Cunliffe concluded his selection with the laudatory if paradoxical remark:

> *Oh commercials, where would we all be without you, without your wit, without your style, your infuriating crassness but above all your entertaining and innovative creativity. Long may they [sic.] prosper!*[5]

Nevertheless, the evidence of such articles cannot necessarily be taken at face value. Contributors made a point of not selecting advertisements already mentioned and kept a certain critical distance by insisting that none of the commercials had ever led them to purchase of the goods in question.

The point of view of creative professionals towards the culture of TV advertising is different. There are various celebrations of technical excellence, from the Clio awards in the USA, which have international as well as American categories, through to the British Design and Art Direction (D&AD) book and the Cannes Advertising Film Festival, held shortly after the International Film Festival itself. What these occasions tend to have in common is a preference to reward one-off innovative productions, at the expense of longer-term campaigns aimed at sustaining awareness, and an inevitable penchant for the remarkable and the out of the ordinary. The same commercials often win prizes at more than one of such ceremonies.[6] Moreover, the link between advertising creativity and more general cinematographic expertise is long-established. Quite apart from the inherent technical similarities between the genres, film directors were attracted to TV adverts.[7] It was Karel Reisz who shot some of Ford's earliest documentaries and television commercials, before moving on to Persil, Mars bars, Chanel and Campari, Lindsay Anderson worked, amongst others, for Guinness and Kelloggs, and Joseph Losey helped market Ryvita, while, more recently, John Schlesinger was responsible for the Conservative party's *Journey* PEB. Ridley Scott directed commercials for Chanel as well as the famous *1984* for Apple Computers and the Hovis *Bike Ride* before moving on to *Alien* and *Blade Runner*.

The advertising business as a whole has a more hard-headed approach to commercials and the biennial *Advertising Effectiveness* awards of the IPA seek to emphasise their contribution to the efforts of the industry, both individually and in multi-media operations. The *Advertising Works* series, in which successful agency submissions are reprinted, has the further advantage of highlighting promotions which otherwise would escape more general notice.[8] The other significant point stressed by the IPA awards is the interaction between TV ads, column inches in the print media and coverage in radio and television programmes. Media exposure is both a boost to the effectiveness of campaigns through free publicity and an aid to the memorability of the commercials. The free air time accorded to the Save the Children Fund's *Skip Lunch* appeal has been mentioned above, but the same campaign also attracted the *News of the World* 'Gazza' appeal, photo calls by the England Football Squad and newspaper cartoons by Heath and Alex. In 1991, Oxo's advertisements starring Lynda Bellingham excited such attention that the company's PR files contain over 200 articles concerning the campaign, most of them from national publications, although no television advertising has matched the impact of Wonderbra's magazine and outdoor adverts of 1994 which accumulated 18 television features at a putative air time cost of over £3 million in four months.

The different criteria for memorable advertisements are not mutually exclusive: it is possible to score highly in the fields of popular appreciation, innovation and effectiveness. A classic example was the Martians used by Cadbury's Smash in the 1970s. Faced with a similar product in Mars Wonder Mash, Cadbury's agency combined humour, animation and a clever final line to see off the competition. As Tim Bell puts it:

> *Wonder Mash lost, because it wasn't about being right, it was all about hearts and minds. There is no doubt that Wonder Mash was logically correct and absolutely communicated the product's benefit, but nobody liked it as much as Smash, despite the fact that frequently Wonder Mash was cheaper.*[9]

Intertextual and cultural references

(a) Personalities

Commercials are a compact and concise form of expression and for communication to be fully achieved a number of symbolic and half-hidden references may be included, in order to appeal to different parts of the target group or indeed to the television audience as a whole. Within the British context, such allusions are nearly always locally or culturally determined. It is therefore no surprise that the personalities used to endorse products, or more generally to promote them, should be people familiar to the TV viewer, for whom recognising a character or voice is a means of becoming involved in the ludic interaction between sender and receiver. The use of known presenters is therefore both a part of the communication process and a confirmation of the Britishness of the message which is conveyed.

Moreover, the actual appearance of the personality on screen is not essential. The familiarity of a voice is a first point of contact between advertiser and viewer, but the correct choice of delivery can do much more. Accents frequently give an impression of social class or education, which may reflect favourably on the product. Tone can serve to increase the emotional appeal or more simply to add surprise and comedy and, last but not least, actors are sometimes chosen for no other reason than their ability to speak their lines correctly and effectively. William Rushton, known to some as a member of the *That Was The Week That Was* team, or to others through his appearances in panel games such as *I'm Sorry I Haven't a Clue*, had, for example, the voice of a story teller which accorded well with the commercials he recorded for Opal Fruits and Golden Churn. When National Savings requested his services, his rich and reassuring tones were designed to appeal to an audience of mostly retired people in search of a clear message of security and congratulation at making the right choice of investment. Voice-overs can also help to create personalities, as was the case when Kenneth Williams lent one of the more up-market of his various stage accents to the role of the dragon Clifford for Listerine mouthwash. Researchers concluded that:

> *Clifford's appeal is based on its originality, humour and wit. The dragon is inherently memorable and appealing.*[10]

It seems reasonable to assume that the many viewers who must have recognised the voice of Kenneth Williams would have associated the cartoon character with some of the positive qualities of the actor himself.

When the personalities appear before the camera, recognition is easier and the potential effect is naturally greater, but in some ways less predictable. Ideally, familiarity should not be the only consideration and some sort of identification with the subject being treated is desirable. Thus Irene Handl warning elderly pedestrians how to cross the road and Lulu promoting Camay soap were chosen both for their inherent reputations and their apparent affinities with the intended recipients of the message. In comparison, the selection of Benny Hill to promote Schweppes tonic or Tony Hancock to advertise eggs seemed almost arbitrary, while the advertisement for Goodyear tyres to which the former Metropolitan Police Commissioner Robert Mark lent his weight went to the opposite extreme. The commercial owed everything to the name and substantial reputation of the former policeman and nothing to his photogenic qualities or communicational gifts. The danger of a well-known personality is, of course, that he/she will dominate the commercial to such an extent that the product itself is completely forgotten. The example of John Cleese is a case in point. By the 1980s, as Torin Douglas remarks, the comedian was in such demand for commercials that *it was suggested there should be a new creative award 'for the best use of John Cleese'.*[11] This jocular proposition was not carried out, but the potentially damaging high profile of Cleese had (and still has) to be set against his undoubted abilities as a communicator.[12]

Recent advertisements seem to have found a solution to this dilemma. Barclaycard devised a series of narrative advertisements in the early 1990s, in which Rowan

Atkinson played not himself, or any of the other comic personas he had already embodied, but the new role of a Foreign Office official, whose incompetent behaviour allowed the benefits of the card to be more clearly revealed. Latham was still a comic figure, of course, but he operated within the confines of the scenario devised for the product. The Alliance and Leicester Building Society ads starring Stephen Fry and Hugh Laurie was a similar example. The interaction between the two comics was part of the plot and part of the attraction for the viewer, but their roles were devised strictly according to the needs of the product.

> *Each execution contrasts the simplicity of the Alliance & Leicester with the complexity and risk of the alternatives ... Stephen Fry represents the over-confident, pompous and arrogant buffoon who tries to do things the complicated way but comes unstuck ... Hugh Laurie, on the other hand, represents the sensible Alliance and Leicester customer who gets a reliable result with none of the fuss.*[13]

(b) Television sources

Other kinds of intertextual references appeal equally to the general competence of the viewer or to his general knowledge of culture and particularly popular culture, which will help him both to recognise the allusions and to identify with them. Although advertisers like to describe commercials as mini films, the most common source of intertextual inspiration is not the cinema, but the medium of TV itself. In the early days of advertising, attempts were made to make commercials in settings which resembled television studios, and even to copy, more or less openly, popular game shows or documentaries. Such devices are still occasionally repeated, but the associations now tend to be less explicit and the most obvious comparisons are those of commercials with television's own soap operas or situation comedies. Apart from emphasising the link between advertisements and programmes, aimed at similar audiences and transmitted at the same time, commercial series or serials have the added advantages of adaptability, topicality and the possibility of some sort of character and plot development. Moreover, the sheer number of such commercials makes them a familiar and integral part of television culture.[14]

In this necessarily a brief examination of the advertising series, it is impossible to go beyond a general outline and a few salient examples. The oldest of these long-running commercials, for PG Tips and Oxo date back, respectively to 1956 and 1957, but here the similarity ends. The Oxo series was finally discontinued on 31st August 1999 and fell neatly into two phases, based on the names of the two housewives who were presented, Katie (1957 - 1975) and Lynda (1983 - 1999). In fact, the series was not continuous and there was a conscious repositioning for the 1980s. Katie helped to escape from the gloom of the post-war years and introduced the cooking of new foods in the 1960s, visiting America to discover the attractions of hamburgers, before returning to make good value dishes in the dreary early 1970s. The Lynda campaign was much more controversial, by virtue of its less cosmetic portrayal of family life, with more independent and free-thinking children, developing characters (one of the regulars was a vegetarian), moments of domestic crisis and more fragmented eating patterns. The PG Tips series, by contrast, has been almost totally uniform in approach. Technical developments of the product have been few, the introduction of tea bags in the 1980s and of triangular-shaped bags in the 1990s, and the uninterrupted transmission of advertisements based on a single communicational idea is proof of the validity of one of David Ogilvy's eleven commandments of advertising, namely that if you manage to create good advertising you should stick to it until it loses its effectiveness.

The unchanging creative formula, with its paradigmatic variations, is proof of the continued acceptability of tradition alongside innovation in advertising: the infinitely flexible model permits the advertiser to react rapidly to events while retaining a familiar and well-loved format. The first advertisement featured a chimpanzees' tea party, a common zoo attraction in the 1950s, filmed with lavish table settings in a real stately home, accompanied by the music of Greensleeves and a voice-over commentary from Peter Sellers. In the first 30 years of the series, some 100 different commercials were screened, although the Piano Shifter and the Tour de France cyclist of the 1970s are probably the best known and were used in flashbacks in the advertisements of 1983 to 1985. Topical relevance can often be seen; the Tour de France commercial came at the time of debate over Britain's EEC entry, while a 1999 ad exploited a school situation, possibly designed to reflect the increased importance of educational questions under the Blair government. The campaign received the Grand Prix at the IPA Advertising Effectiveness Awards of 1990, and the report for the judges emphasised both the initial interest generated by the commercials and their continuing popularity which helped PG Tips to maintain its position of brand leader.[15] The PG commercials are equally significant for having initiated the practice of employing animals to market unrelated products, which has become a feature of British advertising, but chimpanzees have the additional advantage of lip movements onto which words can be dubbed to heighten the comic effect through mimicry and parody. The series is a classic example of entertaining advertising being effective.

Television in the 1980s and even more in the 1990s showed an increasing trend towards the development of mixed or hybrid genres, and the same tendency became more marked in the commercials of this period. The 1980s witnessed the start of soap opera type commercials with the arrival of Renault 25 and Gold Blend adverts. In these cases, the viewer was presented with recurring characters, a man and a woman, in an evolving scenario which had some relation to everyday life. For the Renault 25, a luxury product, the centre of interest was the progress of the professional lives of a cool and calculating married couple with a different stage in their career advancement being marked with each episode. By the nature of the teasingly slow love affair between the eligible pair of neighbours, Gold Blend was able to make its key idea last a little longer. Each commercial was short enough for much to be left unsaid and for the development of the couple's apparent attraction into a loving relationship to cause a deal of suspense. Understandably, each advert served to promote the product itself, thus taking up further time which could have been devoted to the couple. In accordance with the implicit conventions of advertising, the ending was happy and public interest in the campaign was satisfied with the joint publication in 1993, by Corgi Books and Nestlé UK, of a novel *Love Over Gold*, written by Susannah James and loosely based on the characters of the series.

Television comedy has proved, if anything, an even more fruitful area for the attentions of advertising imitations. The classic example is no doubt that of Maureen Lipman's series for British Telecom. The central figure, Beattie, was a comic character in her own right, with her tendency towards busy-bodying and garrulous interference in the dealings of others and the commercials served both to give a much-needed human face to the privatised telephone company and to provide information about new facilities and arrangements, such as the numbering changes of the early 1990s. As a Jewish mother/grandmother, Beattie found herself typically in a number of situations involving the long-suffering members of her extended family. Writing in *The Listener* in November 1989, after the publication of the book, *You Got an Ology*, based on the series, Jonathan Sale emphasised the comic quality of the commercials:

> *If you can name me a situation comedy which achieves in 30 minutes what this pulls off in as many seconds, I'll pay your fare to the Cannes Advertising Film Festival.*[16]

Other advertisements, especially for products for men, adopted methods close to those of television sketch comedies or the activities of stand-up comedians. Heineken's *refreshes the parts ...*, Black Label's *I bet he drinks ...* and the *Happiness is a cigar called Hamlet* series all played on the interaction between a stereotypical format and a number of unlikely or implausible events, while the Foster's lager commercials featuring Paul Hogan found their humour largely within the bluff frankness of the presenter himself. The absence of women in these commercials can perhaps be attributed both to the social and television phenomenon that there were few (successful) women comics and to the target audience of the commercials. All of these series enjoyed lasting popularity and were, for some viewers, almost as appreciated as the types of programmes which they imitated.

By the 1980s, the use of comedy had become a fully accepted trick of British television advertising culture, reflecting both the mock serious or ludic nature of the genre and the effectiveness of the device for establishing successful communication with the willing viewer. In an article in the *Daily Telegraph* in 1990, Jane Thynne commented:

> *Advertising has become a two-way process – people are willing collaborators in the game, as long as they are kept interested and their intelligence is not insulted.*[17]

Significantly, David Ogilvy raised the preference for humour (and entertainment generally) in advertisements almost to the status of a national characteristic, at least when compared to practice in the United States. *British commercials*, he wrote, *tend to be less direct, less competitive, more subtle, more nostalgic, funnier and more entertaining*. In the same vein, Ogilvy quoted his American partner Bill Taylor as observing:

> *There seems to be a realization in England that maybe, just maybe, the product being sold is* not *the most important thing in the consumer's mind … Realizing this, the British are able to present their product to the consumer in perspective. They joke about it, sing about it, and often underplay it. In short they have a sense of proportion.*[18]

(c) Literary and cinematographic references

Television is not the only source of intertextual references, but most of what is borrowed by commercials belongs very much to the realms of popular rather than high culture, if only because the audience's familiarity with the allusions made is essential to their success in achieving a feeling of identity. Few products could treat with the same seriousness as Mr Kipling cakes such ideas as Keats' 'mists and mellow fruitfulness' or a Dickensian Christmas, but this product's advertising was known to be strongly based on nostalgia. The Stella Artois pastiche *Jacques de Florette* (1990) contained numerous echoes, for the specialist of French films, of Claude Berri's adaptation of Pagnol's novel *Jean de Florette*, but for most British viewers the immediate identification with Provence had its origins in Peter Mayle's bestseller *A Year in Provence* and the television adaptation which followed it. Much the same argument applies to the visual arts in commercials. The works of painters such as Constable and Lowry are sufficiently nationally well-known to be instantly recognisable and used as part of a common cultural heritage, while modern art, with its associations in the popular mind with intellectual avant-gardism, was the victim of one of the more cutting of the Foster's lager commercials (1986).

Films and cinematic references, more demonstrably an element of popular culture, are a substantial source of inspiration for advertising, even though, almost by definition in the light of the brevity of commercials, actual borrowings are few. Such well-known stars as Charlie Chaplin and Buster Keaton have made brief appearances and have fulfilled the essential role of attracting the viewer's attention and/or sympathy by their familiarity. The mode of pastiche and parody is more common, however, with certain types and periods of films being particularly subject to such treatment. The 1980s fashion for adverts reminiscent of the USA of the 1950s was reflected by scenes recalling the settings of films of the period. Holsten lager made the parody explicit by creating a series of advertisements, to which it ascribed the generic name, 'a Holsten Pils Production', using carefully dubbed footage showing British comic Griff Rhys Jones apparently playing alongside such stars as Marilyn Monroe, Barbara Stanwick and John Ford. Closer to home, the clean-cut figure of James Bond and the visual tricks and stunts of the Bond movies were the source of inspiration for the exploits of the Cadbury's Milk Tray man, while more direct borrowings in the 1960s featured William Franklin as a Schweppes secret agent and Gillette showed two agents fighting for survival and the favours of a beautiful woman by the means of a duel as to who had the closest shave.

These types of references tend to go in phases as advertisers seize on the good ideas of others. The events in Eastern Europe in the late 1980s and early 1990s gave the added spice of topicality to the intercultural references being employed. A 1985 Levi's scenario portrayed a young man smuggling jeans into a bleak, grey totalitarian country, but the ex-Soviet Union soon became the setting for less sombre events. Rover showed a British diplomat driving from Berlin to take up his post in Moscow while Rowan Atkinson's *Mole* advertisement for Barclaycard in 1991 ridiculed the shady world of Cold War espionage. Another trend was the use of scenes evoking the period of the Prohibition in the United States for the promotion of alcoholic and non-alcoholic drinks. The alcohol-free beer Barbican (1988) reproduced details of a raid on a speak-easy, filmed with dim lighting and stereotypical hard-nosed policemen, although the message of the commercial ultimately proved enigmatic, as is often the case of such borrowings. The final shots showed the product being poured or thrown away rather than consumed and it is tempting to wonder how far such images, despite their obviously recognisable intertextual context, actually constituted a positive promotion of the product. Red Rock cider's early 1990s campaign was more indirect in its approach, with the parodic element being strongly evident. American and British film and television conventions were cheerfully mixed from the moment the police were seen arriving, in the first commercial, in a large truck marked POLICE towing a trailer labelled MORE POLICE. These adverts owed their originality to an extended series of plays on words based on recognisable detective film jargon, with examples such as *sister* (at which a nun was observed), *book her* (followed by the question, *Are you available on the fifteenth?*) or *cover me* (at which the detective's colleague put a coat over his head).

Folk memories and self-image

Much of the complicity and connivance created by commercials is attributable to what one might loosely call popular memories, the kind of experiences which remain subconsciously within the British viewer's mind, reinforcing the impression of common identity, or adding further layers of meaning, essential or redundant, to the message that is being conveyed. Many such elements are only vaguely familiar, while others are sufficiently obvious to be taken automatically as part of a portrayal of British life and society, even though it must be emphasised that such details are no more than part of a recreation of a life-like setting for promotional purposes. Such cultural markers as pillar boxes or double-decker buses, along with, for instance, shop names and pub signs, are generally representative of the British scene, while the types and architectural styles of houses may go beyond simple familiarity to connote social class. Rural scenes are less easy to typecast and to define as being visibly British, although the impression of beauty and tranquillity and the presence of waterways and anglers (coarse fishing being the country's major participation sport) may be held to be representative of the 'green and pleasant land.' Actually recognisable locations are not necessary for the process of identification, even if the symbolic value of identifiable sights, especially in London, may immediately convey the message of authenticity desired by advertisers. Car advertisements of the late 1980s and early 1990s exploited the national dimension by displaying the models speeding comfortably along mountain roads in various parts of the United Kingdom. Purely aesthetic considerations may be allied to popular memory: fine buildings like Longleat House and Cricket St Thomas can still be admired, even though they now form part of larger leisure complexes, while Ginsters' Cornish Pasties combined the beauty of the small fishing port of Mevagissey with the traditional associations of the West Country and its more leisurely and attractive pace of life. The post-cease-fire *Advertising for Peace* commercials in Northern Ireland took the significance of place one stage further. The emphasis on the splendours of the coastal and inland landscape of the Province reinforced the message, strongly suggesting that acting with senseless violence when one lived in such a charming area was tantamount to sacrilege. The Mourne Mountains, the Sperrin Mountains, Whitepark Bay, Devenish Island, Strangford Loch, and the communities of Portaferry, Portrush were among the celebrated sights of Ulster which featured in the campaign.

The self-image of the British citizen is another factor of considerable significance. In the case of government advertisements and those for charitable causes, the notion of social responsibility is essential for the correct reaction to be achieved, but elsewhere the picture of the Briton, with his sense of humour and of fair play, his traditions and his much-loved and sometimes faintly ridiculous pastimes, has positive connotations and represents a further way of creating confidence between advertiser and public. Familiarity and expectation are both part of the process and certain well-established figures are naturally associated with a particular and usually self-deprecating view of society. Such stereotypes as the hesitant or embarrassed clergyman, the monocled, gin-drinking retired colonel, the henpecked husband, the bossy wife and the silly secretary are recognisably the common stuff of popular jokes and their predictable actions serve to confirm the viewer's expectations, even though such caricatures are by no means all exclusively British. Similarly the quainter of customs, such as the distractions at a Country Fair or the activities of Pearly Kings and Queens and even of the pub pianist have all excited amusement, and it is certainly possible to detect a development in their treatment: pursuits with an old-fashioned flavour now tend to be treated with humour and a modicum of ridicule, which would probably not have been the case in previous years. On the other hand, if a degree of self-mockery is a marked British characteristic, it has its limits in advertising. The term 'British' or 'English' added to a product name is now once more part of its attraction, after a period when national pride was at a low ebb.

These examples serve to show that self-image is a multi-faceted question about which it is difficult to be categorical. The British, like other nations incidentally, see themselves as animal lovers and numerous advertisements for dog and cat food associate the animal with aspects of daily life, from the wide-open spaces of the British countryside, complete with green fields and dry-stone walls, to scenes of the more domesticated bliss of the well-kept interior or garden of the Englishman's home (or castle). A touch of authenticity is frequently added by references to pedigree breeds or to the name and residential area of a cat owner. Beyond this, animals are considered as members of the family and even as an extension of the personalities of their owners, as well as being symbolically associated with positive values. Thus, cats embody the love of comfort, dogs represent companionship and the picture of domestic bliss was well captured by a solid fuel heating commercial of 1988 in which a bulldog, a cat and a mouse were shown luxuriating on the same carpet. Animals themselves are a well-established feature of British commercials.

> Since advertising began, animals have sold objects. A winsome wide-eyed puppy sitting by a phonograph sold gramophone records. A shaggy dog called Duke is immemorially associated with a brand of paint. Pretty cats lick their whiskers on screen just long enough for the advertiser to get the message across.[19]

Some advertisements for motor vehicles have taken the argument one stage further by granting animal characteristics to cars. Vauxhall's Car Pet (1990) presented a Nova capable of walking to heel, of stopping and of growling aggressively while, a few years before, Renault had enhanced the identification process by emphasising the names customers gave to their models.

Sport

The love of and/or participation in sport is another British characteristic which is widely exploited in advertising. As Peter Bromhead remarked in 1980, The British are great lovers of competitive sports; and when they are neither playing nor watching games, they like to talk about them, or when they cannot do that, to think about them.[20] If the play up and play the game spirit of Newbolt's poem, with its patriotic fervour, now has an exaggerated and old fashioned feel, other notions such as team spirit, common endeavour and fair play are not completely moribund, while the anchoring of sport in popular consciousness, as a source of entertainment and interest is unshaken. From the advertisers' point of view, the positive concept of mens sana in corpore sano, along with the favourable notions of excellence and success, remains as solid as ever, while, as a communicational vehicle, games and sports seem to offer a substantial variety of treatments and the possibility of appealing to a range of different social groups. The linking of sport with humour and good humour is a strong argument. The sight of two huge American basketball players discussing the merits of Bounce conditioner and a rival product (1988) was incongruous in the extreme, while the picture of an American college footballer embarrassingly losing his Levi's jeans and his dignity in a commercial filmed in 1993, but depicting 1921, was a further source of amusement.

Interest in sports news goes beyond the back page of newspapers and events on the football field, in particular, can achieve heightened importance. In 1997, Pizza Hut attracted attention by featuring a trio of unfortunate England

170

footballers, Chris Waddle, Stewart Pierce and Gareth Southgate, all of whom had failed to score with penalty kicks in important international qualifying matches. The national reaction to these disasters lay somewhere between sympathy and contempt, and the advertiser profited from the notoriety of the incidents, among a substantial section of the population at least, by deliberately building into the dialogue of the commercial a large number of words containing the syllable mis-. Adverts for sports equipment itself, with the exception of the boom in footwear and clothing brought about by the rapidly growing interest in fun running, tend to be relatively rare except on dedicated sports channels, but one of the commercials featured in the IPA Effectiveness Awards for 1996 proved to be the exception and illustrated that sport was not necessarily an extra in advertising, but could indeed hold centre stage on its own merits. The commercial in question was for Reebok boots and played heavily on the registers of tradition, nostalgia and popular memory. It consisted of footage showing, or purporting to show, playing in the same team, Manchester United stars and household names from previous years. These included Johnny Carey and Charlie Mitton, from the 1940s, Harry Gregg and Bobby Charlton, both survivors of the 1958 air crash which decimated the original Busby Babes, stars of the 1960s and 1970s, such as Nobby Stiles, George Best and Denis Law, and a representative of the 1980s in Steve Copple, all alongside the 1990s' Ryan Giggs.[21] The latter, the viewer was informed by a voice-over from Bobby Charlton, would have been in any selection of the club's best side and would have been wearing Reebok boots. Beyond the obvious appeal to fond memories, the ad achieved general sports page coverage by its contentious claim to present the 'greatest' Manchester United team of all time and thereby to resolve the vexed question of comparing players of different generations.

Most sporting references are much more limited in scope, being restricted to celebrity endorsement or recommendation, sometimes with scant respect for the sports personality in question. Olympic champion Steve Ovett suffered the indignity of being beaten in a race with a schoolboy who had eaten a sandwich made of Champion Bread (1989), while in 1997, footballer Gary Lineker was dressed as a schoolgirl, complete with gymslip and pony-tails, to ensure the promotion of Walkers crisps. Sports figures can have their serious side, too. In the 1970s, England footballer John Hollins discouraged cigarette consumption amongst youngsters, by the simple and striking message that, if he had smoked, he would never have represented his country, while the Northern Ireland Office commercial *Stars* featured a number of celebrated individual and collective sporting achievements,[22] hoping to find within popular memory material to instill a sense of local pride. Last but not least, sports can help the advertiser to link his product to the collective identity of specific groups. Men can generally be targeted in this way, individual sports can be associated with ideas of social status, gentility and elegance, while for black teenagers in particular, the presence in commercials of role models such as Daley Thompson and Linford Christie was, however stereotyped, a valuable point of contact.

Music and language

Television commercials need to convey a message which may be simultaneously comprehensible to a variety of different audiences of varying competence at decoding the information presented and of a wide range of interests and education. The choice of music and language is a vital part of this process, as both are communicational vehicles in their own right and can be used in various ways to enhance comprehension, to create a mood and to encourage recognition and recall.

The relation between music and adverts is in fact complex. The initial use of music in commercials came through jingles, some of which, as mentioned in chapter two, were based on the tunes and rhythmic patterns of nursery rhymes and rapidly passed into collective memory. Advertising in fact still uses well-known tunes to which appropriate promotional words have been added, while interaction between the genres is sustained by the number of songs which have been specifically composed for commercials, only to be subsequently marketed as popular music in their own right.[23] In all these cases, familiarity and recognition can be important considerations, but additional benefits may also be forthcoming. The 'authenticity' of the 1980s adverts featuring 1950s American settings was strengthened by recordings of music of the time. More than this, song lyrics may actually be appropriate to reinforce the message of commercials. The examples are numerous: the mood of Nimble bread's balloon advert from 1965 was captured by the strains of *She flies like a bird*, the strident masculinity associated with the dockyard scenes of Tennent lager's advert of 1990 was strengthened by the sound of James Brown's *It's a man's world*, while Leon Redbone's adaptation, *Untwist again* was ideally suited to the late 1980s Intercity train advertisements which emphasised relaxation and an esoteric, oneiric atmosphere.

Advertising music can also have an identifying role similar to that of theme tunes of television programmes and commercials sometimes borrow directly from that source. C & A's adverts for ski wear were accompanied by the tune from the BBC's *Ski Sunday* programme, while Guinness presaged the arrival of a Polynesian war canoe on a peaceful English river by the music of *Hawaii Five O* and Carling Black Label featured a squirrel performing remarkable tricks of acrobatics to the theme of *Mission Impossible*. Classical compositions are particularly suited to this task and are now readily associated in the public mind with commercial products, although the process is not new. In the 1960s, the words *The Esso sign means happy motoring* were sung to an air from *Carmen*; *O sole mio* was transformed into *Just one cornetto*, while Bach's *Air on a G string* is indelibly linked to the catastrophes befalling various Hamlet cigar smokers and Dvorak's *New World* symphony evokes nothing more clearly than the old-fashioned merits of Hovis bread. Most importantly, music of all kinds has the potential for emotional as well as mnemonic contact with the viewer, but it is clear that the effects are frequently subjective, may even be intimate and are not necessarily well-suited to general analysis. At a collective level, the positive associations of music were nevertheless exploited in the attempt to create a sense of community in Northern Ireland through the songs of Van Morrison and by the playing of the Londonderry Air.

The use of particular types and categories of language is another familiar aspect of television advertising, as of other forms of promotion, with the obvious distinction that the interchange between spoken and written word and the reinforcement, and, more rarely, the contradiction, of words by pictures gives an additional communicational option to advertisers. Ease of comprehension is a key attribute and the relatively few commercials translated into English from other languages suggest that there is a marked preference for shorter words and simpler constructions in home-produced adverts than in some of their foreign counterparts. In any case, as some advertisers have demonstrated, verbal messages are not always essential. *Le Piat d'Or*, in the 1980s, stressed its (positive) French quality, not only by a typical scene apparently shot in a meridional wine-growing region, but also by the nasal sounds emitted and gestures made by the protagonists, who communicated exclusively by these means, and Sony has demonstrated the force of its slogan, *Nothing sounds like Sony* in a number of non-verbal commercials.

These are not the only techniques which advertisers have at their disposal. Accent too can be a means of nuancing or strengthening the message. Foreign voices can serve to emphasise the exotic or unusual quality of the products on offer or sometimes to suggest British national superiority, while commercials for Fosters and Castlemaine XXXX lager chose authentic Australian actors to promote what was presented as an Australian product, albeit brewed under licence in the UK. Local and regional accents can also play a role by arousing a sense of complicity or identification. Until the ceasefire, the words of the *Advertising for Peace* campaign in Northern Ireland were spoken, exclusively in local tones, although the actors shown on screen were not familiar to viewers in the Province. On the other hand, a variety of accents can be used to suggest diversity and therefore universal interest, as well as bringing more subtle associations. As Jim Davies remarks, one of the earliest Guinness campaigns (1956):

> ...featured a plummy bartender confiding that, 'The chaps from the factory down the road like to drop in for a Guinness when they knock off. Wonderful how it bucks you up when you're tired.' Not surprisingly, it was redubbed with a more palatable accent for regions outside the home counties.[24]

Moreover, accent frequently gives a hint of social class or status and, in this respect, it was something of a surprise when a National Westminster Bank commercial featured a financial adviser with a marked Geordie accent as an integral part of a strategy aimed at closeness with the viewer. More typically, food products wishing to stress their traditional origins often use the tones of rural areas such as the West Country or Bernard Matthews' Norfolk.

In fact, the linguistic devices used in commercials are frequently only too familiar to the viewer. The slogan has particular value, while accumulations, repetitions, comparatives, superlatives and other intensifiers, ready recourse to imperatives and the motif of identification produced by the alternation between the pronouns 'you', 'we' and 'they' are all part and parcel of standard techniques. Occasionally neologisms (notably compound adjectives) and hypallages can be found, and the careful use of rhythm, rhyme and deliberately ambiguous terms is standard practice. The dynamism suggested by verbs and the emotional overtones of adjectives are fully appreciated. As Geoffrey Leech points out, it is the latter which represent a field of considerable interest,[25] although generalisations are dangerous and it should be remembered that the text of any commercial is the product of a deliberate copy strategy. Direct-to-camera promotions frequently use more careful language than dialogue advertisements where the incoherences of 'normal non-fluency'[26] add to the effect of realism and promote identification with the characters involved. Genuine stylistic or linguistic effects nevertheless remain relatively rare occurrences and reflect no more than an occasional desire on the part of the advertiser to achieve a particular and memorable impact. The Esso Blee Dooler of the 1960s was copied by the similar spoonerisms of Cadbury's Spirals (1989) with such errors as *the thick plottens, Watson*. Red Rock cider, as indicated above, indulged in a series of extended plays on words, while first Perrier and then the water privatisation campaign profited from the polysemic value of the letter and sound -o- by such combinations as *swalleau* and *H²Owner*, but such examples are not frequent.

Taken as a whole, commercials manage to appeal to and to modify popular expectations and to develop to match the changing world. As the distinguished broadcaster John Humphrys wrote recently, they mark each generation and tend to remain in the collective or folk memory:

> *Forty years on from the start of commercial television it is impossible to exaggerate the effects of those advertisements. Even now I can remember many of the jingles. We all repeated them the way youngsters would once have repeated nursery rhymes. I still wonder where the yellow went when you brushed your teeth with pepsodent and why Murray Mint should be the too-good-to-hurry-mint. By today's standards they were truly dreadful, but we were fascinated by them ... Then we were riveted by them. They were the entertainment, just as much as the programmes that surrounded them.*[27]

The general evolution of commercials towards greater brevity, with improved lighting and filming techniques and the recourse to virtual images and animation, is an inevitable result both of the developments in television and film-making themselves and of a different relationship with the viewer. The latter is now more visually literate, recognises and appreciates the use of humour, understands the complexities of dialogue and narrative commercials, but also needs to be treated with greater care. David Ogilvy summarised the need for mutual respect with typical succinctness, *the more people trust you, the more they buy from you*.[28] Barry Day made a similar point about the need for advertisers to acknowledge the viewer's competence:

> *Unless consumers believe that the advertiser understands them, there is little else to be said. Thus the clues and cues, the minutiae of daily life – the little things that make*

up that life, the way people dress, talk and behave — are all part of the communications vocabulary.[29]

Martin Davidson's observation of a general movement in commercials towards creative advertising and humanist contact with consumers in the 1990s[30] confirms the same impression. The change of the status of advertising, which we have observed, from a direct promotional tool into a positive attribute of the product itself and of its brand image is a further sign of a radical shift in viewpoint.

Television advertising is often ephemeral and is, for some commentators, a 'magpie genre', thanks to its propensity to borrow from other sources and to exploit the idiosyncratic and the topical in its quest to appeal to diverse aspects of British collective culture. As we have seen, it has its own conventions and feeds upon itself in a more or less overt way: the copying and parodying of ideas from other promotions and other domains and the frequent series with their paradigmatic variations are all examples of the introspective tendency of advertising culture. The balance between evolution and familiarity is one which British television ads have been constantly obliged to reconsider and some surprising variations can be observed. Changes in product placements and in goods and services themselves or in external circumstances almost inevitably bring the need for amendments in the promotional techniques. Cars, for example, constantly need to modify their appeal to encourage regular purchases, but long-established brands such as Babycham have moved with the times. The product's eminently respectable 1950s adverts gave way, in the later 1960s, to suggestiveness and innuendo, before returning to moral correctness in the 1970s and 1980s. In the 1990s, the more dynamic and modern image of New Babycham took over. On the other hand, advertising series undoubtedly appeal to the loyalty of the public and sometimes have a surprising longevity, and few brands have exhibited the restlessness of Guinness, whose changes of agency and constant search for innovation have sometimes occurred at the expense of much-appreciated ideas.[31] All in all, though, the constant construction and reconstruction of advertising techniques has not gone beyond the norms expected by society itself. Television commercials, with the obvious exception of government ads, are rarely designed to shock, the genre remains strictly regulated, boorish behaviour and nudity still seem to be generally considered as undesirable and probably counter-productive and the use of the obscure or esoteric, which causes difficulties of comprehension for the average viewer, is still limited. It would seem that, whether or not advertising accurately reflects trends in society, advertising culture follows the conventions that this society seems to expect.

Notes

1   Dominic Strinati explains the view thus: *The villain of the piece was a media-produced mass culture, aimed at a mass and passive consuming public, and systematically poisoning and corrupting what had once been a genuine and authentic popular culture*, Dominic Strinati, "The Taste of America", in Dominic Strinati and Stephen Wagg (eds), *Come On Down?*, London, Routledge, 1992, pages 48 - 49.

2   Deborah Philips and Alan Tomlinson, "Homeward Bound: Leisure, popular culture and consumer capitalism", in Dominic Strinati and Stephen Wagg (eds), *op. cit.*, page 41.

3   Richard Hoggart, *The Way We Live Now*, London, Pimlico, 1996, page 99.

4   Jane Hewland, "Ad Break", *Spectrum*, Summer 1994, page 9.

5   David Cunliffe, "Ad Break", *Spectrum*, Autumn 1994, page 15.

6   For example, in 1990, Vauxhall Motors Nova advert *Car Pet* won two gold awards (Creative Circle and Cannes Festival) along with a silver at the British TV awards and a silver crayon from D&AD.

7   *Making commercials became a well-paid art form which attracted leading directors*, Jeremy Potter, *op. cit.*, page 209.

8   The 1986 publication contained details, for example, of a campaign in Devon by a local double-glazing company, AGS Home Improvements, whose simple direct-to-camera promotions helped secure increases in sales of 21 per cent in 1985 and 40.5 per cent in 1986.

9   Tim Bell, "The Agency Viewpoint 3", in Brian Henry, *op. cit.*, page 448.

10 Terry Bullen, "Listerine and Clifford: a breathtaking success", in Paul Feldwick (ed), *op. cit.* 1990, page 137.

11 Torin Douglas, *op. cit.*, page 139.

12 Cleese's appearance for Sainsbury's as an aggressive and loudly-dressed salesman (1999) attracted the hostility of staff and customers and the commercial was rapidly withdrawn.

13 Will Collin, "Alliance and Leicester Building Society — Advertising Effectiveness 1987 - 1991", in Chris Baker, *op. cit.*, page 366.

14 The use of the plots of soap operas to raise social questions and therefore to inform the public of such issues has long been a feature of British broadcasting.

15 According to the report presented to the IPA, the ads achieved the following results in public attitude surveys between 1981 and 1989:

	Market average	Chimps
Amusing	100	139
Better than other teas	100	146
Would enjoy seeing again	100	162

16 Jonathan Sale, "Ad Absurdam", *The Listener*, 9 November 1989, page 26.

17 Jane Thynne, "Best TV Ads Have the Last Laugh", *Daily Telegraph*, 11 May 1990.

18 David Ogilvy, *Ogilvy on Advertising*, London, Guild, 1985, pages 173 - 176.

19 BBC TV, programme entitled *Star Paws* in the *Forty Minutes* series, August 1990.

20 Peter Bromhead, *Life in Modern Britain*, London, Longman, 1980, page 104. My article entitled 'Sport in British TV Ads', in *Revue Française de Civilisation Britannique*, vol.10, no.4, 2000, discusses in greater detail the role of sport in commercials.

21 'Britishness' was a key notion here. Manchester United's current crop of foreign internationals was not shown, while all the home nations were included: Charlton, Stiles and Copple are English, Gregg and Best are from Northern Ireland, while Scotland and Wales were respectively represented by Law and Giggs.

22 The commercial included, for instance, Snooker World Champions Dennis Taylor and Alex Higgins, Olympic gold medallist Mary Peters, world boxing champion Barry McGuigan and motor cyclist Joey Dunlop but also the skill of the Irish Rugby team, featuring a try by Ulsterman Mike Gibson, and a goal scored for Northern Ireland by Norman Whiteside.

23 The best-known example is Coca Cola's 1971 song, *I'd like to buy the world a coke*, which became a world-wide hit with the altered lyric *I'd like to teach the world to sing.*

24 Jim Davies, *The Book of Guinness Advertising*, London, Guinness Publishing, 1998, page 144.

25 *The study of noun vocabulary is particularly unrewarding. This is because the majority of nouns in consumer advertising copy are concrete and refer directly to the product, to features and parts of the product [....] adjective vocabulary, on the other hand, can be highly informative.* Geoffrey Leech, *English in Advertising,*

London, Longman, 1966, page 57.

26 This term was created by Geoffrey Leech and Michael Short in *Language in Fiction* (London, Longman, 1981). It covers clichés as well as structural and grammatical errors, hesitations and false starts.

27 John Humphrys, *The Devil's Advocate*, London, Hutchinson, 1999, pages 98-99.

28 *op. cit.*, page 149.

29 Barry Day in Torin Douglas, *op. cit.*, page 9.

30 *op. cit.*, page 45.

31 Under S. H. Benson, Guinness progressed from poster-based adverts, via animation, to live action commercials in the first year. J. Walter Thompson (from 1969) was notable for the *Ages of Man* commercial, for pub-based comedy and introducing the toucan to Guinness's television advertising. Allen, Brady and Marsh's short-lived *Guinnless* campaign gave way in 1985, after only two years, to Ogilvy and Mather's *Pure Genius*, which was followed by a substantial number of brief commercials featuring the *Man with the Guinness* Rutger Hauer and finally by the *Black and White* series.

Conclusion

In British television advertising, the questions of cultural identity and communication are closely interwoven. The successful transmission of messages depends on the specificity of the information to be conveyed, on the techniques employed but also on an awareness of underlying cultural factors. The evolution of communicational methods is undeniable, and even comparatively easy to follow; the preceding chapters have illustrated the increasing importance of such major factors as creativity and innovation, the borrowing from and adaptation of an ever-widening range of sources, vastly improved visual and filming techniques, the preeminent role of humour, and the development of commercials from simply being a means of transmitting a sales message into a positive factor enhancing the brand image of the product or service in question. What is also clear is that adverts do not stand still and that old ideas only rarely return in exactly their original form. The best schematic illustration of the process would be not a circle, but a spiral, with similar-looking features reappearing, but at a different and usually superior level. This trend corresponds to the increasing competence and sensitivity of the viewer, and to the need for advertisers to continue to attract and maintain attention in an age of mushrooming viewing opportunities offered by new channels.

If there can be some measure of agreement concerning communicational methods, the question of the truthful representation of cultural identity in commercials remains controversial. In his comments in the BBC's *Washes Whiter* series, social historian Paul Hewison put forward a very different view from that expressed by advertiser David Putnam, claiming that far from being an element of a country's self-perception, adverts were *a perfect copy of a world and a way of life which never existed*. The two opinions would indeed seem to be incompatible, but this may be because the hopes and expectations of the two commentators are essentially divergent, if equally valid. It is undoubtedly true that adverts act as an archive, recording empirically observable events and physical changes, but also as a barometer indicating feelings, dreams and aspirations, those of the television viewer, of course, but equally those of commercial enterprises as well as of other opinion formers. That this should be the case is perhaps inevitable. Television itself is a medium of information, education and entertainment and adverts reflect in their various ways these three contradictory but not mutually incompatible aims, the more so as the sheer range of products and services to be promoted allows of just such a variety of treatments.

There are perhaps two further arguments to consider. With rare exceptions, commercials do not pretend to tell more than a partial truth and they may be seen as part of the illusory, therapeutic effect of television, which produces a comforting spectacle based on familiarity, on the combining of a variety of different factors, in short on what might be generally viewed as 'Britishness', in a world of rapid change and of ever-encroaching globalisation. They are, moreover, and this offers further reassurance, obliged to conform to a relatively explicit and specific set of regulations. Television and television adverts are a meeting place for all sorts of diverse concepts and appeal to the divergent tendencies, myths, dreams, illusions... of a fragmented society in which, according to French anthropologist Marc Augé, the mass media confuse the public by the 'fictionalisation' of reality. Commercials are part of the established pattern, one might even argue, of the ritual of television. The 'normality' they recreate is firmly based, as we have seen, on a judicious blend of elements which are recognisable and therefore comprehensible to the British viewers, but the influence they wield over behavioural patterns is considerable, for manipulation is a process which may be suspected or go unnoticed... If British television adverts of the last 45 years have in reasonable measure satisfied public expectations and commercial interests, it can only be a cause of conjecture how they will cope with the challenges of the 21st century. At the very least it is clear that the developments in programming, technology and viewers' demands will inevitably lead to the established principles of commercials being much more frequently called into question.

Bibliography

- Abastado Claude, *Messages des médias*, Textes et non-textes CEDIC: Paris, 1980.
- Adorno Theodor, "La télévision et les patterns de la culture de masse", in Beaud Paul *et al.*, *Sociologie de la communication*, Réseaux, CNET, 1997.
- Baker Chris (ed), *Advertising Works 7*, Henley-on-Thames: NTC, 1993.
- Baker Chris (ed), *Advertising Works 8*, Henley-on-Thames: NTC, 1995.
- Balle Francis, *Médias et société*, Paris : Editions Montchrestien, 1992.
- Barendt Eric, *Broadcasting Law, A Comparative Study*, Oxford: Clarendon Press, 1993.
- Beaud Paul *et al.*, *Sociologie de la Communication*, Réseaux, Issy-les-Moulineaux: CNET, 1997.
- Berger John, *Ways of Seeing*, London: BBC Publications, 1972.
- Bernstein David, *The Television Commercial*, London: The Advertising Trust, 1986.
- Billington Rosamund *et al*, *Culture and Society, A Sociology of Culture*, London: Macmillan, 1991.
- Booker Christopher, *The Neophiliacs*, London: Pimlico, 1992.
- Briggs Asa, The History of Broadcasting in the United Kingdom, Vol V, Competition, Oxford: OUP, 1995.
- Brochand Bernard, Lendrevie Jacques, *Le Publicitor*, Paris : Dalloz, 1989.
- Bromhead Peter, *Life in Modern Britain*, London: Longman, 1980.
- Brown Mary Ellen, *Television and Women's Culture, The Politics of the Popular*, London: SAGE Publications, 1990.
- Bullmore Jeremy, *Behind the Scenes in Advertising*, Henley-on-Thames: NTC, 1991.
- Butler D. E. and King Anthony, *The British General Election of 1966*, London: Macmillan, 1966.
- Cathelat Bernard, *Styles de vie*, tome 1: Cartes et portraits, Paris: Les Editions d'organisation, 1985.
- Cathelat Bernard, *Styles de vie*, tome 2: Courants et scénarios, Paris: Les Editions d'organisation, 1985.
- Charlot Monica (ed), *La transmission des valeurs par la télévision britannique*, Paris: Presses de la Sorbonne Nouvelle, 1989.
- Cook Guy, *The Discourse of Advertising*, London: Routledge, 1992.
- Cornu Geneviève, *Sémiologie de l'image dans la publicité*, Collection E.O.Sup, Paris: Les Editions d'organisation, 1990.

- Curran James and Gurevitch Michael, *Mass Media and Society*, London: Arnold, 1996.
- Curran James and Seaton Jane, *Power without Responsibility*, London: Routledge, 1991.
- Davidson Martin, *The Consumerist Manifesto, Advertising in Postmodern Times*, London: Routledge, 1992.
- Davies Jim, *The Book of Guinness Advertising*, London: Guinness, 1998.
- Dickason Renée, *Sport in British TV Ads*, in *Revue Française de Civilisation Britannique*, vol.10, no.4, 2000.
- Dickason Renée, *Radio et télévision britanniques*, Rennes: Presses Universitaires de Rennes, 1999.
- Douglas Torin, *The Complete Guide to Advertising*, London: Macmillan, 1984.
- Durand Jacques, "Rhétorique et image publicitaire", *Communications*, n°15, Paris: Editions du Seuil, 1970.
- Dyer Gillian, *Advertising as Communication*, London: Routledge, 1986.
- Eco Umberto, "Sémiologie des messages visuels", Communications n°15, Paris: Seuil, 1970.
- Empson William, *Seven Types of Ambiguity*, Harmondsworth: Penguin, 1961.
- Featherstone Mike, *Consumer Culture and Postmodernism*, London: SAGE Publications, 1991.
- Feldwick Paul, *Advertising Works 5*, London: Cassell, 1990.
- Feldwick Paul, *Advertising Works 6*, Henley-on-Thames: NTC, 1991.
- Fiske John and Hartley John, *Reading Television*, London: Routledge, 1978.
- Fiske John, *Introduction to Communication Studies*, London: Methuen, 1982.
- Fiske John, *Television Culture*, London: Routledge, 1987.
- Fletcher Winston, *A Glittering Haze*, Henley-on-Thames: NTC, 1992.
- Gauthier Alain, *The Semiology of the Image*, British Film Institute Advisory Document, London: British Film Institute, 1976.
- Geraghty Christine and Lusted David (eds), *The Television Studies Book*, London: Arnold, 1998.
- Goldman Robert, *Reading Ads Socially*, London: Routledge, 1992.
- Hargie Owen, *A Handbook of Communication Skills*, London: Routledge, 1986.
- Henry Brian (ed), *British Television Advertising, The First 30 Years*, London: Century Benham, 1986.
- Hoggart Richard, *The Way We Live Now*, London: Pimlico, 1995.
- Humphrys John, *The Devil's Advocate*, London: Hutchinson, 1999.
- *ITC Advertising Standards and Practice Code*, London: ITC, 1997.
- *ITC Factfile 1997*, London: ITC, 1997.
- *ITC Programme Code 1997*, London: ITC, 1997.
- Jakobson Roman, *Six leçons sur le son et le sens*, Paris: Minuit, 1976.
- James Susannah, *Love Over Gold*, London: Corgi Books, 1993.
- Jhally Sut, *The Codes of Advertising, Fetishism and the Political Economy of Meaning*

in the Consumer Society, London: Routledge, 1990.

- Leech Geoffrey, *English in Advertising*, London: Longman, 1966.
- Leech Geoffrey and Short Michael, *Language in Fiction*, London: Longman, 1981.
- Macdonald Myra, *Representing Women, Myths of femininity in the popular media*, London: Arnold, 1995.
- McLuhan Marshall, *The Medium is the Massage*, New York: Bantam, 1967.
- McNair Brian, *An Introduction to Political Communication*, London: Routledge, 1999.
- Marwick Arthur, *British Society since 1945*, Harmondsworth: Penguin, 1996.
- Mattelart Armand, *La publicité*, Repères, Paris: La découverte, 1990.
- Méredieu (de) Florence, *Le film publicitaire*, Série Essais, Henri Veyrier, 1985.
- Myers Kathy, *Understains*, London: Comedia, 1986.
- Negrine Ralph, *Politics and the Mass Media in Britain*, London: Routledge, 1989.
- Nevett Terry R., Advertising in Britain , London: Heinemann, 1982.
- Ogilvy David, *Ogilvy on Advertising*, London: Guild, 1985.
- Philo Greg, *Seeing and Believing: The Influence of Television*, London: Routledge, 1990.
- Phipps Sue, *A Woman's Place? – The Portrayal of Women in Advertising*, London: Advertising Association, 1991.
- Pontoizeau Pierre-Antoine, *Manuel de Communication*, Collection U, Paris: Armand Colin, 1991.
- Potter Jeremy, *Independent Television in Britain, Volume 3, Politics and Control*, Basingstoke: Macmillan, 1989.
- Robertson Geoffrey and Nicol Andrew, *Media Law*, London: Penguin Books, 1996.
- Rosenbaum Martin, *From Soapbox to Soundbite*, Basingstoke: Macmillan, 1997.
- Sauvageot Anne, *Figures de la publicité, figures du monde*, Paris: PUF, 1987.
- Scammell Margaret, *Designer Politics*, Basingstoke: Macmillan, 1995.
- Schlesinger Philip, *Media, State and Nation, Political Violence and Collective Identities*, London: SAGE Publications, 1991.
- Sendall Bernard, *Independent Television in Britain, Volume 1, Origin and Foundation*, Basingstoke: Macmillan, 1982.
- Seymour-Ure Colin, *The British Press and Broadcasting since 1945*, Oxford: Blackwell, 1991.
- Sked Alan and Cook Chris, *Post-War Britain, a Political History*, Harmondsworth: Penguin, 1993.
- Smith Anthony, *British Broadcasting*, Newton Abbot: David & Charles, 1974.
- Storey John, *Cultural Studies and the Study of Popular Culture, Theories and Methods*, Edinburgh: Edinburgh University Press, 1996.
- Tennyson Fionnualia (ed), *Advertising Breaks*, London: Advertising Association, 1992.

- *The Media Pocket Book 1992*, London: The Advertising Association & NTC Publications Ltd, 1992.
- *The Media Pocket Book 1994*, London: The Advertising Association & NTC Publications Ltd, 1994.
- *The Media Pocket Book 1997*, London: The Advertising Association & NTC Publications Ltd, 1997.
- The Media Pocket Book 1999, London: The Advertising Association and NTC Publications Ltd., 1999.
- *The Polity Reader in Culture Theory*, Cambridge: Polity Press, 1994.
- Thompson John B., *The Media and Modernity, A Social Theory of the Media*, Cambridge: Polity Press, 1995.
- Truxillo Jean-Paul and Corso Philippe, *Dictionnaire de la Communication*, Paris: Armand Colin, 1991.
- Watson James and Hill Anne, *A Dictionary of Communication and Media Studies*, London: Edward Arnold, 1993.
- Watts Duncan, *Political Communication Today*, Manchester: Manchester University Press, 1997.
- Williams Raymond, *Television, Technology and Cultural Form*, London: Routledge, 1990.
- Williamson Judith, *Decoding Advertisements: Ideology and Meaning in Advertising*, London: Marion Boyars, 1978.
- Wilmshurst John, *The Fundamentals of Advertising*, London: Heinemann, 1985.
- York Peter and Jennings Charles, *Peter York's Eighties*, London: BBC, 1995.

Index